Praise for *Ideas for Action*

"There's a long-running conversation about what's wrong with our world and how to fix it. *Ideas for Action* fills in on the 'backstory' that can help you to join that conversation."
　—Jeremy Brecher, author of *Strike!* and *Globalization from Below*

"The world is in dire need of hope. Right now people are encouraged to be suspicious, authoritarian, belligerent, and hateful rather than to be hopeful. As intellectuals and scholars we are needed more than ever, especially by young people, to shine a light on the possibility of social change. Professor Kaufman does just that in this book. In her own words, she hopes to 'stimulate thought and encourage wondering'—two things we are in desperate need of. A wonderful book well worth reading and giving to others."
　—Aída Hurtado, author of *The Color of Privilege*

"*Ideas for Action* makes it plain! This is an excellent and very readable overview of what's wrong with the world and about how we can work to make it better. Kaufman explains a great deal—capitalism, globalization, racial and gender inequality, the threatened environment—in a way that is both accessible and sophisticated. She never loses sight of the practical issues: the need for change, and ways to make change for the better. I particularly liked her treatment of racism as an injustice to everybody. *Ideas for Action* will be a great textbook for many courses in many subject areas."
　—Howard Winant, author of *The World Is a Ghetto*

"Having cut her teeth in the 1980s Central American solidarity movement and continuing today as a local tenant rights activist, Cynthia Kaufman weaves her story into a brilliant and seamless theoretical work on radical activism in the United States. Although Kaufman holds a doctorate in philosophy, and her deep and extensive knowledge of political theory from Karl Marx to Stuart Hall is clearly presented, this book is no academic monograph, rather a manual for organizers and for the people. Kaufman's modest yet sure voice is that of the best of feminist and social justice writing today."
　—Roxanne Dunbar-Ortiz, author of *Outlaw Woman*

"What is remarkable about Cynthia Kaufman's book, *Ideas for Action*, is how it steps back from our day-to-day struggles to gain historical and theoretical perspective, and then moves forward again to use these perspectives for the solution of specific, immediate problems. The book ranges broadly over many contemporary problems, and manages to be both theoretical and practical in the analysis of these problems."

—Howard Zinn, author of *A People's History of the United States*

"This is an extraordinary book, made attractive by its optimism, passion, and brainpower. *Ideas for Action* is unblemished, stimulating and unusually bold in its critiques and alternatives. It's a profound and panoramic exploration work of the most powerful and practical ideas needed for a true, radical social change. Professor Kaufman not only points us to the right direction, but also articulates those practical steps in the context of a troubling globalized neoliberal politics."

—john a. powell, Director of the Haas Institute for a Fair and
Inclusive Society, UC–Berkeley, and author of *Racing for Justice*

Ideas for Action

Relevant Theory for Radical Change

Second Edition

Cynthia Kaufman

Ideas for Action: Relevant Theory for Radical Change, 2nd Edition
Cynthia Kaufman

© Cynthia Kaufman 2016
This edition © PM Press 2016

PM Press
PO Box 23912
Oakland, CA 94623
www.pmpress.org

Cover design by John Yates/stealworks.com
Layout by Jonathan Rowland

ISBN: 978-1-62963-147-9
Library of Congress Control Number: 2016930957

10 9 8 7 6 5 4 3 2

Printed in the USA by the Employee Owners of Thomson-Shore in Dexter, Michigan.
www.thomsonshore.com

This book is dedicated to the students I
work with at De Anza College. Their passion
for a better world, intellectual curiosity,
and love of life continue to inspire me.

Contents

Acknowledgments

I'D LIKE TO THANK SOME PEOPLE FOR READING AND COMMENTING ON drafts of this book. Some gave extensive comments on many drafts, others pointed out errors or weaknesses of analysis, still others simply gave encouraging feedback that kept me going. I'm grateful for all of it. My network of supportive readers included: Carlos Davidson, Kai Lundgren Williams, Marcy Darnovsky, Michael Goldhaber, René Francisco Poitevin, Greg Smithsimon, Wickie Stamps, Jed Bell, Adam Welch, Chad Makaio Zichterman, Binh Ly, Gene Coyle, Blair Sandler, Michael Rubin, Jan Arnold, Tom Athanasiou, Eddie Ytuarte, Raj Jayadev, Jackie Reza, David Kim, Nicky González Yuen, Mimi Ho, Rebecca Gordon, Nora St. John, Elizabeth Mjelde, Jed Mattes, Loie Hayes, Jen Myhre, Isaiah Nengo, Maximus Grisso, Josef Ferreira, and my editor at PM Press, Romy Ruukel. Special thanks to Carlos Davidson for his infinite faith in this project and my ability to do it, and to Rosa B. Davidson for helping me to finish on time.

Preface to the Second Edition

WHEN SOUTH END PRESS WENT OUT OF BUSINESS IN 2014, AND I GOT A new contract with PM Press, I was thrilled to be able to take this as an opportunity to do a second edition and update this book. For me, it has been an interesting experience thinking about what has changed significantly in the past fifteen years.

The 9/11 attack on the World Trade Center happened just as I was finishing the first edition. I added a bit about that, knowing that big changes would come as a result. At that time, many of us suspected that there would be a chilling of social movement and a clamping down on civil liberties. None of us could have predicted, though, just how devastating the war on terror would be, or the extent of government spying, state-sanctioned torture, and Guantanamo. Also horrific has been the way that attack would be used to unleash major ground wars in Afghanistan and Iraq, and the ways that has led to a deep destabilization of the region.

At that time, the war on drugs had been in place for many years, and the age of mass incarceration of black and brown people had begun, but few of us saw the depth of that problem. Now as I complete this second edition, there is widespread understanding of the extremely high levels of incarceration in the United States and a broader understanding of its causes. It looks as though we may be seeing the beginning of the end of mass incarceration. And a movement to challenge the widespread killing of black and brown people by police is growing.

At the time of the first edition, I was very clear that capitalism needed to be named and challenged by social justice advocates in ways that it had not been in the United States for many years. As I write this, there is a growing sense that there needs to be large-scale and rapid change in the economic structure of society.

When I wrote the first edition, I had a sense that the world was beginning to change and I was beginning to believe that, as the Zapatistas say, "another world is possible." But at that time, it seemed as much wishful thinking as hardheaded analysis. I now see a world full of crisis and trauma, but also a world increasingly unmoored from old structures and stabilities, and one where the crises, especially the climate crisis, make it such that serious change has to happen in a very short period of time.

People are beginning to talk about a "great turning" as people all around the world are busy challenging capitalism and building solidarity economies; setting up structures of accountability to limit the actions of multinational corporations; electing governments that stand up against global capital; and undermining the influence of the fossil fuel industry. It no longer seems unrealistic to posit an alternative to capitalism. In fact viable, socially just, and environmentally sustainable alternatives are growing quickly in many countries, including in the United States.

Whether things work out well or not, the next twenty years will likely be significantly different from the recent past. Just as the Soviet Union and many of the neighboring states it had dominated changed their political structures significantly in a period of a few years beginning in 1989, so we may be entering a period when change that seemed unimaginable a few years ago becomes our lived reality.

I hope this book will be a helpful guide for some of the people working to birth that new and better world.

Introduction to the First Edition

WHEN I WENT TO MY FIRST MEETING ABOUT THE GROWING WARS IN Central America, I was nineteen years old and had never been involved in a political group before. At that time, my reaction was a simple humanitarian horror that people were being murdered and that my government was on the side of the murderers. Before I knew it, I was being recruited to form a chapter of the Committee in Solidarity with the People of El Salvador in the area north of Los Angeles where I lived.

I had no idea what I was doing, or how to go about forming an organization. Fortunately, I was put in touch with a few other young and inexperienced people from the local community college who had already begun to organize. They had just arranged an educational forum on El Salvador. One of the speakers lived in my community and had been very involved in the movement to stop the Vietnam War. As I listened to his stories of doing social change work back in those days, I realized how much our group could benefit from the involvement of people with more organizing experience.

Through this work, I got to know many people who had been involved in the radical social movements of the 1960s and others who had come directly from the revolutionary movements of Central America. I felt fascinated by the ideas and histories that appeared to be second nature to more seasoned activists. They had a whole vocabulary of historical events, famous people, and political positions that I had never heard of. They talked about the Russian Revolution, Emma Goldman, mysterious countries I didn't know existed; they argued over violence and pacifism; people would be dismissed as out of touch, with labels such as "sectarian" or "Maoist." At first I found it all very intimidating. How could I be a part of this movement if I had no idea what they were all talking about?

As I became more involved, my understanding of the world was completely shattered. Where I had once believed that the US government was democratic and that it promoted democracy around the world, I began to see it as controlled by evil forces and wreaking havoc on the world. In order to make sense out of my new awareness, I began to read. I read books about anarchism, Marxism, the Spanish Civil War, and feminism. My reading was scattered, and the more I read the more, I realized, I still had to learn.

The most important thing I gained from all of this reading was a new framework for understanding the world. I no longer saw the United States as a benign force for good, nor did I see it as simply a force of evil. I began to gain a new, fairly coherent picture of the world that included concepts such as imperialism, colonialism, corporate influence over the media, and ideology. These concepts were crucial for forming a new sense of meaning.

At the time when I became involved, there were many people around me who had been involved in the movements of the 1960s. And though many had come to see limits in what they had accomplished, they nevertheless had seen some major social transformations—the end of the eight-years-long Vietnam War, for one—happen before their eyes and as a result of their actions. As that time recedes into history, and textbooks and TV movies portray '60s activism as nothing more than naïveté and a bad fashion statement, the possibility that social movements can make a positive difference is increasingly hard to believe.

Mainstream media rarely represent social movements without distorting them—and the theories associated with them—beyond recognition. Still, when activism becomes too widespread to ignore—as it did in 1999 when tens of thousands of protesters shut down the World Trade Organization (WTO) meeting in Seattle—popular dissent and the possibility of making a difference becomes obvious even to the mainstream. Yet the intellectual tools needed to turn this discontent into a plan for action remain virtually inaccessible. Those interested in reading about politics find few contemporary theorists whose writing is easily understood. In meetings as well as in written materials, newcomers encounter people who use information and political jargon as a weapon to gain social status and intimidate others. And they see how intellectuals sometimes put themselves above people with less education. One easy response to all this is to become anti-intellectual, yet the fact is that we are always using ideas and theories. If we don't reflect on them, we are likely to be using ideas that will not serve us well.

As people begin their engagement with movements for social justice, they often struggle to understand what they are doing and why they are doing it. Without some basic literacy in social theory, it is easy to be confused about what sorts of issues one should be working on, how this work will ever end up making a difference, and how the things one doesn't like in the world are related to each other. Confronted with the corporate corruption of our government and declining avenues for democratic change, many people choose to drop out of politics altogether. Popular media portray cynicism as cool. The majority of Americans feel hopeless, ineffective, or both.

Understanding the issues from a historical point of view and using theory to analyze them can be very empowering. If we know the places where people's thinking has gotten stuck in the past, we are less likely to repeat their mistakes. If we understand the references people are using, we are more likely to challenge and question, and less likely to be intimidated into agreement. If we understand the underlying issues in a given political situation, we are in a better position to analyze it for ourselves and to understand what should be done.

When I first began to study radical ideas and history, I had to remind myself that I was never going to know about everything. I needed to get used to the situation of knowing that there was a lot I didn't know, and many theoretical issues about which I wasn't sure of my opinion. That is a lesson I carried into the writing of this book. The book presents issues that I'm still wondering about and great debates that I can see both sides of.

There aren't any simple answers to political questions, but there are tools and points of reference that can enrich our understanding of what is going on. I hope this book offers a coherent analysis of the issues and theoretical innovations of current US social justice movements and encourages you to investigate further. People can disagree about important issues and still be on the same side politically. They can accept some ideas from a thinker while rejecting others. When activists use a black-and-white framework, with theorists already pegged as either good or bad, they don't push themselves to do the hard but rewarding work of putting the world together in a way that makes deep sense for themselves.

There are habits of mind that I think are important for a healthy engagement with the political world. One of the most important is openness.

When we think we have all the answers, it is easy to become dogmatic and authoritarian. The other is humility. By this I mean holding on to a sense that no matter how much we know, other people have experiences and perspectives that we have much to learn from. This openness to complexity can also serve us well in political situations, where we learn to value the multiplicity of perspectives that different people bring to a situation. If I believe that there are simple political truths, then I am likely to make judgments about other people before I have really listened to their perspectives.

A vision of the world that includes the possibility for change requires a major reorientation in how we see the world. The biggest reorientation we need is one that enables us to see the ways that ordinary people, when they work together, can make huge changes in their society.

We are encouraged to see history as being made by amazing individuals, by the inevitable flow of things, or by government action. The fact that ordinary people acting together to achieve goals is a crucial part of the history of human society is rarely part of the picture we are given. Yet if we look at the positive changes that have been made in the recent past, almost all were the result of collective struggle.

Women didn't just get the vote in modern electoral democracies when the time for it was inevitable. Rather, thousands of ordinary women, and men who supported their cause, in countries all around the world, organized and agitated to get the vote. The elementary school version of the civil rights movement is that Martin Luther King Jr. made it all happen through the sheer force of his personal morality. What's too often left out is that King himself operated in the context of a broad popular movement made up of many ordinary people pushing for what they believed was right. The movement made King as much as King made the movement.

We can see these distortions in the way that Rosa Parks's story is told. Many people learn in school that Rosa Parks was an African American woman in Montgomery, Alabama, who was so tired coming home from work one day that she refused to give up her seat on a bus to a white rider. She was jailed for her action, which led to a boycott of the bus system that lasted more than a year until segregated seating was abolished.

What we aren't told is that Parks was an activist who had gone through organizer training at the Highlander Folk School in Tennessee, that she was a member of the NAACP, and that King and his organization were looking for a case to draw attention to the issue of segregation. While it wasn't especially uncommon for African Americans to resist giving up their seats—conflicts over segregation happened all the time—what was special about Parks's case was that she was part of a movement to challenge segregation. Rosa Parks was not an amazing individual when she took her action. She was a person of conscience acting as part of a movement. When she refused to give up her seat, she didn't know how the situation would play itself out, but she knew she could count on the movement to back her up.

When we're in the heat of a movement, we often don't know the importance of what we're doing. Partly that's because it really is unpredictable how our actions will add up to lasting social change. But we also lack the most basic information about how the actions of those working for change in the past have added up to many of the things we take for granted in our lives.

The eight-hour workday was one of the major goals of the labor movement from the nineteenth century when the struggle began until it was enacted in the twentieth. In contrast with the US Labor Day in September, people throughout the rest of the world celebrate International Workers' Day on May 1, to commemorate the May 1886 demonstration for the eight-hour day in Chicago's Haymarket Square and the four anarchists, whom the Illinois authorities hanged for their alleged association with a bomb that exploded at that demonstration.

The Haymarket incident was just one of the many events that took place as thousands of ordinary labor movement activists fought to achieve the eight-hour workday. Surprisingly few people in the United States have any idea that it was the labor movement that enabled us to have some reasonable time off from work.

Probably most of the people involved in the movements that have shaped our lives for the better doubted their abilities to make a difference and were ridiculed or persecuted for thinking that they could make a difference. Yet ordinary people acting together for common goals have accomplished incredible amounts. There is nothing magical about making social change happen. What is required is a sense of hope that it is possible to make a difference, and some understanding of the world that helps orient our choices about what kinds of actions to take.

It is easier to see how our actions can make a difference when we can see how the actions of others have made a difference in the past, and when we can understand activists as ordinary people like ourselves. Once we see the ways that the work of social change activists has had a significant impact on our lives, from the eight-hour workday to the rights of people of different races to eat together in restaurants, a cynical worldview that says we can't make a difference begins to look less appealing. Why settle for a world in which we feel powerless to affect the problems around us, when we can connect ourselves to the people and movements that are responsible for making a better world?

In order to see the ways that people acting together can make the world a better place, we need to be able to see through the mystifications of mainstream culture, and we need new forms of knowledge and access to histories that have been deeply buried. By giving an introduction to that alternative world, I hope that this book will provide access to a way of being in the world that is hopeful and inspired. Armed with the tools people have used to make a better world, you will be in a position to counter cynicism in your own life and in the structure of the world around you.

CHAPTER 1

Thinking about Liberation

HOW MANY TIMES HAVE YOU HEARD THAT WE CANNOT HAVE A SOCIETY based on cooperation because people are naturally greedy? The idea that human nature is unchangeable and that it is basically selfish or antisocial is used over and over again to discourage people from challenging our current social order. It is one of the mechanisms used to promote cynicism and destroy hope.

But is it so? Dominant ideas about human nature are often dated back to Adam Smith, one of the most important theorists of capitalism. In *The Wealth of Nations*, published in England in 1776, Smith writes that people are naturally self-interested. The best society, he argues, was one that made good use of this fact. "It is not from the benevolence of the butcher, the brewer, or the baker that we expect our dinner, but from their regard to their own interest."[1] He imagines society as a collection of these self-interested, small-business people, with social goods achieved through the invisible hand of the market. If we simply allow markets to work, people will be able to get what they need.

The idea of the sufficiency of the market has expanded into the idea that when people pursue profit they are doing something good for society. It lives on in the idea that social policies not based on self-interest and the free workings of the market are bad for all members of society. Social programs must make the best use of the unavoidable truth that people only act out of self-interest. If we appeal to any values other than self-interest, we are being idealistic, unrealistic and starry-eyed.[2]

What is human nature?

One of the complications in thinking about human nature is that the very question, "What is human nature?" implies that we can look at people as they are, outside of any specific culture. When we ask what human nature is, we are asking, "What are people like underneath all of the layers of cultural conditioning?" But one of the most fundamental things we can say about human beings as a species is that we live together in groups, and that we get our senses of meaning, identity, purpose, desire, etc. from our cultures.

Smith makes a mistake that is common among social theorists. He looks at people in his society and extrapolates to make judgments about how all people are. As a middle-class person, writing at a time when capitalism was stabilizing as the dominant economic system in England, Smith saw the world in individualistic terms. But people in different societies experience reality in very different ways. And it turns out that the greediness hypothesis isn't even a good characterization of people in a society dominated by capitalist processes.

If we ask ourselves what motivates us to take care of the people in our families or our friends, what makes us help people in our communities or volunteer for organizations, we can see that our motivations are very complex. Of course, we could say that even if I rush into a burning building to save my neighbors, I am acting greedily because I am looking to feel good about myself. That sort of argument, while common, does not seem very helpful. If I want to really understand my motivation in helping my neighbors, it seems simpler to say that I have a sense of right and wrong, of what good people do and of what it means to be the kind of person I want to be, or that I have a big heart and I am acting out of a sense of care and empathy. These motivations are all mixed up in the social order and in how meaning is generated from it. Thus, we need a richer theory of human nature than the one that is accepted as common sense in the dominant culture.

At best, the greediness hypothesis explains how people are expected to operate in business. It doesn't explain how they act in all other spheres of life. Because Smith's theory of human nature takes people as they are expected to act in a modern industrialized society as the basis for his view of how they always are, his views seem like an excellent description from within this society. So if we think the way most of the social forces around us want us to think, Smith's philosophy will seem natural and normal. It's hard to criticize Smith's view because we live in a society that is organized around the assumptions that he made. Much of what we are taught in school, shown by the media, and told by our friends and neighbors supports the view that people are greedy consumers, and that it is good to be that way. If we want to challenge this view, we are facing an uphill battle against ideas that seem like obvious common sense.

But alternative, and more hopeful, ways of looking at the world have always existed alongside this dominant set of ideas. Exciting social movements have challenged the way society is organized, and fascinating thinkers have helped create different ways of understanding the world. Unfortunately, most people are not taught about the ways that these movements have made major contributions to a better world. The thinkers associated with them are not widely known in the United States. And, to the extent that these thinkers and movements are represented in popular culture, they are seriously misrepresented.

One example of this is the nineteenth-century German philosopher and social activist Karl Marx. Most people know Marx as the father of communism, but aren't aware that many people had theorized communism before him, and no nation had a communist government in his lifetime. Extrapolating from what they've been told about the Soviet Union, they suppose that Marx advocated an authoritarian state that would rule over every aspect of people's lives. For many people, the name Marx conjures up images of a gray and boring world, in which people work all the time and are controlled by the police.

Marx didn't write much about how he imagined life would be in a communist society, but in the following paragraph he envisions a society in which people can do what they want:

> In a communist society, where nobody has one exclusive sphere of activity but each can become accomplished in any branch he wishes, society regulates the general production and thus makes it possible for me to do one thing today and another tomorrow, to hunt in the morning, fish in the afternoon, rear cattle in the evening, criticize after dinner, just as I have a mind.[3]

When people read Marx for the first time, they are often surprised to find him writing persuasively about the ways that capitalism crushes the human spirit through mind-numbing work and a lack of control over our lives. He was deeply interested in freedom and human fulfillment.

Marx was born in 1818 into a middle-class Jewish family. His father was a banker who converted to Christianity, wanting to escape the discrimination Jews experienced in Germany at that time. Karl Marx studied philosophy and received a doctorate for a thesis that focused on early Greek thought. He never worked as an academic, though. His interest in politics drove him into journalism, a field he worked in for the rest of his life.

While there are weaknesses in Marx's work that can help explain how it was used by others to justify authoritarian state rule, there is nothing in Marx that argues for a strong state or that advocates drudgery.

Marx offers us ways of looking at the world that help us to see how it can be made better for everyone. His is a hopeful vision of the ways that misery can be eliminated from people's lives, and that all of us can bring forward that vision. His ideas have inspired generations of activists, even though his image in the dominant culture is a negative one.

Similarly with anarchism. In popular culture, anarchism is often presented as a philosophy of total destruction and gratuitous violence. Sometimes it is portrayed as even less than that, as merely a fashion statement made by alienated young people. Yet many powerful anarchist social experiments, such as the Mondragón network of cooperatives in Spain, have shown how a human society based on cooperation is possible. Anarchists have been involved in many movements for social justice and were important leaders in the United States fight for the eight-hour workday.

Because our textbooks, newspapers, and talk show hosts often misrepresent the thinkers who have played important roles in changing society, we are kept ignorant of the forces that have helped foster movements for social justice. The dominant set of ideas that rule our society encourage us to have a passive view of our place in the world and a pessimistic view of the possibilities for change. Once we break free of this dominant set of ideas, a whole world of possibilities for changing the world opens up before us.

Liberation

Understanding the possibility of human liberation requires us to risk upsetting the very foundations of how we see the world. The dominant view argues that to be liberated is to be freed from social obligations that get in the way of our pursuit of our own interests. So, for those who accept Smith's idea of people as basically self-interested, capitalism is the ideal society. In contrast to Smith, many other theorists argue that human nature is basically about caring for others. Seeing people as altruistic social beings, they argue that the best society is one that allows this goodness to run the social order. If human beings are basically good, then it makes sense to argue that the best society is one that allows people to do what they want to do.

Emma Goldman was a leading thinker in the anarchist expression of this viewpoint. Born into a working-class Jewish family in Russia in 1869, she immigrated to Rochester, New York. Forced by a tyrannical father into a loveless marriage, Goldman became interested in radical politics through following the case of the Haymarket massacre.[4] She left her family and bad marriage and moved to New York City, where she became involved in the anarchist movement. Goldman advocated for access to birth control, an end to repressive attitudes about sexuality, and freedom from state control. In 1919, she was deported to Russia as a result of her opposition to the draft for World War I.[4]

Goldman envisioned a life in which we would be much freer to follow our desires and in which the happiness of each member of society would matter. Goldman defined anarchism as "the philosophy of a new social order based on liberty unrestricted by man-made law; the theory that all forms of government rest on violence, and are therefore wrong and harmful, as well as unnecessary."[5]

Anarchists such as Goldman played a major role in the development of the US labor movement. They inspired the particular sorts of antiauthoritarian activism that were popular in the 1970s and in youth-based radical circles since.

Much of the value of anarchist thinking to movements for social justice has been its insistence on paying attention to people's lived experiences. Where Marxists can sometimes argue that something is good for society on the basis of a theoretical argument, anarchists almost always ground their views on the value that a change will have for the actual lives of people. Goldman was an important contributor to this tendency. The famous slogan, attributed to Goldman, "If I can't dance, it's not my revolution," expresses this sentiment. When told that it was unbecoming for revolutionaries to dance, Goldman replied by stating that "I want freedom, the right to self expression, everybody's right to beautiful, radiant things."[6] For her, a joyful life was one of the goals of social transformation and, like many anarchists, she believed that we should be living the kind of life we are working toward as much as possible. This view—that how a movement is structured influences its results—is at the root of much US social justice politics developed during and since the 1960s.

Goldman argues that people should be able to develop their inner potential, free from distorting and constraining social systems. There is no conflict between the individual and society, she claims, when people are able to develop freely. "The individual is the heart of society, conserving the essence of social life; society is the lungs which are distributing the element to keep the life essence—that is, the individual—pure and strong."[7] Anarchists and procapitalist thinkers such as Smith are on opposite ends of the spectrum with their views about greed and human nature. Where Smith sees people as selfish, Goldman believes that without government to oppress us, people will find ways to get along.

Yet Goldman and Smith share a certain stress on the individual. Not all anarchists are individualists, but many are. There is a strong tendency within the anarchist tradition to suppose that when left alone people will fulfill their potential. This tradition is in contrast with another tendency within the anarchist tradition, often called social anarchism, which works hard to find ways to have people work together to create social forms that everyone can live well within.[8]

Goldman shares the weakness of many anarchists of not looking too deeply into the complex ways that society influences our desires and senses of self. Procapitalist thinkers and some anarchists, such as Goldman, take liberation to mean being free from social fetters.

Thinkers from many non-Western traditions argue that this idea of people being best understood as fundamentally individual is particular to the European tradition.[9] Contemporary philosopher Segun Gbadegesin claims that we are all born into a network of social relationships. Gbadegesin is a professor of philosophy at Howard University and he is from Nigeria. Most of his work focuses on ethics and medicine, but he has also written several essays on ethics from the perspective of traditional Yoruba values. Gbadegesin argues that social relationships begin to influence us even before we are born. Describing life in a communal society, such as the Yoruba of Nigeria, he writes,

There need not be any tension between individuality and community since it is possible for an individual to freely give up his/her own perceived interest for the survival of the community. But in giving up one's interest thus, one is also sure that the community will not disown one and that one's well-being will be its concern. It is a life of give and take. The idea of individual rights, based on a conception of individuals as atoms, is therefore bound to be foreign to this system. For the community is founded on notions of an intrinsic and enduring relationship among its members.[10]

While a Western reader might think that this leads to a lack of individuality, Gbadegesin argues that in a society where people are bound together by networks of deep relationships, the social order changes and adapts to make way for the needs of all members of society. This allows for more individual differentiation than a society based on abstract and general rules for behavior, such as the dominant culture of the West. Thus, for example, most US school systems are designed for students who can sit still for hours at a time. Those who can't are given drugs to make them able to do so. The school system rarely takes the particular needs of the individual student into account. Instead, in many aspects of life, we are treated as interchangeable units, rather than as specific people with different desires, abilities, and personalities.

Small-scale communal societies are often more able to respond to individual differences. According to Gbadegesin, if someone is acting in antisocial ways, the Yoruba ask themselves what they have done wrong to make it so that this person's way of being isn't in harmony with the needs of the community.[11]

Of course, small-scale societies have ways of controlling people and many limit people's possibilities especially in terms of gender and sexual identities. Gbadegesin's point isn't that these societies are ideal, but simply that they can allow for greater levels of individual difference than we sometimes imagine, and in some cases allow for more individual difference than do large-scale societies in which people are treated as interchangeable units.

Freedom from interference, freedom from domination

One way to characterize the difference between Smith's idea of liberation and Gbadegesin's is that Smith sees liberation as based on freedom from interference by others. In this view, we are the most free when people leave us alone. Both Smith and Goldman see freedom this way. This is what people in the United States usually mean when they talk about freedom. Conservatives often focus on things such as freedom from taxes. Anarchists often focus on things such as freedom from invasive drug laws or, in Goldman's case, freedom from repressive laws regulating sexuality.

Gbadegesin, on the other hand, sees freedom more as *freedom from domination*, where freedom is defined as the ability to realize your desires in community with others. An example of this would be freedom to have access to housing and health care. Most people in the United States do not see this as a freedom or a right, but rather as something one has the opportunity to earn. On this view, freedom is seen as freedom from domination. Followers of this view argue that there are many forms of domination that limit our ability to live well and do what we want, and that many of them do not involve people intruding on us.

In general, thinkers on the left who have been influenced by Marxism usually define freedom as freedom from domination, whereas liberals, conservatives, libertarians, and some anarchists are more inclined to define it as freedom from interference. Karl Marx developed a powerful critique of the limits of the freedom from interference approach in his early writing *The Economic and Philosophic Manuscripts of 1844*. These notebooks were written when Marx was twenty-six and had just moved to Paris. He moved there from Germany, where he had been a journalist and had gotten into trouble with the authorities for violating censorship rules imposed on the paper he worked for. The notebooks, which were not published until over eighty years after they were written, are some of Marx's most philosophically rich work. In them, he argues that the dominant idea of freedom—freedom from interference—is based on an assumption of individualism that grows out of capitalist social relations.

The equation of freedom with freedom from interference encourages us not to look at the ways that society offers us some options and not others. Thus, if I am homeless, a person using the freedom from interference idea of freedom might say I am free as long as no one tells me what to do. According to the freedom from domination idea I am not free if I have to spend every day begging to keep from starving to death. There is a system of domination keeping me from being able to meet my needs.

Marx's theory of human nature tries to avoid making any claims about people's natural character. Instead, he claims that people are social beings, and that how we experience our world and ourselves is fundamentally tied up with the forms of our society. For example, if we live in a consumerist society, we might find our deepest pleasures by going to the mall. If we live in a small-scale communal society, we might find ourselves fulfilled by helping our neighbors build a house and having a party afterward.

In Marx's early work, he claims that human beings are defined as a species by our social consciousness.[12] One way of understanding this idea is to look at language. Language is an important part of the human thought process. The language we use comes to us as a result of the uses of generations of people before us. The things we think and say are influenced by the meanings words have come to have over time. People are constantly expressing their consciousness through these communal symbols, and having their meanings interpreted by others. This process of mutual understanding and misunderstanding always happens in a social context in which some meanings are more obvious to people than others.

When I use the word "free" to describe how I feel when I dance, I am not simply expressing an individual truth. Rather, I experience my own personal truth through the concepts and systems of meaning of centuries of English users before me. I am influenced by the ads I see on television and by the ways my friends feel about dancing. I am influenced by this history of Western ideas of freedom, even if I have never heard about them. We carry culture and history with us very deeply in ourselves in ways we are not even aware of. Our individual sense of meaning always takes place and is developed in the context of the systems of meaning embedded in the society we are a part of.

Marx argues that when human beings live in a society that does not allow them to engage in this creative process of having intentions and realizing them, we are oppressed. For him, the sign of liberation in a society is when people are able to be creative and realize their dreams. One of the problems with a capitalist society for Marx is that in working as a wage laborer, the employee is alienated from his or her "species being"—from his or her human nature. Most people must sell their ability to work to an employer in exchange for a wage, and in the resulting work, we turn ourselves into commodities—things to be bought and sold. Our life activities, the actual movements of our physical bodies, and our thoughts and intentions become the possessions of our bosses who can direct our activity the way they like.

> The worker therefore feels himself only outside his work, and in his work feels outside himself. He is at home when he is not working, and when he is working he is not at home. His labor is therefore not voluntary, but coerced; it is *forced labor*. It is therefore not the satisfaction of a need; it is merely a *means* to satisfy needs external to it.[13]

For Marx, labor, like all other aspects of life, should be something that has meaning for us. The things we do to meet our basic needs should be part of the expressive whole of our lives.

The things we do to meet our needs do not have to be drudge work. One way to imagine this is to think about the things many people in a society dominated by capitalism do as hobbies. We often garden, make furniture, cook food. These activities are not unpleasant, or "work" by their nature. Marx says these things become drudgery, or work, when the social relationships around them are such that other people define the conditions of the activity and control its results.

Another way to think about this is to imagine a small-scale society in which farming, cooking, making objects, and taking care of children are all part of a network of social relationships that have inherent meaning. In our own society, even the unpleasant work, such as taking care of garbage, doesn't seem miserable when we are doing it as a favor to a friend. When human activity takes place in the context of mutually desired social relationships, none of it necessarily feels like work.

Before there was class society, there was no such thing as "work." Work, meaning an alienated and meaningless way of meeting our needs, is a modern invention.

An advantage of Marx's theory of liberation is that it does not rely on a theory of human nature that says anything more than that human beings are social and creative beings. When we can express ourselves—and meet our material and emotional needs—in a society in which others do not have unilateral control over us, we are free.

Marx's theory also helps to explain the rise of the theory of human nature as individualistic and greedy. In a society that has a large amount of capitalist activity people are put into conflicting relationships with one another, and the success of some is based on a lack of social control on the part of others. In such a society, people's interests are in conflict, and looking out for oneself comes to mean not looking out for others.

But if human beings are not necessarily greedy, how did we get into a situation in which society is built upon the powerful and deeply embedded hierarchies that we see all around us? Many anthropologists argue that for the vast majority of our time on Earth, human beings have lived in relatively egalitarian societies. Why not now?

The Marxist anthropologist Marvin Harris writes about the systems of social organization that many societies have developed that foster and reinforce social equality. These relatively egalitarian societies, he argues, have systems of restraint on power. As societies became larger in scale and more populous, the "opportunity to break away from the traditional constraints on power would increase."[14] It seems implicit in Harris's view that unless power is somehow constrained, it will tend to concentrate.

We might infer from this that Harris is saying that human beings naturally desire to increase their power. This seems to support Smith's view of human nature as greedy.

Another way of interpreting this, however, is that human societies are complex, and they generate individual people with a variety of different needs, interests, and desires. Finding ways to weave these desires into a whole that works for everyone is a real challenge. Once hierarchies of power develop, they have a tendency to be self-reinforcing. If there is a hierarchy, those in positions of power have more ability to transform the social order in ways they prefer. And once things go out of balance, it is easy for them to become more so. It becomes very easy for some members of a society to begin to structure the social order in ways that meet their own needs and not the needs of others.

In the United States, a large part of the funding for public schools comes from property taxes. This means that the schools in wealthier neighborhoods are generally much better than the schools in poor neighborhoods. Getting a better education opens up more career opportunities for the wealthy, which leads to greater wealth. Such a funding scheme would never have been proposed by the poor.

When the ways of running a society are in the interest of some members of society but not others, and these become structured into the social order through patterns of expected and allowed behavior, we have a system of domination and inequalities of power.

Power, ideology, and interests

Anyone interested in liberation needs to have an idea of what he or she wants to be liberated from. If people were more simple beings, it might be possible to say that we want to be liberated from those things that make us unhappy, like lousy jobs, for example. But human happiness is a tricky thing. Most of us have had the experience of desiring something we know is bad for us. Am I liberated when I can buy the sport utility vehicle I see on TV? Am I liberated when I can have the clothes that I think will make me beautiful? Can I call myself liberated when I am able to spend all my rent money on drugs? If our desires can be manipulated, then liberation is not such an easy thing to understand.

Often we approach this question by saying domination exists when there are unequal relations of power. In English we have two basic uses of the word "power": power *to* and power *over*. Power *to* simply means ability, as in, I have the power to be heard. Power *over* means something more like domination. It is more than simply the ability to influence someone. If we are discussing what to have for dinner and I convince you that lasagna would be a good idea, I have persuaded you; we wouldn't say I dominated you unless I somehow coerced or manipulated you. When we talk about having power over someone, we mean the ability to influence them in a way that is not in their interest, often without their awareness of it.

Antonio Gramsci developed a rich theory of the nature of domination and its relationship to systems of ideas. Gramsci was an Italian communist who, in the 1920s, was simultaneously challenging the developing fascist movement in Italy and the authoritarian direction that the Soviet Union was headed toward under Stalin's leadership. In 1926, he was imprisoned by the fascist leader Benito Mussolini and wrote most of his important work while in prison.

Born in 1891 into a poor family on the rural island of Sardinia, Gramsci received a scholarship to study in Turin. There he encountered industrial society for the first time in his life. He was instantly swept up into the political movement brewing in Turin.[15]

Gramsci had a serious malformation of the spine, which led to other health problems. His ill health, along with poor living conditions in prison, led to his early death in prison at the age of forty-six. When he died, he left many articles that he had written for political periodicals and thousands of pages of notes that he wrote in prison. These form the basis of his most important theoretical work, eventually compiled and published in English under the title *Selections from the Prison Notebooks*.

In the *Prison Notebooks*, Gramsci asks some interesting questions about how we can tell when we are being dominated, given how flexible our sense of what we want out of life can be. He claims that when this power is exercised through violence, it is clear that a person is being dominated. But what about when force is not used?

Gramsci claims that systems of domination always include two elements: force of the dominant and consent of the dominated. The element of force is made up of military or police power, or individual acts of violence, but a system of domination that relied only on violence or threats of violence would be unstable and hard to maintain.

Because of this, systems of domination usually also contain some element of consent, or control through a system of ideas or what is known as ideology. When we are taught that we live in a democratic society and that if we don't like something about our government we can change it through our vote, we come to accept the actions of our government as legitimate. People hold onto this view and use it to convince themselves and others that we should not criticize the government because the government reflects our point of view and our interests. And people hold onto the view that our system is democratic, even when they know that money influences the electoral system much more significantly than our individual votes do, even when they know that only a minority of potential voters feels invested in choosing among the candidates on the ballot.

To give another example, if women are raised to believe that their own sexual desires are shameful and insignificant, then they are likely to accept a sexual system that puts heterosexual male pleasure as the goal of sex. Even today, many women are taught that allowing their husbands to penetrate them is simply a marital duty. Until relatively recently, a man could not be charged with raping his wife, since his sexual access to her body, regardless of her unwillingness, was assumed to be part of the marital contract. The sexual revolution of the late twentieth century has only partly dispelled this myth. Many women still believe that it is more important, easier, or safer to focus sex on pleasing a man than it is to follow their own sexual desires.

People come to accept their own domination when the ideas prevalent in their society lead them to forget what they lack and to believe in the rightness or the naturalness of the present order of power and privilege.

Gramsci uses the term *hegemony* to describe the way that idea systems come to legitimize or support the interests of the ruling groups in society. As the views of the dominant groups come to be widely accepted, they turn into *common sense*. Gramsci distinguishes this hegemonic worldview from what he calls *good sense*: the ability to see things as they really are.[16]

Gramsci's ideas help us understand how systems of domination become embedded in the world of ideas. His work reminds us that systems of domination are not simple and mechanical. But if he is right about this, then how do we distinguish good sense from common sense? How do we know when our thoughts are ideological and in the interest of the ruling class, and when they are good sense, based on our own interests?

A Gramscian view might argue, for example, that it is good sense when people who are gay or lesbian fight against homophobia. But then how do they decide what sorts of demands are in their interest? Many queer activists have advocated for legalized marriage. Some see marriage as a prerequisite for joining the mainstream. Others argue that even if you aren't interested in marriage, it is important to make it legal because to allow it to be illegal is to accept legal discrimination. Others in the queer movement have rejected both of these arguments as too assimilationist, arguing that much of what is important in queer politics is a rejection of mainstream sexual values in general, including marriage.

These differences were hotly debated in the recent past by activists and different people took different positions based on their life experiences and their political thinking. It isn't easy to say that one is objectively right and the other is objectively wrong, that one is based on good sense and the other is mired in ideological consciousness.

Gramsci argues that political questions such as these can be answered by doing careful analysis of the objective nature of the system of domination. In his own anticapitalist work, he uses Marx's critique of capitalism as the foundation for his analysis. He posits that working-class people can learn to see through the confusions of ideology and come to have good sense through studying the work of intellectuals who have carefully analyzed social reality.

But if these intellectuals are also a part of the society they are trying to study, then how can they know that they are seeing things as they really are? No matter how much analysis people do, they are always theorizing from a particular position. Although Gramsci was critical of some authoritarian tendencies among Marxists, this idea—that some group of people know what's right for others—is in itself authoritarian.

This weakness in the Marxist tradition has spawned a number of alternative traditions that are more skeptical about our ability to know our interests and to distinguish operations of power from what is liberatory.

One of the more important of these traditions is postmodernism, a body of theory that questions the ways that meaning becomes settled and looks at the categories we use to analyze society. Postmodernist thinkers tend to criticize the ideas developed in Europe in the period of the Enlightenment. Many postmodernist theorists see themselves as social justice advocates, though many activists criticize postmodernist thought as overly academic.

Michel Foucault was one of the most important proponents of postmodernism. Born in France in 1926, he was deeply involved in the radical movement that was centered in the French universities and swept the country in 1968, and he helped found an organization that worked to get the voices of prisoners heard by French society as a whole.

In addition to teaching at the Collège de France, he spent much of his time teaching at UC Berkeley, and in the 1980s came to prominence as one of the most important radical theorists of his time. Foucault was fascinated, in both his intellectual work and in his personal life, with the complex relationships between sexuality and power. He found a fertile social laboratory in San Francisco among gay men who were pushing the boundaries around sexuality, power, and sadomasochism. Tragically, for Foucault and for many thousands of gay men, that scene was also one of the epicenters of the emerging AIDS crisis that the Reagan administration ignored for years as hundreds of gay men died. When Foucault died from AIDS in 1984, the syndrome was still not well understood and Foucault himself may not have known the cause of his fatal illness.

Challenging traditional theories of the self which is to be liberated, Foucault writes, "What troubles me with these analyses which prioritise ideology is that there is always presupposed a human subject on the lines of the model provided by classical philosophy, endowed with a consciousness which power is then thought to seize on."[17] Foucault challenges the idea that there was a place of clarity to which a thinker could retreat in order to come up with an analysis of what is in his or her real interest. Marxists, he claims, use a theory of power that is too simplistic. Whereas Marxists—even Gramscians—see power as something that comes from the outside and represses or limits a person, in Foucault's view, power is more diffuse and deeply embedded in our psyches and in our sense of our own bodies.

Power is implicated in the creation of our sense of self, our desires, and beliefs. Systems of power make people want to drink Coke, desire heterosexual romance, and believe that America is the best country ever. According to Foucault, systems of power actually create who we are. Because our very systems of desire are constructed through complex social processes, we cannot look deeply into ourselves and know our true interests beyond the reach of ideology.

The idea that we can know our interests in a simple way relies on the idea that there is some clear set of things that are good for us. It is tempting to say that we all share some basic interests, such as food, shelter, good human relationships, etc. But, given how deep the reach of culture is in creating a sense of who we are and what we need, our interests are always deeply socially mediated, wrapped up in the systems of meaning and values of our society. What food people desire and what kinds of social relationships they find satisfying are radically different in different cultures and for different individuals.

Our inability to say in any simple way what is in people's interest raises difficult issues for people interested in liberation. If we have a simple idea of what we see as in people's real interest, we'll feel we can say clearly what kinds of changes in society will lead toward liberation. This theory led to an unfortunate arrogance on the part of many social justice activists. If I have a system of analysis that helps me see through the distortions of common sense, and I feel I can see what is in people's real interest, I will be tempted to put my own judgments of what is good for people above their own.

Knowing ourselves

This idea that people don't know their own interests is sometimes referred to as *false consciousness*. The theory of false consciousness says that people can have a consciousness that thoroughly distorts their view of reality and makes them believe that things that are bad for them are really good for them. It says that people's understanding of the world around them is distorted by the workings of ideology and power.

The concept of false consciousness is similar to *internalized oppression*. According to that idea, people in subordinate groups have a tendency to accept the dominant worldview and the terrible things it says about one's own group. As a result, for example, oppressed people will often believe the reasons the dominant culture gives for why their conditions are bad in society. If Asian Americans believe that they are members of a model minority that succeeds by not challenging society, then they are less likely to rebel than if they believe that Asian American success has come through the hard work of political struggle.

Internalized oppression is a concept that developed out of the anti-racist and antisexist movements of the 1970s. False consciousness is a similar concept that has its roots in the Marxist tradition.

It is hard to reject completely the idea of false consciousness. People often do seem confused about the world they live in and act in ways that seem against their own interest. For example, many studies have shown that elementary school teachers, even female ones, typically pay less attention to girls than they do to boys. This has led many girls to believe, especially in fields such as math, that they are not as smart as boys are. If I ask a group of girls if they want their algebra teacher to treat them differently, they may say that there is nothing wrong, that they are happy the teacher does not pay them more attention.

Because sexist ideology has so influenced their consciousness, they may really prefer not being singled out by the teacher. In some ways it is hard, when looking at a situation like this one, not to make a judgment that the girls are confused about what is going on, and that they would be better off accepting *my* analysis of what is going on and challenging the system of oppression under which they live.

But perhaps this particular group of girls may have different concerns that I am not aware of and that are more pressing than that of being ignored by their math teachers. Maybe, they see the boys acting out and thus winning only negative attention. Perhaps they feel empathy and solidarity with their teachers. Maybe, along with boys in their school and with their teachers, they are outraged by a lack of access to books in the school. If they were to get involved in challenging a system of domination, maybe the class-based oppression that caused their school to be underfunded would be the thing that was closest to their hearts. It might be that because of my own social positioning, I see the sexism in the situation acutely, but miss the class-based oppression.

It is important to remember that as the person making the analysis of what needs to be changed in society, I, too, am a social being. There really is no way to think myself outside of my social reality and get to the truth of what is good for all other people. What we believe is good for us is always tied up in our experience of the world and what we've been taught to expect. For that reason, liberation is always a dynamic issue, related to lived experience and shot through by a variety of structures of domination, such as racism, sexism, and capitalism.

Another example of how the analysis of false consciousness can get us into trouble is the way that many white social justice advocates have talked to people of color about racism. Armed with their own analysis of the nature of class and race exploitation, whites have sometimes tried to "raise the consciousness" of people of color by showing them how they are being victimized by the current social order. This strategy can run into trouble because one of the ways that the racial system works is to symbolize whites as social agents, or people who make things happen, and people of color as voiceless objects. In US history textbooks, the people who make things happen are almost always white, and the actions of people of color are often overlooked, as in discussions of slavery that claim that African Americans never rebelled against it. For many people of color, the analysis framed by white social justice advocates isn't very appealing, and it actually reinforces the oppressive view that they are nothing more than passive victims.

If I try to get someone involved in social change work, I need to engage that person on the basis of what matters to him or her. If I tell people what they need and that their own perceptions are wrong, they're not likely to follow me. Or if they do follow me, they might not trust their own judgments, since I'm the one with the analysis. The possibility of corruption in that case is enormous.

Theodore Adorno had an interesting perspective on this problem. Adorno was a German Jew who was a part of a group of radical theorists working in Frankfurt, Germany, before World War II, which became known as the "Frankfurt school." As the Nazis came to power in Germany, Adorno and many other members of this group fled to the United States. Members of the Frankfurt school were deeply disturbed by the authoritarianism of the Soviet Union, and because they were writing at the time of the rise of fascism in Europe, they also were deeply pessimistic about the possibilities for making a better world.

In his book *Negative Dialectics*, Adorno develops a way of thinking about social criticism that is very skeptical of our ability to make grand claims about the world. It argues, instead, that we should build our analysis on our own feelings of dissatisfaction, what he called negation. These negations, he argues, should be taken as the beginning point of social analysis because they tend to work like grains of sand in the machinery of society.[18]

Adorno engaged in a critical way with the part of the Marxist tradition that had been influenced by the nineteenth-century German philosopher G.W.F. Hegel. Hegel argues that there are deep conflicts in human society and within each of us, which he calls contradictions. These are conflicts within our consciousness and within social reality. One of the contradictions is a basic conflict that usually exists between the individual and society. Often, what individuals want for themselves and what they know is good for society are in conflict with one another. Another important contradiction Hegel discusses is that between reason and emotion. He argues that for most of human history, reason, or what people think is right, is in conflict with what they want, their emotion.

Hegel believed that these contradictions were inherently unstable, and that the imbalances that grow out of people trying to live with these contradictory needs and impulses lead to social change.

This type of analysis is referred to as *dialectics*. A dialectical analysis is one that assumes that society is full of internal conflicts, and that attention to these conflicts can help us see the ways that society is prone to change. When analyzing something, it argues that we should look to the internal contradictions implicit in that situation.

Hegel believed that there was a natural working out of these contradictions that was the main motor of human history. Human history was defined by the need of these contradictions to work toward resolution. Hegel saw human history as moving in a linear way toward progress. Progress meant the resolution of these contradictions in human existence. While Marx was critical of Hegel's theories in many ways, he adopted this particular set of ideas.

Adorno argues that there is no one direction to history, no single direction that all of human societies are headed toward. He uses Hegel in a limited way. He uses the ideas of the dialectic and of contradictions to analyze the splits in the world of our lived experience. He argues that we should look at the contradictions, or internal inconsistencies between what we want and what is possible, between our desires and our reason, as sources for our analysis of where society should go. We can look to people's desires and see in them critiques of the social order.

Adorno called his view *negative dialectics* because he did not accept Hegel's view that there was a positive direction in which we could see history moving. Perhaps because he was writing at such a pessimistic time in world history, Adorno thought it was not helpful to think about utopia, or our ideals of where we want society to go. Instead, he believed that the best we could do was to pay attention to what we could see that was wrong with the present world.

Progress, pessimism, and utopia

There is quite a bit of difference among advocates of social change about the role played by positive ideas of utopia. For much of the early part of the twentieth century, Marxists operated with a strong image of an ideal socialist state that they were working toward. Anarchists have also had a variety of utopian ideas, usually of independent, small-scale societies, that they have used to keep a clear sense of the direction they want society to go in. After the failures of the Soviet model, and of many utopian communities of the 1970s, many social change advocates began to operate, like Adorno, with a clear sense of what they were against, and not much of a sense of what they were for.

For those with a strong sense of a utopian vision, it is hard to imagine people working for social change without one. Yet many activists in the present are content to work only in a negative way. Those who follow this path usually do have some intuitive sense of what they are working toward, but it is based on their experience of what feels good in human life, as opposed to postulating the ways that such another world would be organized.

Adorno advocated that our analysis should start from our criticisms of our present social order rather than what we imagined of the future. According to this way of looking at things, the social theorist must be very cautious in making judgments about what would constitute the liberation of any given group of people in society. It is important to engage in a dynamic analysis of what each person says and feels about the world around him or her, and to engage in careful reflection on how it all fits together. This is not an easy task, and requires a delicate balance between listening to the expressions of people as individuals and a careful analysis of the complex realities of social relationships.

Gramsci had argued that radical social theorists should have a close relationship to the people they see as in need of liberation; ideally they should be in the same situation. He called these people "organic" intellectuals, meaning that they were connected to those they were analyzing as if they were parts of the same organism. He believed that social theory should grow out of a close relationship to social movements.

The feminist movement of the 1970s saw an amazing development of theory. The movement required a deep rethinking of the roles of men and women in society, and of how we think about power and oppression. Thousands of women and men participated in developing those ideas, and the ideas developed in close relationship with the movement.

There are times when theory grows organically along with a movement. At other times, movements grow using ideas borrowed from the past, and people developing theories do so without deep connections to social movements. When it is at its best, radical social theory grows out of the careful articulation of and reflections on the expressions of those actively involved in movements for social change.

We are entering a period where there are renewed senses of optimism on the left. The Zapatistas movement in southern Mexico played an important role in opening up people's imagination when in 1994 they declared that "another world is possible." As the climate crisis develops many people see the possibility of deep social transformation as necessary, and therefore perhaps possible.

Oppression and intersectionality

One of the more useful concepts that has come to be central in the liberation movements of the latter part of the twentieth century is oppression. The word "oppression" describes a systematic imbalance of power. We use it to help orient our analysis and to look for the places where unequal relations of power are built into the social order. Relationships of power become embedded in the laws, the values, the expectations, and the norms of society. When a group is systematically mistreated, we call that oppression.

We can easily see that racial and ethnic minorities, women, and the disabled and poor are oppressed in various ways, but how did these oppressions originate and how can these groups achieve liberation? Theorists often have argued that one type of oppression is fundamental and others are secondary, and thus that political action should focus on the fundamental oppressions rather than the secondary.

Some Marxists have believed that class relations constitute the "base" or basic structure of society. In contemporary capitalist society, racism developed to divide the working class, and sexism developed to create a family structure that would produce new workers for the industrial economy. In a similar vein, some radical feminists have argued that all types of oppression derive from patriarchy—a system of male domination. The claim was that patriarchy structures society along competitive and aggressive lines. Other types of domination grow out of the basic problems caused by this competitive structure.

This search for the fundamental oppression has led to a ranking of oppressions. Secondary oppressions were seen as distractions. So, for example, if patriarchy or capitalism is the most fundamental problem, then women or the working class must unite to fight it, and those who raise questions about racism—either in the movement or as an issue that needs attention more broadly—are likely to be seen as divisive.

While most people on the left have moved past the tendency to try to reduce one type of oppression into another, it still is difficult to understand how types of oppression are related to one another. We often assume that all types of oppression work in exactly the same way. Thus we suppose that all of the lessons that we have learned about sexism can be applied to our analysis of, say, racism. We simply switch the specifics, but keep the analysis the same. This has led some white women to presume that, because they understand sexism, they are also experts in analyzing racism, which is usually not the case. With more specific analysis, it becomes clear that racism and sexism do not work in exactly the same ways.

But neither should we think of each form of oppression as completely separate and unrelated to the others. If, for instance, racism, homophobia, and militarism affected society only in distinct methods and spheres, how can we understand the lives of racist, homophobic soldiers? This tendency to see types of oppression as essentially separate has led to two problems.

One problem is that if we look at each type of oppression one at a time, we usually end up privileging the dominant members of the oppressed group we are looking at. For example, in most discussions of women's issues that don't consciously take race, class, sexuality, and physical ability seriously, the generic form of woman is assumed to be a white, middle-class, heterosexual, able-bodied woman. If we think of women this way, then we are likely to develop plans for action that take only this type of woman's needs into consideration.

This need for a multifaceted approach became apparent in the reproductive rights movements. There was a time in the 1970s when the fight for reproductive rights was focused solely on gaining and protecting legal access to abortion. Many women of color claimed that while they were also interested in abortion rights, their communities were subjected to forced sterilization. For them, the right to have children was also a feminist goal. If women in the movement had insisted that all women experience sexism in the same way, this issue might not have come to light.

The other problem is that if we think of types of oppression as fundamentally separate, we are then tempted to understand their interrelationships by supposing that we can merge them together. So, for example, if being a woman lowers one's wages and so does being African American, then one would expect a hierarchy in which African American women are at the bottom end of the wage scale. However, in her essay "Multiple Jeopardy, Multiple Consciousness," Deborah K. King writes,

> Given our subordinate statuses as female and black, we might expect black women to receive the lowest incomes regardless of their educational attainment. However, the returns of postsecondary education, a college degree or higher, are greater for black females than for white females. A similar pattern is not found among

males. In this three-way analysis, black women are not consistently in the lowest status, evidence that the importance of the multiple discriminations of race, gender, and class is varied and complex. In the interactive model, the relative significance of race, sex, or class in determining the conditions of black women's lives is neither fixed nor absolute but, rather, is dependent upon the sociohistorical context and the social phenomenon under consideration.[19]

King's study points to the need for a careful analysis of the relationships between oppressions. If we want to be able to understand the ways that each of us is influenced by a variety of oppressive and empowering social forces, we have to develop a way of understanding systems of oppression as distinct, yet deeply interrelated. In 1989 African American legal scholar Kimberlé Crenshaw used the term "intersectionality" to name the complex, and sometimes unpredictable ways that multiple systems of oppression impact us.[20] Without this understanding, we are likely to fight over whose oppression is the most important. With this understanding, we are in a much better position to form meaningful coalitions between groups of people and to develop effective plans for action.

Michael Omi and Howard Winant's book *Racial Formation in the United States* develops a theoretical framework for understanding racism that can be used for a general discussion of oppression. They argue that race is a socially constructed category, and that there is no biological basis for the notion of race. Still, they claim, race is real in the sense that a person's identification with—and assignment to—a racial category has enormous social consequences. Racial identity deeply affects how people live their lives. Race consciousness is interwoven in the fabric of society. The concept they use to explain how racial dynamics are developed in a society is *racial formation*.

> We define *racial formation* as the sociohistorical process by which racial categories are created, inhabited, transformed, and destroyed. . . . We argue that racial formation is a process of historically situated *projects* in which human bodies and social structures are represented and organized. . . . A *racial project is simultaneously an interpretation, representation, or explanation of racial dynamics, and an effort to reorganize and redistribute resources along particular racial lines.*[21]

Omi and Winant believe that racism becomes embedded in the structure of society through the actions of people over time. Racism is built into the fabric of society in how resources are distributed, in how cultural meanings are created to represent different people, and in how people come to explain and understand the reasons why social systems are what they are. They see racism as a set of material and cultural practices that get woven into the social fabric over time.

Slavery is an example of a hegemonic racial project; the entitlement of European Americans to own African Americans as slaves was established and legitimized by the actions of many people over time. The reality of slavery then left a legacy that racists and antiracists have had to deal with. For Omi and Winant, racial projects can be racist or antiracist. The civil rights movement is an example of what they call a democratic racial project—one aimed at reworking the power relations that had devolved from slavery. As different groups compete to institutionalize and prevail in society, society comes to have a particular set of ways that race is structured into it. This structure never can be analyzed simply and without taking into consideration the operations of history. The accidents of history, of how a particular event plays itself out in reality, have an important role in the development of the racial formation of society.

According to this approach, society is structured through human action. People *create* meanings, and they do things to make certain ways of operating in society the common practice. These actions, or projects, become institutionalized and begin to determine the actions of other people and groups of people. This is how social structures are formed.

Omi and Winant use this analysis to explain racism, but we can extend the idea of racial formation to other systems of oppression. Their basic insights—that social structures form over time through historical accidents, through the work of groups of people trying to make things happen in society, and through the struggles over the meanings of these structures—can be used to analyze the ways other systems of domination are structured into society.

A social structure is a pattern according to which some aspect of society operates. A social structure can be a set of attitudes, a mechanism for the distribution of resources, or a pattern for the development of forms of identity. These patterns are developed and made stable by a variety of mechanisms, usually having something to do with power.

In order to understand a social formation, we must look at its histori-cal roots. No predetermined rules can tell us how a system of oppression will develop. Real people making things happen, historical accidents, and the complex interactions of many different systems of oppression influence how an oppression formation will develop. This makes analyzing oppression formations complex and means that to analyze them we need to look at the details of how things have come to be what they are.

This means that we cannot come up with one theoretical explanation of how two types of oppression interact and then derive our analysis in some logical fashion. Rather, we must see the interrelationships between types of oppression as determined by history and the outcome of social struggles.

For example, the societies that engaged in the early appropriations of slave labor and indigenous land in the Americas were already structured through sets of power relations that had gender built into them. Men did certain things and women others. In the Spanish and Portuguese colonies, the colonists were almost entirely men, whereas British colonists included men and women. This led to very different racial formations in the United States and in Latin America. In the United States, the attempt to protect the purity of the white race led to the theory of *hypodescent*, in which one drop of blood from an African family member meant that a person was not considered white. In the Spanish and Portuguese colonies, where white women were not a part of the equation, a much more complex system of different gradations of racial purity developed.[22]

These differences in the gendered structures of the two colonizing so-cieties influenced the ways that racism developed in these two places. The sexist dynamics of each society were embedded in all its social relations, and as a racial set of power relations began to be played out, racial projects were influenced by gender projects and vice versa.[23]

The ways that systems of power relations influence one another is un-predictable. Sometimes different forms of oppression reinforce one another. In the United States, racism in the form of immigrant bashing is often used to divert attention from the real causes of economic hardship. Vincent Chin, a twenty-seven-year-old Chinese American, was killed by two men involved in the auto industry, one a supervisor, the other a laid-off autoworker. The two men were heard grumbling that it was because of people such as Chin that the one man had lost his job.[24]

The loss of jobs in the US auto industry was blamed on Asians, rather than on the bad decisions made by US auto manufacturers. Since the murderers focused their rage on Asians, rather than on the owners of the auto plant, racism ended up reinforcing class-based oppression; the class-based cause of unemployment was allowed to go unchallenged. In this example, racism helped to reinforce class-based oppression. But the opposite is often true as well. Sometimes one system of oppression helps to undermine another. For example, the ways that capitalism pulled more women into the paid workforce in the 1970s helped support women's demands for more equality in the workplace.

While it would make coalition-building easier if forms of oppression always supported one another, and fighting one oppression automatically undermined the power of the others, reality is not that neat. Instead, I would claim that it is imperative for those working for social justice to fight all forms of oppression, both because of a shared goal—a world without oppression—and because when people in one group support those in another, those alliances can be used in future struggles to strengthen both movements.

Conclusion

While the rest of this book deals with issues of liberation and oppression, it doesn't offer clear answers as to what is liberating and what is oppressive. It's important to be careful in defining what counts as liberation for members of different groups in society. Ideas about liberation have to be developed through social movements. Many people find the concepts of liberation developed in these movements to resonate with their own desires and to be inspiring. The following chapters will hopefully help make sense of those visions of liberation.

Chapter 2

Capitalism, Freedom, and the Good Life

In 2002, I was involved in a struggle in Oakland, California, where I lived, to protect the rights of tenants. For the previous decade, the economy in the Bay Area had been booming. Despite the collapse of the computer and internet-related industries, a lot of money had poured in, and many people who had lived here for generations were displaced by well-heeled newcomers.

In Oakland, we had a moderate form of rent control. The landlord could raise our rent only about 3 percent a year, but whenever an apartment went vacant, he or she could raise it to whatever the market would bear. My landlord evicted one of my neighbors, then turned around and rented out the apartment for $600 more a month. African Americans were leaving the city at an alarming rate, many returning to the South.

The organization I worked with, Just Cause Oakland, passed an ordinance that made it illegal to evict people unless they had done something illegal or destructive. As I talked with people on the street about the issue, the tenants eagerly grabbed the petition out of my hands. They were angry and afraid of losing their place to live. But many people I gave the petition to felt differently. They rented out property, and they'd say, "It's my property, shouldn't I be able to do with it what I want?"

I found it difficult to counter those arguments in a way that made sense to property owners. Belief in the rights of property owners runs deep in this society. Many of the landlords claim that if tenants want more security they should buy their own homes. They also argue that rent control is the problem. If we were to just let the market work, there wouldn't be such a difference between the rents people pay now and the amount a new tenant would pay. And they believe that if the market were able to do its work, then, somehow, there would be homes available at the prices people could pay.

This is Adam Smith's theory of "the invisible hand of the market": when markets are allowed to operate, resources appear where they are most needed as if put there by an invisible hand. In the housing market, this theory assumes that some landlords will always choose to rent their properties more cheaply than others.

Yet Smith himself knew that markets could accomplish only some social goals. Markets will not provide goods to people who have *no* money. They won't make it profitable to provide decent homes for the poor, at least not when the wealth gap is as extreme as it currently is in the United States, when the wealthy are willing to pay incredible sums for center-city condominiums. And markets will never promote forms of life that have nothing to do with buying and selling.

The reaction to Oakland's anti-eviction petition was the clearest example of a class difference that I had seen in years. You could predict with incredible accuracy what viewpoint someone held by knowing which class position he or she occupied. The experience also reminded me of how intensely the dominant view of freedom is mixed up with capitalism.

For the landlords, the law we were trying to pass would indeed limit their freedom. To them, freedom means the ability to do what they want with what's theirs. Landlords believe that the tenants are free to buy homes if they want. And if they can't afford homes, they are free to get a job or go to school to get a better job so that they will be able to do so in the future.

One of the amazing things about the views of freedom that develop in a society dominated by capitalism is that those views focus on the freedoms of those with power. The freedom to live in your rented apartment without fear of eviction somehow doesn't count. That's because people thinking according to a capitalist logic associate freedom mostly with largely the freedom of property owners to dispose of their property as they please. This is supposedly fair because everyone has the right to own property. So we are all equal. This way of thinking hides the mechanisms that make it easy for some people to own property and harder for others. And it hides the ways that other sorts of freedoms are limited by this primacy of property.

Those of us brought up in a society dominated by capitalist logics are taught from an early age that capitalism equals freedom, that a free-market economy is the only way for society to produce wealth. We are surrounded by a dazzling array of efficient machines and cool products. We are told that capitalism allows anyone—with effort—to have everything he or she dreams of. And we are told that the alternatives involve poverty, stagnation, boredom, and a police state.

Capitalism has led to an unprecedented development of useful machines, technological abilities, and an endless supply of desirable consumer products. No one in the nineteenth century could have dreamed of the things we now take for granted, from smartphones to Botox, prosthetic limbs to chicken nuggets.

The idea we are generally taught is that capitalism is the magic machine that has given us all of these things, and freedom, too. Capitalism means a free market—and, somehow, a free society.

Early ideas about capitalism and freedom

People didn't always associate capitalism with freedom. When it was first coming into being in England in the seventeenth century, many people saw capitalism as taking away their freedoms. For them, members of the rising capitalist class were thieves. While many people worked as serfs under brutal conditions of feudalism during this time, peasants who lived outside of the feudal estates could be relatively self-sufficient. Those living on land known as the commons, which officially belonged to the king, were permitted to build cottages, gather firewood, hunt, and even farm. With the rise of capitalist agriculture, these common lands were increasingly fenced or otherwise enclosed by the aristocracy and entrepreneurs. Deprived of their farming and grazing land, the only option left to the poor was to sell their time for wages. Working for wages was an entirely new arrangement, and the formerly independent and largely self-sufficient laborers resented it tremendously. According to David Mulder, "Vulnerable to fluctuations in price and wage, dependent on seasonal work, housed in rude one-room cottages, shunted to the fringes of the manor, landless wage laborers had no stable niche in the rural economy."[1]

Gerrard Winstanley was one of the most renowned anticapitalists of this early period. He was a writer and organizer and a founder of the movement known as the Diggers. Winstanley had a vision of a society in which everyone had access to the resources each needed to have a decent life. He saw capitalism as taking away this access and forcing people to be even more dominated by the wealthy than they had been before. In 1648, Winstanley and a group of thirty to forty people decided to take back the land they believed to be rightly theirs. They occupied a piece of unused land called St. George's Hill in the town of Cobham, building huts and planting crops. They intended to set up a communal society in which everyone would work the land and share what they produced. They hoped that the idea of "digging" would spread to all of England and that people would begin to see the error of private ownership.

Winstanley was a religious thinker and saw private property as sinful. "In the beginning, the great Creator Reason made the Earth to be a common treasury."[2] He believed that the wealthy landowners were only able to have their wealth by forcing others to work for them, and he thought that digging would undermine the whole system of capitalist wage labor.[3]

Winstanley addressed the landowning class when he wrote,

> The power of enclosing land and owning property was brought into creation by your ancestors by the sword; which first did murder their fellow creatures, men, and after plunder or steal away their land, and left this land successively to you, their children. And therefore, though you did not kill or thieve, yet you hold that cursed thing in your hand by the power of the sword.[4]

Just as the Diggers' crops were beginning to bear fruit, English soldiers, supported by local landowners, went to St. George's Hill and destroyed the encampment, injuring several, destroying the huts, and trampling on the crops.

At the time of the Digger resistance to capitalism, there was a three-way battle going on in England between the old feudal aristocracy, the rising capitalist class, and the poor. In the English Civil War, the aristocracy had largely sided with the monarchy, while the rising capitalist class sided with the parliament. They wanted to overthrow the monarchy in favor of a parliamentary system that would act in their interests. In order to have the power to overthrow the monarchy, though, they needed the help of the poor. Many poor people joined Oliver Cromwell's pro-Parliament army because they were told that they were fighting for liberty and access to land for all.

At every step of the way, though, the wealthier members of the movement ended up betraying the interests of the poor people's organizations.[5]

One of the most brilliant theorists of nascent capitalism was John Locke. Locke was born in 1632. He was trained as a medical doctor, but made his living for much of his adult life as assistant to the Earl of Shaftesbury—one of the important leaders of the English Parliament. He spent many years in France in exile because his ideas were seen as undermining the power of the monarchy. Locke is most famous for developing theories of natural rights and individual freedom.

And yet, he was an investor in the transatlantic slave trade and helped write the constitution for Carolina, a document that included slavery.[6] As advisor to Shaftesbury, he advocated for the "enclosures," which threw poor people in England off their land, and he advocated for the expropriation of the lands of indigenous peoples.

From around 1600 through 1850, many European thinkers were interested in ideas of freedom, democracy, individual rights, progress, and politics based on reason rather than traditional authority. This period, called the Enlightenment, has been seen as the birthplace of much that is good in the European tradition. Until very recently, social justice advocates have mostly seen their work as extending the values of the Enlightenment.

Yet anticolonial thinkers have long pointed out that there is a deep contradiction between Enlightenment values and the practices of the very thinkers who espoused them. Many of the same people who supported capitalism and Enlightenment ideas also supported colonialism and slavery.

During the Enlightenment, Europe was engaged in some of the most brutal practices in its history: slavery and colonialism. The rise of capitalism in Europe also exacerbated brutal forms of inequality and poverty. As a result of the enclosures, large numbers of previously independent peasants were thrown off their land. Even with the increasing destitution, there remained a shortage of people willing to work under the conditions offered in the new factories. This is one of the reasons England developed the poor laws that effectively outlawed not working for a wage. Poor people were routinely picked up by the police for sleeping outdoors, for not having any obvious means of support, and for vagrancy. They were turned over to poor houses where they were forced to work.

In Locke's work, we can see all of the complexities and contradictions of a proslavery Enlightenment. In his *Two Treatises of Government*, Locke makes a powerful argument against the legitimacy of monarchy and feudalism. In the process of making that argument, he lays the foundation for a justification of capitalism, colonialism, and slavery. What is amazing about Locke's work is that he justifies these things all in the name of freedom. Locke constructs his argument by asking us to imagine we are in a "state of nature" in which people are "all equal and independent [and] no one ought to harm another in his life, health, liberty, or possessions."[7]

This state of nature is what philosophers call a "thought experiment." Locke makes no claims that it ever existed, rather, that we can know our true state by imagining this possibility. Locke argues that this state of independence is our natural state. He wants us to think of ourselves as individuals first and as members of families and of society second. This undermines any sense of social solidarity and mutual obligation and challenges the idea that the world belongs to all of us to figure out how to use and share. In his justification for private property, Locke argues that although God gave us all the Earth to share, those who make the most of God's gifts deserve them the most.

In England in this period, there were many landlords interested in "improving" their property—in making it more profitable. New agricultural techniques made this development possible, and new class relationships allowed these wealthy landowners to rise to political power. Locke was a part of that "improving" class.

In her book *The Origin of Capitalism*, Ellen Meiksins Wood points out that the word "improve" in English comes from a French root that meant doing something for profit.[8] According to Locke, the indigenous people of the Americas did not have a right to their land because they were not generating excess for the market. The same could be said for the poor in England. The land belongs to those who can make the most profit from it or to the capitalist landlords.

Locke's theory of natural rights is another aspect of his argument that helps support the domination inherent in capitalism. He claims that those with *reason* will all be in a state of nature with each other—meaning that they will all respect each other's natural rights to life, liberty, and property. Some people, however, cannot be expected to use their reason to come to this conclusion. These people are like lions of the forest and cannot be trusted. Because of this, these people are in a state of war with the rest of humanity, and "reasonable" people can do whatever they want to protect themselves.[9]

It was this argument that Locke used to justify slavery. The idea that some people are rational and to be treated with respect, while others who think differently cannot be trusted, is a fundamental part of the ideology of the Enlightenment.

Locke wants us to see society as an aggregation of independent, reasonable people, all with their own land, entering into contracts voluntarily, as all parties desire them. We are to see these independent people as meeting in an imagined state of nature. By asking us to think in this way, Locke is asking us to wish away history, and he is helping us develop the habit, very important as capitalism develops, of not seeing the complex realities of social relations.

Locke's philosophy, by positing the state of nature, encourages us to look at people as if they had no history. According to his view, people chose to enter into and exit from contracts. In reality, people are often forced by circumstances and by the law into situations that they do not choose.

This habit of making history invisible and supposing that we are all born free and equal is another important part of capitalist ideology. When people complain about inequality, we are told that everyone has the same chance to become wealthy and that wealth is based on our ability and desire to work hard. This leads to the idea that those with wealth should be able to do what they want with the wealth, without any obligations to others. Of course, those without wealth are also free to do what they want with their wealth, never mind that they don't have any.

The vision of society as an aggregation of individuals with no history is, of course, a myth. Even in a society with a large capitalist sector, there are networks of relationships that bind us together. What is unusual about life in such a society is that these interconnections are erased by the dominant ways of thinking. We end up not seeing the social mechanisms that give some people more opportunity to succeed than others. And we end up not noticing the ways that we are all coerced to compete in a particular set of economic relations that we do not choose. Nor are we encouraged to see the ways in which people cooperate and help one another in all spheres of life.

An Enlightenment belief in progress might encourage us to think that Locke and his capitalist class made the world better by overthrowing feudalism. This view, however, would leave out the fact that at that time in England there was a far more radical alternative: that of the Diggers and many other radical anticapitalists.

According to the British historian Christopher Hill,

> There were, we may oversimplify, two revolutions in mid-seven-teenth-century England. The one which succeeded established the sacred rights of property (abolition of feudal tenures, no arbitrary taxation), gave political power to the propertied (sovereignty of Parliament and common law, abolition of prerogative courts), and removed all impediments to the triumph of the ideology of the men of property—the protestant ethic. There was, however, an-other revolution, which never happened, though from time to time it threatened. This might have established communal property, a far wider democracy in political and legal institutions, might have disestablished the state church and rejected the protestant ethic.[10]

People who were a part of this second revolution knew full well the prob-lems with capitalism; they saw members of the emerging capitalist class take their land.

The origins of capitalism

Historians have disagreed fundamentally about how capitalism came into being and why it arose first in Europe. Historian Janet Abu-Lughod points out that it is very easy when we are trying to explain how something came into being to think about it as if it were inevitable. She notes that at the time of Europe's rise to world power, the shipbuilding and military technology and the credit and trade systems of many other parts of the world were more sophisticated than those of Europe.[11]

In the period stretching from 1250 to 1700, many countries were in-volved in the mercantilist system, in which the rulers of a country would invest money in commercial trade operations. This system mostly brought luxury goods, such as spices and textiles, to the elites. Ferdinand and Isabela's funding of Columbus is a well-known example. In many cases, these government-sponsored operations involved a combination of com-mercial and military interests.

Abu-Lughod argues that in the century between 1250 and 1350, a complex network of trading relationships integrated scattered towns along several trade and sea routes "that stretched all the way from China to northwestern Europe. In this world system—whose core lay in near and farther Asia—Europe was but a recent and still marginal participant."[12]

In her analysis, the rise of capitalism can be explained as the slow development of these trading relationships to a point where they become powerful enough to dominate the economies of many societies. As the trading systems of the East fell from their position of dominance, due to internal weaknesses, traders from Europe rose in their influence. The European traders were more predatory and more interested in short-term gain than other participants in this world system had been. "More than anything else, then, it was the new European approach to trade-cum-plunder that caused a basic transformation in the world system that had developed and persisted over some five centuries."[13]

The conquest of the Americas was an important part of the rise in European dominance within the world trading system. In a famous passage from *Capital*, Marx wrote,

> The discovery of gold and silver in America, the extirpation, enslavement and entombment in mines of the aboriginal population, the beginnings of the conquest and plunder of the East Indies, the turning of Africa into a warren for the commercial hunting of blackskins, signalised the rosy dawn of the era of capitalist production. These idyllic proceedings are the chief momenta of primitive accumulation. On their heels treads the commercial war of European nations, with the globe for a theatre. . . . The different momenta of primitive accumulation distribute themselves now, more or less in chronological order, particularly over Spain, Portugal, Holland, France, and England. In England at the end of the 17th century, they arrive at a systematic combination, embracing the colonies, the national debt, the modern mode of taxation, and the protectionist system. These methods depend in part on brute force, *e.g.*, the colonial system. But they all employ the power of the State, the concentrated and organized force of society, to hasten, hothouse fashion, the process of transformation of the feudal mode of production into the capitalist mode, and to shorten the transition.[14]

In his book *The Making of New World Slavery*, Robin Blackburn argues that the money generated through the slave trade was an important part of the capital accumulation that allowed England to take off in its capitalist development. Marxist theorists have argued vociferously about the level of importance of slavery in the early development of capitalism.

In an influential article, "The Origins of Capitalist Development: A Critique of Neo-Smithian Marxism," published in 1977, Robert Brenner claims that it was mainly changes in the internal agricultural and political systems of England that led to the development of capitalism in England. For Brenner, the development of capitalism is primarily motivated by the development of means to improve the productivity of labor, such that an owner can make more profit from the same amount of labor time.

Marx believed that this increase in the productivity of labor was the genius of capitalism. It was what made capitalist forms of production more effective than those that had come before, and it was what led to the spread of capitalism and its ability to take over other methods of production.

While both Blackburn and Brenner use Marxist analyses, Brenner is more of a traditional Marxist, focusing on class struggle as the main motivator of historical change:

> The origins of capitalist economic development, as it first occurred in England, are to be found in the specific historical processes by which, on the one hand, serfdom was dissolved (thus precluding forceful squeezing as the normal form of surplus extraction) and, on the other, peasant property was taken or undermined (thus opening the way for the accumulation of land, labor, and the means of production). Clearly, this two-sided development is inexplicable as the result of ruling-class policy or ruling-class intention, but was the outcome of processes of class formation, rooted in class conflict.[15]

Blackburn argues that while it might have been possible for capitalism to develop in the way that Brenner says, the agricultural and political transformations that Brenner outlines were deeply impacted by the wealth coming into England through the slave trade. It was the money from these investments that allowed this class of individuals to rise to political and economic power in England.[16]

Capitalism and government

The vision of free individuals entering into voluntary contracts also makes invisible just how important the government and collective action are to the construction of a procapitalist way of viewing the world. Markets, like any other social form, need to be created. An economy dominated by capitalism is not simply one in which people are allowed to do as they please.

Capitalism requires a working banking system, a legal system including police, and military forces. It cannot develop without a tradition of buying and selling land, without roads, bridges, and a large number of people who have no choice but to sell their time for money. And there must be capital to be invested.[17]

In his novel *Devil on the Cross*, Kenyan author Ngugi Wa Thiong'o describes capitalism as a club of robbers and thieves. One friend explains to another,

> Believe me when I say that theft and robbery are the measure of a country's progress. Because in order for theft and robbery to flourish, there must be things to be stolen. And in order that the robbed may acquire possessions to be stolen and still be left with a few, they must work harder to produce wealth. History shows us that there has never been any civilization that was not built on the foundations of theft and robbery.[18]

In the early phase of capitalist development, budding entrepreneurs accumulate their capital through expropriation, often outside of or on the fringes of the law. The law itself is used to set up systems that favor the capitalist class. The expropriation of Native American territory is a good example. At a treaty council with the Shawnees and Cherokees in 1825, one US government representative, wanting them to move west of the Mississippi, stated, "The United States will never ask for your land there. This I promise you in the name of your great father, the President. That country he assigns to his red people, to be held by them and their children's children forever."[19] Yet soon after the treaty was signed, the US government began to push them off that land as well.

The government used brute force to coerce the indigenous peoples to sign treaties that would "legalize" the situation until the United States was interested in gaining more land. Then force would be used again, followed by another treaty. Thus, the treaties worked to stabilize the situation but were never meant to function as real agreements.

This process of land expropriation is still going on at a rapid pace today, and it should be seen as a part of the expansion of capitalist processes into ever-increasing areas of the world. As I write this, oil companies in Nigeria and in Colombia, to name just two examples, are in bitter fights with indigenous peoples over access to land. The indigenous people want to maintain rights to use the land they have considered theirs. Multinational oil companies, along with national governments and international financial agencies, go into these places and simply take the land, often justifying it on the grounds that they are improving it.

The companies buy and sell their oil on the free market, and they posit that they should be free to take the land and do as they please with it. But the freedom of the indigenous people to live the lives they want on their land and without environmental destruction doesn't enter the picture.

The process of taking what has traditionally been used in common and making it private is called enclosure. Marx had argued that this sort of brute taking was important for the origins of capitalism. Once capitalism got going, he argued, it proceeded mostly by the exploitation of labor. In recent years, anticapitalist theorists have focused on how a continued process of enclosure of the commons is a large part of capitalism.

Currently there are movements all over the world to protect the internet from privatization, to protect the public's assess to water, to keep electric utilities from being privatized. Transnational organizations are also fighting against the patenting of traditional crops and medicines, as what had been knowledge shared by a community comes to be owned as the private property of individual companies. David Harvey calls this enclosure "accumulation by dispossession" and argues that it remains a very significant part of how profits are made under capitalism.[20] Ken Saro-Wiwa was a leader of a movement among the Ogoni people of Nigeria that is trying to stop the oil companies from taking oil and leaving nothing but environmental destruction in their wake.[21] He was executed along with several other Ogoni leaders by the Nigerian government. The freedom to organize to advocate for the needs of his community was not one of the freedoms to be found at that leading edge of capitalist development.

Capitalist economy/capitalist society

If democracy means the rule of the people, then clearly Saro-Wiwa wasn't living in a democracy. Yet there is an amazing tendency in the modern world to talk about capitalism and democracy as if they always went together.

This link between capitalism and democracy can be seen in Locke and Smith. Their ideas of capitalism are built upon the image of small traders engaging in free exchanges, with no one telling anyone else what to do. Locke argued that this free trade was enhanced when there was a government that did nothing more than keep irrational people from disrupting people's ability to trade. Thus, for him, government should be minimal, and capital should be able to do what it wants. Because he was opposed to monarchy and the ways that monarchical control went along with traditional feudal economic relations, he supported the idea of political democracy.

One concept that is often used to make the bridge between capitalism and democracy is "free trade." Capitalism involves trade, and an increase in the volume and social importance of trade usually goes along with the development of capitalism. And somehow, we are told, the freer trade is, the freer society is. This ends up being translated in the contemporary world into the idea that when markets are free, people are free, and economic freedom is linked to democracy.

How this is all connected to democracy is a bit blurry. Capitalist class processes are, in fact, compatible with a variety of political forms. There are capitalist forms of appropriation taking place in the social democracies of northern Europe, in Castro's Cuba, in the People's Republic of China, and in the oil fields of Nigeria. If by democracy we mean a society in which the people rule, then it isn't clear that allowing the owners of the means of production to operate without constraints means that people are ruling their society. In fact, the opposite is often the case. One of the biggest limits on democracy in the United States is the influence of large donors on our elections.

Even though there is no *one* set of political institutions that go along with capitalism, capitalist class processes do end up having important implications for other aspects of how society as a whole is organized. In situations where the owners of the means of production have significant amounts of economic control, they end up being able to control the political, cultural, and legal systems. They use their influence in society to maintain this control at any cost. We see this in the way money influences the US political system. We also see it in the way the health care industry has fought to keep medicine run as a profit-making enterprise, the way the oil industry has dominated foreign policy, and the defense industry's advocacy for belligerent and machinery-using wars.

William Robinson uses the word "polyarchy" to describe the political system many of us live under in which a transnational ruling class has a huge amount of power to set the rules under which we live, while we have nominally democratic governments.[22]

Freedom for the market

Capitalist thinkers often point to the market as the core of capitalism. In a market, people are able to buy and sell from one another as they please. No one is under any obligation to anyone else. The interplay of buyers' and sellers' needs and desires determine what products are exchanged for what prices.

Adam Smith argues that one of the beauties of a market mechanism is that, over time, producers will make what people want to buy, and buyers will find what they are looking for, without any bureaucracy. Producers learn what buyers want, and those best able to give the buyers what they want will stay in business. No one is forcing anyone to do anything against his or her will—we are all in the marketplace voluntarily and the prices our goods get are the natural prices they deserve.

But the market is one aspect of a capitalist process. Equally important is the structure of relations of production. And those relations are not structured according to freedom and equality. If we look at capitalism from the point of view of production rather than consumption, we see that there is much less freedom. Laborers in an economy dominated by capitalism have one product that they can sell: their labor. If they are lucky, they can get an education that will improve the price that they will get for their labor, but unless they earn in surplus of their needs, they will never own the means of production. The owners of the means of production have far more power and control than do those who have nothing to sell but their labor.

The economic historian Karl Polanyi, writing in the early part of the twentieth century, argued that the development of capitalism wasn't so much about the freeing of markets as it was about the separation of the market out of the fabric of more complex networks of social relations. Polanyi was born to a middle-class family in Austria and raised in Hungary. He came to intellectual maturity within a group of radical intellectuals in Budapest. Working as a journalist and a tutor for his early life, he was offered a position at Columbia University in New York in 1947. He was never able to work at Columbia as a regular professor, though. His wife, who had been a radical activist involved in a failed revolution attempt in Hungary in the 1920s, was denied a visa to the United States. Polanyi wrote several important books and commuted from Canada to New York as a visiting professor for the rest of his career.

In his groundbreaking book *The Great Transformation*, Polanyi points out that in noncapitalist societies it doesn't even make sense to say that they have an economy.[23] There is no clear separation between political, economic, familial, and religious parts of life. In feudal or tribal societies, the things people do to meet their needs are wrapped up in webs of social relationships. There is not a separate part of life called "the economy."

Before the European conquest of the Americas, for example, the Iroquois had developed complex ways to resolve interpersonal conflict, political controversies, and questions such as how goods should be distributed and where and when to hunt. The aspects of these decisions that were economic were not separated out from the aspects that had to do with family relationships, political structures, or spiritual considerations.[24]

Polanyi argues that while most societies have had some sort of market, only when capitalist processes gain dominance does a market become something with a degree of autonomy from other social processes. While precapitalist societies engaged in some trade, Polanyi contends that what is distinctive about capitalism is that it is the first time in human history that there are markets in land and labor. For the first time, these things were sold to the highest bidder. Along with that transformation came the development of the idea of the economy as something having its own rules of operation, and the reality of people being dependent upon the economy for their survival.

With capitalism, we begin to talk about the economy as if it were a machine that must be treated in certain ways for it to be able to keep working. Other social goods become subordinated to "what's good for the economy." We become enslaved to *its* needs rather than seeing it as something we use for *our* needs. The freedom of the economy becomes more important than the freedom of those depending on the economy.

This transformation has huge implications for how life is lived under capitalism. In a society in which market forces predominate, culture becomes commodified. The logic of buying and selling becomes an important aspect of the culture in general. This means that, whereas in other societies people create things for the sheer pleasure of it or in order to gain social status or respect, in a society dominated by capitalism people make things to make money.

In the opening chapter of *Capital*, Marx argues that things can be valued according to their various uses for people, what he calls *use value*, or they can be valued according to the price people will pay for them, their *exchange value*. With capitalism, exchange value comes to predominate over use value; things are increasingly seen as commodities to be bought and sold.[25]

This means that it is difficult for us to relate to things in the complex and rich ways that they exist. In a society dominated by capitalist ways of experiencing the world there is plenty of creativity, but many artists develop their work with an eye to what will make it marketable. Those favoring capitalism say that this is positive, because it motivates people. Those critical of capitalism point out that market forces pressure artists to be noncontroversial, or controversial in very sensationalist ways. And it pressures artists to focus more on entertainment than on making us think or experience life in all its complexity.

Most of us end up seeing ourselves as consumers rather than producers of culture. Only those few people who are successful in producing culture for the market are seen as cultural producers. The rest of us use our creativity in the consumer choices we make. We shop for entertainment, we find our cultural niche by the kinds of products we buy, and we use our creativity to assemble the right collection of consumer goods.

As the economy comes to dominate human life and consumer relations become the core of much cultural production, we also come to believe that what is good for the economy is good for us. In a culture dominated by capitalist ways of understanding the world capitalist society, we are taught that our well-being is dependent on the health of the economy, and we are taught that for the economy to be strong we need to allow the sorts of things that are in the interest of the ruling class—or the owners of capital.

To a certain extent this ends up being true, in the sense that if the economy is strong, there are more jobs. With more jobs, each of us is more likely to have access to the material goods we need to survive. But this is a strange sort of truth. In his essay "Wage Labor and Capital" Marx writes,

> The interests of the capitalist and the worker are, therefore, *one and the same*, assert the bourgeois and their economists. Indeed! The worker perishes if capital does not employ him. Capital perishes if it does not exploit labor power, and in order to exploit it, it must buy it. . . . *To say that the interests of capital and those of the workers are one and the same is only to say that capital and labor are two sides of one and the same relation. The one conditions the other, just as the usurer and squanderer condition each other.* As long as the wage-worker is a wage-worker his lot depends upon capital.[26]

In an economy dominated by capitalist processes when the owners of the means of production are able to sell their goods and make profits, there are more jobs and they often pay better. This is why every Christmas we are told that we should be happy that consumers are buying lots of products: more consumption means more production, which means more jobs.

This, of course, leaves out the facts that consumerism is bad for the environment and that people might be happier if they celebrated in ways other than by purchasing things.

Marx argues that this so-called community of interests between capital and labor exists only to the narrow extent that jobs are available. It doesn't mean that capitalism, as a system, is a good way of life for the working class. It does mean that there is a sort of trap set up, whereby our short-term interests may not be the same as our long-term interests.

These sorts of different interests are often hidden under the idea that we should do what is "good for the economy." Professional economists are constantly telling us about whether the stock market is going up or down and how the Gross Domestic Product (GDP) is doing. All of these are taken as indicators of the health of the economy—as if the economy were an organism whose health were some simple and objective thing that all could agree on. Left out of the picture is the fact that many of the things that are good for business are not good for working people.

One interesting example of this is unemployment. If everyone is employed, then working people are in a better position to demand higher wages from their employers. Low levels of unemployment are good for the working class. But because a low unemployment rate creates an environment conducive to demands for higher wages, it can also cut into profit rates. Thus, we are often told that when unemployment is too low, it is "bad for the economy."

Similarly, economic growth is taken as one of the most important signs of a healthy economy. Yet when the Brazilian economy began to grow at an incredible rate in the 1980s, it was accompanied by an equally incredible growth of the number of people in poverty.

Another example is with environmental problems. A "strong economy" is often accompanied by more polluting factories, an increase in traffic, and an overall lowering of the quality of life. And, because adhering to environmental laws can cut into the profits of individual companies, the laws are supposed to be "bad for the economy."

This raises the question of whether or not there is a better way to analyze what is good for society than by looking at what's "good for the economy." What's the point of having a good economy if the quality of our lives is bad because we can't breathe?

The first important step is distinguishing what is good for people in society from what is in the interest of capital. The idea that we are all interested in a good economy hides the fact that there are many potentially conflicting definitions of a good economy.

The most widely used measure of economic health is the GDP, which measures the total value of goods and services exchanged in a national market in any given period of time. While this may be a good measure of the things that capital wants to get out of the economy, it is a terrible measure of the health of our economic relationships.

Feminists have pointed out that the GDP completely ignores nonmarket contributions to our well-being. So, for example, if I cook dinner for twenty people in a restaurant, I am being productive: I contribute to the GDP. If I cook the same meal for my friends or family, I am not contributing to the GDP, and therefore what I do does not count as economic activity. Productivity is defined in capitalist terms as that which generates profit. Ways of organizing our economic life that do not generate profit, because they are done outside the market or because they are done in ways that serve people's needs better, are considered less efficient and less productive. Even though people in society may feel better when they work fewer hours and do more things for themselves, such as cooking at home, taking care of their own children, and making rather than buying things, none of these activities shows up in the standard economic measures as productive.

In her book *If Women Counted*, Marilyn Waring, an Australian politician and activist, shows how distorted our view of society becomes when we use traditional capitalist accounting methods. We ignore much of the productive work done by women, we develop a bias in favor of market solutions to human needs, and we overvalue things that cause tremendous environmental harm. Waring points out that GDP doesn't differentiate between the economic value of societal goods, such as growing food, and societal bads, such as oil spills. GDP simply measures the quantity of market transactions. Along with many environmentalists, Waring has called for different systems of measurement of economic well-being.[27]

Nobel Prize–winning economist Amartya Sen makes a similar argument in his work on hunger. He points out that many societies with high GDPs have very low standards of living in their poorest communities. The United States is a prime example. Conversely, there are other societies that rely more heavily on nonmarket activities where there are low GDPs, but the quality of life is high. The example he uses the most often to illustrate this side of the equation is the state of Kerala in India.[28]

One alternative way to measure the health of the economy is the Genuine Progress Indicator (GPI). According to economists Jonathan Teller-Elsberg, James Heintz, and Nancy Folbre, rather than following the GDP and measuring only goods and services that have a price in the market, the GPI "adds the value of nonmarket activities such as household and volunteer work and subtracts the costs of pollution, resource depletion, and loss of leisure time."[29] They note, "While per capita GDP tripled between 1950 and 2002, GPI has been stagnating."[30] The states of Maryland and Vermont are now tracking GPI and it is helping them to reprioritize state budget decisions.

Capitalism and freedom

While capitalism is often associated with freedom, it actually puts serious limits on our freedom. Because the productive resources of society are owned privately, wealthy individuals can make the bulk of important social decisions for others. The rich can decide what kinds of things will be made and how they will be produced. They get to decide which geographic areas will be developed, which will be beautiful, and which will be turned into wastelands. They get to decide where there will be jobs and what kinds of jobs they will be.

If I work in a factory and the owners decide to move it overseas to be able to pay their workers less, I have little recourse. My job, and hence my means of obtaining a livelihood, do not belong to me, they belong to my boss. Similarly, how I work and what I do at my job are under the control of the owner. The Bill of Rights protects us in our relationship with the government. A place of work is a private institution, and it is largely at the whim of the owners to decide how we are to be treated. If the government wants to do a drug test on you, the Fourth Amendment to the Constitution says that the government must have probable cause to believe that you have committed a crime before it can test you. But your boss can investigate you just because he or she thinks it's a good idea. Similarly with the First Amendment: it doesn't apply in the workplace. Your boss can tell you that you can't wear political buttons at work, can tell you what to wear and not wear, and can tell you what to say and what not to say.

How your work is organized, what you are able to do at work, and what happens to the things you produce and the money gained in their exchange are all under the control of the owners of your company. One could argue that this is only fair, since the workplace is "theirs." While one can make an argument for that view, whether or not it is fair, it is still the case that while we are working for a wage we are not free. Thus, the freedom that we supposedly experience in a society dominated by capitalism is a peculiar sort of freedom. It includes the freedom to buy what we want, if we have the money; the freedom to try to become capitalist entrepreneurs, if we can; the freedom to buy and sell labor; and the freedom to do what we want with our property.

It does not, however, include the freedom to control our workplaces; free speech or freedom from unwarranted search and seizure at work; the freedom to have time to do whatever we want outside the market; the freedom to have a home to rent without fear of eviction; the freedom to decide how we want society to be organized.

CHAPTER 3

Capitalism and Class

ON SEPTEMBER 17, 2011, A SMALL GROUP OF PROTESTERS CONVERGED ON Zuccotti Park in Manhattan to "Occupy Wall Street." They were responding to call that went viral on the internet to converge on the park and stay there. Those who showed up that day began to set up systems of organization, and they sparked a movement around the country and then around the world. The movement was important for breaking the silence in the United States about the severity of inequality that had developed over the previous decades. The main slogan of the movement was "We are the 99 percent." The overwhelming response to the protests was generated by a widespread sense of outrage at the ways the US economy had almost imploded as banks and insurance companies became insolvent following a bubble in the mortgage market.

Those protests opened the door in the United States to being able to talk about class inequality in ways that had for years been considered unacceptable in mainstream society. As if coming out of a dream, people in the United States began to realize that as the middle class was disappearing, and poverty was increasing, a very small group at the top was richer than ever.

In the United States it's fairly common for a student to have several jobs while going to school full-time. More than forty million people in the United States owe a total of more than a trillion dollars in student debt.[1] Many people with children are out working at a job when they wish they were home with their families. At the same time, the difference is increasing between the wealth of the very rich and the rest of us. As of 2006, the richest 1 percent own 40 percent of all the wealth in the country, and the bottom 80 percent own 9 percent. Having a job isn't enough to guarantee a decent life—44 percent of homeless people have a job.[2] As the number of service sector jobs grows, more and more people work in boring, poorly paid jobs with no hope of escape. Yet in television and movies we are represented as a country of well-fed, well-dressed people, concerned about relationships and crime, but never about how to pay the rent or get childcare. What we see is a nation without economic problems, without classes.

Dominant ideas about freedom reinforce the idea of classlessness. The poor are seen as people who don't work hard enough, who don't have the discipline to run their lives well, or whose lives are hard because they use drugs. In addition to the everyday hardships of poverty, the poor in the United States must deal with the humiliation that goes along with other people's view that they have brought their problems upon themselves. And many poor people have internalized this negative view and blame themselves for their plight.

The idea that there are social forces pushing people into poverty and keeping them there, while keeping others wealthy remains foreign to many people in the United States.

What does class mean?

Typically, when people in the United States talk about class, they mean different levels of income. They talk about upper middle class, lower class, etc. Analysts of capitalism have found it more useful to use a definition of class that instead refers to a person's position in the system of production. Someone who owns productive resources (factories, businesses, capital for investment, land for farming, etc.) is a member of the owning class, also called the capitalist class, or the ruling class. People who don't own productive resources, and so must sell their time and abilities for a wage, are called the working class.

Many people in contemporary US society are not members of either of these two primary classes, yet they play important roles in capitalism. The unemployed and the very poor, for example, serve as a "reserve army" of labor. When there are many people out of work, those with jobs know that if they demand too much, it will be easy for the boss to fire and replace them.

Another large group is the professional class, to which managers, teachers, and doctors all belong. While these people have much more control over their working conditions than do nonprofessionals, their autonomy and political power is limited. For example, the fact that a large percentage of health care professionals dislike managed care has not yet led to the end of corporate control of health care decision-making.

Marx argued that productive relations are more revealing of the real structure of social relationships than are income levels. Income levels have a lot to do with our lifestyle and the types of things we consume, but they don't say as much about our place in the economic and political structure of society.

Besides there being many different classes, there are also many different systems of class exploitation existing at the same time in any given society. Alongside the capitalist aspects of the US economy, some feudal, communist, socialist, and patriarchal class processes intertwine in complex ways. Worker-owned cooperatives, run according to communist class principles of shared profits, exist alongside public schools in which the government allocates social wealth in socialistic ways, and alongside patriarchal families in which women are exploited in terms of household labor.[3] Rather than characterizing our society as capitalist; it is more helpful to say that some aspects of our economy are.

Class struggle

When we look at people's relations to the means of production in a society that has a large amount of capitalist activity we see that most people must work for a wage. When people work, they trade their time and capabilities for money. The owners of the means of production get to set the terms of the relationship and decide what we will do during our working hours. But they don't completely control the situation. In a class-divided society, members of different classes often act in ways that advance the interests of their class.

Marx called that process *class struggle*. He argued that class struggle happens constantly as members of each class jockey to improve its situation. Eventually, he thought, class struggle would get elevated to the level of a revolution in which workers would finally achieve what is ultimately in their highest interest: the abolition of the capitalist system. It seems more productive to think of challenging capitalism as something that we can do all the time in a variety of ways. And one of those ways is class struggle.

In the class struggle that takes place every day, members of the owning class try to get as much profit as they can by controlling labor processes and by cutting back on overhead costs such as health care. They also engage in struggle with society as a whole to improve their situation. Corporations fight for lower taxes; for the government to pay for the infrastructure they need, such as roads; and for the government to discipline the workforce, for example, by making unionization difficult.

Members of the working class will also often work to improve their situation as a class through trying to get higher wages and better working conditions, and by trying to get their governments to provide for social needs.

Labor parties, socialist parties, and unions in much of the world worked hard throughout the twentieth century to win guarantees from the state for basic protections such as health care for all, livable minimum wages, and time off to take care of children. And whenever members of the ruling class fought to take away those protections, the working class fought hard to protect them, often with massive multi-union strikes.

Huge gains were made by the working class in the United States over the course of the twentieth century, largely through the mechanism of labor unions. US working people have often joined forces to gain better conditions. Yet because the working class in the United States is deeply divided along racial lines, and because many of its members believe so strongly in the ideology of freedom, its gains in the class struggle have not been as strong as they could be in the future.

Lack of class mobility

Belief in class mobility is one of the core ideas that keep US working people from engaging in struggle for their class. Many people believe that if they work hard enough they can become wealthy, as can anyone in the United States.

If those of us who are in the working class can move out if we try, then there's no need to improve things for the class as a whole. Our goals become focused instead on improving our own individual situations.

The reality is that most people in the United States work for a wage. While some people do change classes, class situation is largely inherited. The very wealthy pass on their wealth to their children, the professional middle classes pass on education and cultural resources that allow their children to maintain a professional middle-class position. Children of the poor generally go to poorly funded schools, have no resources to start businesses, and don't have the cultural training to easily become members of the professional middle class.

The owning class

For Marx, the basic structure of a capitalist society could be understood as the conflict between the owning class and the working class. The owners, through their ability to control the social resources needed for survival, are in a position of dominance in their relationship with members of the working class. According to Harry Braverman in *Labor and Monopoly Capital*, the owners reap profits when they control the work process in such a way as to get high levels of productivity from the workers.

> Labor, like all life processes and bodily functions, is an inalienable property of the human individual. Muscle and brain cannot be separated from persons possessing them; one cannot endow another with one's own capacity for work, no matter at what price, any more than one can eat, sleep, or perform sex acts for another. Thus, in the exchange, the worker does not surrender to the capitalist his or her capacity for work. The worker retains it, and the capitalist can take advantage of the bargain only by setting the worker to work. It is of course understood that the useful effects or products of labor belong to the capitalist. But what the worker sells, and what the capitalist buys, is *not an agreed amount of labor, but the power to labor over an agreed period of time*.[4]

Thus, it is in the interest of the owners to do what they can to ensure that the workers perform their labor as productively as possible. This often involves the development of time-saving machinery, the development of more efficient ways of doing things, and struggles to get the workers to work harder for the same amount of pay.

In businesses such as fast-food operations, owners profit by having the production process so efficiently organized that practically every move of the worker is planned by engineers. Because little training is required, workers are easily fit into the process and easily replaced if they become less than optimally productive. Generally, in the absence of strong unions, unskilled work means low wages. In higher wage employment, employers profit from the training that goes into the worker, and employers work to make sure people stay on the job and that their skills are put to use. Managers work to make sure each person is working to his or her potential. And managers who don't perform that function usually don't last long on the job.

All this regimentation and specialization makes capitalism an incredible engine for the development of ever more sophisticated ways of producing things. There is profit to be made in developing new machines that automate assembly lines. There is profit to be made in reducing the number of steps from cash register to milkshake machine. And there is profit to be made in prefabricating building trusses. Businesses in an economy with a large capitalist sector are in constant competition with one another, and any business that isn't able to return a reasonable profit loses out in the competition with other businesses.

Members of the working class must also compete in the labor market to survive. If they want to create a situation of security for themselves and their family members, they are coerced to participate in capitalist processes. Linking up in a union allows workers to resist excessive coercion by collectively demanding better conditions. But generally, in an economy that has a large amount of capitalist activity, those who do not own enough resources to employ others have little choice but to sell their labor for a wage and compete with other workers for better jobs.

As a class, owners will tend to bond together to protect their interests. They will use their power to get the state, the media, and the educational system to function in ways that get them what they want. Edwards, Reich, and Weisskopf write in their book *The Capitalist System*,

> The super-rich capitalists associated with the giant corporations constitute the most privileged and politically powerful part of the capitalist class. Through their control of large corporations, they command vast economic, political, legal, and ideological

resources. Since they have the most far-flung interests, they are the most likely to perceive the needs of capitalism as a system and to act upon that perception.[5]

While these super-rich capitalists are in competition with one another, most of them also can see the big picture of their common interests. Paul Sweezy, one of the founders of *Monthly Review*, a Marxist theoretical journal, writes,

> capitalists can and do fight among themselves to further individual or group interests, and they differ over the best way of coping with the problems which arise from their class position; but overshadowing all these divisions is their common interest in preserving and strengthening a system which guarantees their wealth and privileges.[6]

In recent years it has become clear that to really understand the owning class it is best to see it as a transnational force. Sociologist William Robinson describes the way that members of the owning class work to create transnational structures that serve their interests. Some of the most important of those organizations are the International Monetary Fund (IMF) and World Bank (WB). Both were set up by dominant Western powers at the end of World War II, and are largely dominated by the United States and the European Union (EU), a governing body of the countries of Europe that has taken away much of the sovereignty of people in European countries. There is also the World Economic Forum, a club of the World Trade Organization (WTO):

> Global corporate executives, for instance, manage their European capital operations through EU administrative structures, plan investments in North America through the NAFTA, consult with the IMF and WB on Latin American macroeconomic performance as regards their South American activities, coordinate their Asian plans with the Asian Development Bank over infrastructural needs, and so on. These same executives share their worldwide experience and strategies at the annual meetings of the WEF in Davos, Switzerland, over what proposals to bring to the WTO or

the UN, just as IMF and WB officials, central bankers, and private transnational bankers might mingle together each year at the annual IMF and WB meetings in Washington, D.C., to discuss global finances and draw up policy. As transnational capitalists move about the world, their practices integrate these diverse supranational forums into a coherent network.[6]

The owning class works together when needed and across national boundaries to build a framework to make profit making go as well as it can for them. And one of the most powerful tools they have at their disposal is the willingness of governments to enact policies that suit their interests.

One of the most important ways they are able set a structure that allows for maximal profit making in the United States is through its influence over elections. When the Supreme Court decided in 2010 in the *Citizens United* case that campaign finance laws were an inappropriate limit on the free speech of corporations, legally defined as "persons," it opened up our political system to unprecedented levels of spending in elections. Total election spending in 2012 in the United States was $6.3 billion. That's more than double the amount that was spent in 2000.[7] In the United States, individual business people and business-related political action committees (PACs) contributed $1 billion, while labor unions contributed 160 million to political campaigns in 2004.[8] With these figures, it is easy to see why politicians rarely pass legislation that is in the interest of the working class and not in the interest of business.

The US government can be seen as a site of contestation, where working-class people sometimes win struggles and have government policies reflect their interests, and where ruling-class interests sometime win. Throughout the later part of the twentieth century there was much progress in reigning in campaign spending to make the voices of working-class people stronger. When the Supreme Court decided *Citizens United v. Federal Election Commission*, all those years of work were dramatically rolled back. The organization Move to Amend is working to get a constitutional amendment to declare that corporations are not people, and therefore do not have free speech rights.

Besides using the political system to support their class interests, the members of the owning class also use the legal system. In the history of US law, we can see a perpetual struggle over the relationship of the legal system to the class formation. According to Howard Zinn in *A People's History of the United States*,

> The Constitution . . . illustrates the complexity of the American system: that it serves the interests of a wealthy elite, but it also does enough for small property owners, for middle-income mechanics and farmers, to build a broad base of support. The slightly prosperous people who make up this base of support are buffers against the blacks, the Indians, the very poor whites. They enable the elite to keep control with a minimum of coercion, a maximum of law—all made palatable by the fanfare of patriotism and unity.[9]

The legal system largely works to protect the interests of the wealthy. But if it only did this, it would lose its legitimacy. Thus, in practice, it ends up being a site of contestation—a place where people with different interests make demands. Sometimes US labor unions are able to pressure the government to pass laws that protect the safety of people on the job; unfortunately, the ruling class often weakens these laws either as they are implemented or through repeal.

Class and race formations of US capitalism

US history textbooks tend to focus on the story of the Pilgrims and other Europeans who were fleeing persecution. These stories leave the impression that democracy and religious freedom were the founding principles of the United States. If we look more closely at origins of the colonies, we get a very different picture.

The major impulse that drove people from Europe to the Americas in those early years was profit-making. The original purpose of Columbus's first voyage was trade with Asia; once it was realized that that plan wasn't going to work, the next voyages were undertaken to find gold and then to set up colonial, slave-based plantations.

Columbus's voyages were sponsored by the Spanish monarchy as business ventures, much the same as hundreds of other mercantilist projects launched in that period. Columbus set sail at the time of the beginnings of capitalism. Indeed, if we accept Abu-Lughod's interpretation of the rise of capitalism, Columbus's voyages and the integration of the Americas and the African slave trade were critical chapters in the story of Europe's rise to power and of the development of capitalism.

In a powerful and provocative essay called "Columbus and the Origins of Racism in the Americas," Guyanese novelist Jan Carew writes,

> With Columbus' journey to the Americas, the new ethic evolved into full flower. The ideology of the church with its theoretical postulate that all true believers were equal in the sight of God (and this included the new convert as well as the person born into the faith) gave way to the ideology of capitalism which turned human beings, particularly those whose labor was in demand in the newly discovered lands, into commodities, chattels and so many faceless ciphers in a juggernaut of production and profit. Usury, a practice excoriated by the medieval church for centuries, was transformed, expanded, and legitimized, as feudalism, wilting at its roots, lost ground to an ineluctable and predatory capitalism. This new and seemingly invincible system was sustained by a hitherto unsurpassed greed for gold and a passion for discovery, empire building, slavery, and profit making.[10]

The first nonnatives to permanently settle in what is now the United States were "African slaves left in South Carolina in 1526 by Spaniards who abandoned a settlement attempt."[11] Before the Pilgrims landed at Plymouth Rock, the Spanish had settled a third of what we now know as the United States.

The Europeans who colonized the northeastern part of the United States also were engaged mostly in business ventures. Few of the settlements were driven by flight from religious persecution. The London Company and the Plymouth Company were joint-stock ventures that sent settlers to colonize the United States in order to engage in businesses such as logging and trade.[12]

Capitalism has been entwined with issues of race from its very beginnings, but more so in the Americas than in Europe. In England, as capitalism was developing, the working class was almost all white. People of color who were a part of the English economic system lived in faraway colonies. In contrast, as capitalism developed in more racially diverse North America, work and social life were organized along racial lines. Racial formation is such a dominant part of the US historical experience that we often see ourselves more as members of racial groups than as having any class position, a consciousness that often seems strange to Europeans.

In order to have a clear understanding of how class operates in the United States, it is helpful to understand the ways that members of different racial groups have different historical experiences of the workings of capitalism.

African Americans first entered the US economic order as enslaved people. This meant that, while they were doing the work that produced the much of the wealth that the nation's economy was founded on. Their work was not based on wage labor.

Once slavery was abolished, many African Americans found themselves in a situation similar to that of slavery. In much of the South, slavery was replaced with sharecropping. In that system, those who worked the land were paid a share of what they had grown; the rest went to the landlords. If the crop was bad, the farm worker ended up going into debt, needing to pay the landowner for seed, fertilizer, and supplies. This system ended up maintaining many of the economic aspects of slavery long into the twentieth century. Many African American women also worked in the households of landowners or professionals, in forms of domestic labor that combined elements of feudal and patriarchal relations along with capitalist ones.

Barriers to equal participation in the system of capitalist labor still exist for African Americans. Labor unions largely excluded them until the 1930s. White Americans came to see African Americans as not really legitimate workers in the wage system. They have continued to be pushed to the margins of the economic system, often still working in low-wage service jobs. The methods of exclusion have been legion and continue to this day.

While African Americans became integrated into the economy of the United States as a super-highly exploited group, Native Americans have generally been pushed out of the economic order altogether. When the colonists first arrived in North America, they often worked closely with indigenous peoples in order to learn how to survive in this new and strange land. After that first period of learning was over, the mistreatment intensified. While Spanish colonists succeeded in enslaving indigenous people in Central and South America, the Caribbean, and in the US Southwest, the English colonists chose extermination and expulsion as their preferred method of expropriating indigenous resources.

At various times, the US government has tried the strategy of forced assimilation for Native Americans. Much of the rhetoric of the ruling class in the first centuries of colonization claimed that indigenous peoples were backward and that their lives would be improved if they could be trained to embrace Christian beliefs and European habits. Rhetoric aside, assimilation campaigns worked exactly as intended by colonial leaders, breaking down the communal structures that had kept communities together and making expulsion of tribes from their land easier for the colonists to accomplish.

The process of coerced assimilation often focused on indigenous women. In most indigenous societies, women did hard agricultural labor and were important parts of the social decision-making processes. One of the tasks the Europeans set for themselves in conquering the Native Americans was to transform their gendered divisions of labor.

In an essay titled "Distinctions in Western Women's Experience: Ethnicity, Class, and Social Change," historian Rosalinda Méndez González writes that leaders of colonist expansion

> recognized that to break down Indian resistance it was necessary to undermine the tribal and clan social organization of the Indians and to enforce upon them the individual nuclear family, with the husband the authority figure over the women and children. This attempt had the multiple purposes of forcing the Indians to alienate their communal tribal lands, breaking their economic and social clan organization, transforming them into individualist and competitive capitalist farmers, and providing the nuclear family institution through which the ideology of private property, individualism and dominant-subordinate relations could be passed on.[13]

Once land was held by private individuals, those individuals could be coerced through violence, starvation, or bribery to give up their land.

Some indigenous groups, such as the Cherokees, did adapt and develop social forms that were hybrids of European and indigenous ways. For a while, the Cherokees thrived and it looked as if some form of coexistence for groups that bent to European ways might be possible. The cruel lesson from this experience was that as soon as colonists were interested in the land occupied by Cherokees, assimilated or not, they were forced to leave it. And the assimilation process made this easier.

While Native Americans today populate every class and economic strata, indigenous culture and many Native Americans continue to exist largely outside the dominant class system. Life on the reservation is based on a combination of traditional communal tribal economic relations and, where the land is so poor or the social relations so destroyed as not to allow subsistence lifestyles to thrive, dependence on government subsidies. While many nonindigenous people today see as tragic what has been done to indigenous Americans, they also believe that the destruction of indigenous cultures was inevitable, that Native American traditions are incompatible with modern life and will eventually disappear. And yet, while the position of Native Americans in the economic structure remains extremely marginal, there is a dramatic resurgence of Native American culture going on.

There is incredible work going on to reclaim lands, to protect languages and cultural traditions, and to develop economic resources that will lift people out of poverty.[14] In addition to traditional economic activities, many tribes have used their semisovereign status to create commercial gambling businesses, which have generated resources needed to run autonomous cultural, educational, and economic systems. With the development of the casino economy, a new hybrid system seems to be emerging, with the tribal governments collectively owning economic resources that are administered in traditional capitalist ways, exploiting the wage labor of those who work in them.

Asians and Latinos have been largely concentrated at the lower end of the working class for much of US history. Interestingly, when the United States annexed half of Mexico in 1848, members of the Mexican ruling class came along with the poor and the Native Americans. Some of them were absorbed into the US owning class, but most had their land expropriated through complex legal maneuvers. This part of our history is largely ignored, and all Latinos are often assumed to be foreigners and recent immigrants.

Many of the Asians and Latinos who came to the United States in the nineteenth century came as single men working in jobs highly segregated by race and gender. Women from these groups were generally not allowed to immigrate. When the work was completed, the men were expected to leave.

The image of these ethnicities as outsiders has persisted, and it remains one of the core racist concepts used against them. They are often seen as not belonging, and as disloyal to the country.

The role of these groups as outsiders and not as full members of the capitalist economic order was developed in the nineteenth century in ways that helped consolidate whites into a coherent racial group. According to Tomás Almaguer, at that time the ideology of "free labor" unified the interests of whites of different classes: "White Americans of all classes—the European American working class, petite bourgeoisie, and self-employed propertied class—accepted the social world this ideology promoted: an expanding capitalist society based on free labor, individualism, market relations, and private property."[15] "Free labor" was free in the sense that workers were neither enslaved nor indentured; at least hypothetically they could bargain with owners for the terms of their employment. And while it wasn't really free, workers were led to believe that they were free under it.

This racist labor division was the foundation of US capitalist class relations. And while it exploited the white working class, it provided whites a sense of dignity and superiority in comparison to people of color who were forced to participate in feudal and slave-based economic systems. While many Latinos and Asians were petit-bourgeois shopkeepers, traders, and independent miners, in the popular consciousness they were still associated with semi-feudal farm labor and the slave-like conditions of contract labor.

> There emerged during this period a strong symbolic association between different minority groups, on the one hand, and various precapitalist economic formations on the other. White antipathy toward Mexicans, Native Americans, and Chinese and Japanese immigrants was typically couched within the rubric of this "free white labor"/"unfree nonwhite labor" dichotomy: Mexicans became inimically associated with the "unproductive," semi-feudal rancho economy that European Americans rapidly undermined after [California's] statehood; Indians with a "primitive" communal mode of existence that white settlers ruthlessly eradicated through violence and forced segregation; and Asian immigrants with a "degraded" unfree labor systems unfairly competing with and fettering white labor.[16]

Blacks were associated with slavery and with the virtual slavery of sharecropping.

The hostility of the white working class toward inclusion of people of color in their organizations—and in their sense of solidarity as a working class—helped to keep these racist "precapitalist" systems of labor in existence. When the Social Security Act was passed as part of New Deal legislation in 1935, it specifically excluded farm labor from its protections.[17] Farm labor was instead regulated under the Farm Labor Standards Act, which was much weaker. This separation continues in some forms to the present day and partially accounts for horrendous working and living conditions for farm laborers, most of whom are people of color. The legal standards for working hours, health, and safety in farm labor are all much lower than for the rest of the working class.

White racial unity and the lack of class consciousness

Racist ideology, promoted by socially conservative and procapitalist groups, leaves many whites believing that they are more deserving of the benefits of society than people of color, and that people of color are given social benefits that come out of the pockets of whites. These beliefs lead to a white unity that tends to blunt the edge of class divisions.

The mid-nineteenth century—when there were large immigrations from Europe and the nonwhite population expanded with the annexation of the Western states and Asian immigration—was also a time of expansion and consolidation of the concept of the white race. The concept of the white race expanded to include immigrant groups, such as the Irish, Germans, Jews, and Slavic people, who had previously been excluded from the definition of white. Before that time, each of those groups had been discriminated against by the dominant English and Protestant groups. Conflict with Mexico, and to some extent the rise of Chinese immigration, made it possible in the 1840s and 1850s for leading Democrats to develop racial schemes that gathered all European settlers together as whites against the "colored" races.

The idea of white unity also helped bridge the differences between whites of different classes. This consolidation of the white race has had very important implications for the development of the class structure of the contemporary United States. There has been some degree of unity among people who see themselves as white, and this unity crosses class lines. This racial unity among whites has ended up helping the ruling class keep many white people loyal to the capitalist system as privileged workers within it.

Historically, many social justice advocates have argued that attention to race divides the working class. They claim that the most important conflict in a capitalist society is between the owners of the means of production and the workers. They argue that the path to class liberation is unity, and unity is achieved by focusing on what working people from different races have in common.

Eugene Debs was the very successful leader of the Socialist Party toward the end of the nineteenth century. He was imprisoned for speaking out against US involvement in World War I and received almost a million votes when he campaigned from his prison cell to be elected US president. In discussions of race, Debs shared the view of many social justice advocates of his time.[18] He argued that attention to race was unnecessary: "We have simply to open the eyes of as many Negroes as we can and do battle for emancipation from wage slavery, and when the working class have triumphed in the class struggle and stand forth economic as well as political free men, the race problem will disappear."[19]

Others have attempted to build class unity between the races by teaching whites about the ways that racism is bad for the white working class. Keeping African Americans out of unions, for example, meant that blacks were available to be used as strikebreakers. Their exclusion kept them from feeling solidarity with the striking workers. This lack of multiracial unity leads to an inability of the working class to advocate for its interests as a whole.

In 1948, black communist organizer Harry Haywood wrote,

> It is not accidental that where the Negroes are most oppressed, the position of whites is also most degraded. . . . "Keeping the Negro down" spells for the entire South the nation's lowest wage and living standards. . . . Sharecropping has drawn into its orbit tens of thousands of white workers. . . . Political controls which are aimed primarily at the disenfranchisement of the Negro have also resulted in depriving the mass of the poor whites of their right to a ballot.[20]

There are many ways racism keeps the white working class from acting in ways that are in the interest of the working class as a whole. Politicians are able to mobilize white workers' resentments against "undeserving poor people who sponge off the system." In 1996, then president Bill Clinton set out to get rid of the system of support that existed at that time for giving small payments to mothers to support their children, generally called "welfare." One of the main strategies his supporters used was to promote the image of the undeserving welfare cheat. In popular consciousness, this person was typically a black female, even though the majority of people on welfare at that time were white. Antiblack racism was mobilized in ways that hurt poor whites as well as poor people of color.

Similarly, racism has been used to mobilize resentments against undocumented immigrants in ways that hurt the working class. Arguing that US citizen workers have a "right to jobs" and undocumented people don't, the government uses these distinctions to crack down on undocumented people when they attempt to unionize and count on racist resentments to prevent white workers from coming to the aid of immigrants. Yet the presence of large numbers of nonunionized workers in any given industry drives down wages, hurting all people in those sectors, no matter what their race or nationality.

When US automakers were beginning to develop their global approach to manufacturing, anti-Asian racism developed among white, African American, and Latino workers. The mainstream media deflected blame for the loss of jobs from the actions of the US-based manufacturers and focused on the rise of Asian manufacturers. A violent wave of anti-Asian hysteria hit the country, and little attention was paid to the failure of the US manufacturers to anticipate North Americans' desire for smaller, more fuel-efficient cars. In the midst of this hysteria, Vincent Chin was murdered in Detroit in 1982 by two white men angered at the loss of jobs in the US car industry.

While not challenging the claim that racism divides the working class, the white historian David Roediger adds a twist to this analysis. In his book *The Wages of Whiteness*, Roediger asks: If racism has no positive benefits for the white working class, why is it so persistent? He points out that while whites may lose in some basic economic ways, they also gain. There is a social wage paid to white workers for their whiteness.

As a case study, Roediger traces the history of the Irish in the United States as they moved from being considered members of an inferior race to being included as white. As this transformation took place, their social status and access to political power increased dramatically. Roediger argues that the white working class has historically used its position of power to keep ahead of people of color. He argues that working people in the United States must take racism very seriously and uproot it from their consciousness, for it is only through concerted efforts at antiracism among whites that a real unity can develop among members of the working class.

Gender and class

While people of different races are woven into the class formation in different ways, each of those racial groups also includes gender differences. Women and men are positioned differently in the class formation. The main forms of gender difference that are built into the US class formation have their roots in the gender ideology that the dominant European groups brought with them to the Americas. Men were to be in business and government, and women were to be the wardens of the home. While the early white settlers in the northeastern part of the United States lived in societies where women and men worked together without a distinct separation of spheres, according to Jeanne Boydston, the roots of a gendered separation between public and private came with the colonists from England.

> A largely subsistence oriented people, the New England Puritans defined the household as "the economical society" and understood that family survival required the wife's work. In the garden, the barnyard, and the larder as much as it required the husband's work in the fields and meadows and barn. . . . At the same time, colonial society contained the ideological foundations for later denial of the economic worth of wives' labor. As ministers reminded women, husbands—not wives—were the public representatives of the household. . . . Wives' subordination was embedded in the English common law that the Puritans brought with them to New England. As *femme covert* a wife's legal identity was subsumed under that of her husband, who was recognized as the owner of her labor-time.[21]

As the industrial economy developed, men's labor increasingly subsumed women's and made it invisible. In working-class families, men worked for a wage in capitalist enterprises. Women of all races often did too, but they also did much work that was unpaid. Boydston argues that women contributed as much as men to the economic survival of working-class families of the nineteenth century. We can only see their full contribution when we take into account not only their wage labor, but also their unpaid efforts such as childrearing, housework, gardening, nursing the old and sick, scavenging, bargaining, and bartering with neighbors.

Boydston argues that this invisibility of women's work was to the advantage of the industrial employers. Marx had noted that a worker needs to be paid at least the amount it takes to keep him or her alive. Boydston expands on this by pointing out that if a wage earner is living off of the unpaid labor of a wife, the owner benefits along with the husband in the exploitation of her labor.[22]

Along with capitalist forms of appropriation, there has existed a patriarchal form of appropriation. We will look at this in depth in Chapter 6. For now it is worth mentioning that much of the important work that women of all races have done traditionally has been done in the household. Even when they have worked in wage labor, women have done a vastly disproportionate amount of household labor. The concepts we use to analyze economic activity have been developed with capitalist production in mind and largely do not account for the productive activity that takes place in households. Thus, the work done to take care of people's basic personal, emotional, and childcare needs is largely economically invisible.

Domestic labor is not considered real work when it is not paid. When it is paid, as with much of the work that has traditionally been done by women of color working as laundry women, nannies, housekeepers, and cooks, it often takes place at the margins of capitalist labor. Paid domestic work rarely ends up being counted in the official economy as productive labor.

As part of the New Deal that President Roosevelt brokered to get the country out of the Great Depression of the 1930s, a whole set of protections for workers was put into place. White southerners were worried that having those protections apply to domestic workers and farm laborers would be very disruptive to the deeply exploitative labor relation that existed in the South at that time. As a result they fought hard, and Congress came up with a compromise that allowed for protection of many forms of labor, but excluded domestic and farm labor. To this day, farm labor and domestic labor are not covered by the same set of laws as other form of labor. Ira

Katznelson's book on that history, *When Affirmative Action Was White*, shows how this and other New Deal policies has specific and intentional racial implications that helped lead to the development of a white middle class, while keeping people of color in poverty.[23]

As a result this "informal" labor is thus done without the basic protections that have come to be associated with capitalist labor relations in the United States, such as health and safety standards, laws on overtime, paid time off, etc.

As capitalist industrialization developed, the idealized role for a white woman was that of homemaker. She was supposed to provide for the personal maintenance of the worker and the reproduction of the working class. Marxist feminists have argued that in the dominant ideology of capitalism, the man is responsible for production, while the woman is responsible for reproduction—reproducing the workforce.

The trade union movement in the twentieth century fought hard for the ability of male workers to support their wives and children at home. They demanded a "family wage," meaning a wage large enough to support a whole family. For much of that century, the idea that a worker's wages were supposed to be enough to support a family was an assumption built into most union contracts.

Beginning in the 1970s, demands for a family wage became harder to win. As real wages (that is, wages adjusted for inflation) began to go down dramatically, fewer families were able to maintain their former standard of living on one income.

Modern capitalist societies are based upon the norm of the heterosexual nuclear family. Nuclear families are more compatible with capitalism than are extended family structures. As opportunities for work move geographically, nuclear families can uproot and settle down someplace else far more easily and quickly than can extended families. The idealization of the romantic heterosexual couple is a part of the social glue that holds this family structure together.

In reality, the ideal of the heterosexual nuclear family with a female at home accurately reflects only wealthier whites. Relatively few white working-class men have been able to "provide for their families" in this way; likewise, since men of color have systematically been denied work that paid a family wage, only a small percentage of women of color have the luxury of being stay-at-home wives and mothers. The connection between women and the household has meant that women have been excluded or marginalized from the better paying forms of capitalist labor. Jobs that have traditionally been women's jobs typically pay less than traditionally male fields, and when women work in the same jobs as men, they are often paid less.

As people work increasingly long hours in the United States, many middle-class families and the wealthy hire more people to take care of the needs of the home. In the book *Global Woman: Nannies, Maids, and Sex Workers in the New Economy*, Barbara Ehrenreich and Arlie Russell Hochschild argue that there is an increasing global shortage for care, as women from the poorer countries of the Global South migrate to the Global North, and end up taking care of the children, elderly, and homes of people in the Global North. Women in those countries, who stay, then often have the children and elderly of those who migrate to care for.[24]

Trade unions

The struggles over racism among sectors of the working class and the complex positions of women in a capitalist economic structure raise challenges for organizing among the working class. One of the main organizing strategies that members of the working class have used to challenge capitalism is the trade union. In Chapter 4, we will look at other ways of challenging capitalism. For now, we will look at the complex and often contradictory roles played by unions.

As the industrial capitalist economy developed, so did trade unions. Early trade unions were modeled after the craft guilds of the Middle Ages in Europe. In these, skilled workers controlled the conditions of their labor, trained new members of the guild, and restricted entry into the guild. The early unions were organized by "craft" rather than by workplace. Craft unions attempted to protect the benefits that come from having specialized skills. These craft unions usually worked to improve the conditions of a "labor aristocracy" made up of skilled white men, and to protect their members' jobs and status from the rest of the working class. A more progressive tendency also developed that attempted to unify the working class, including people of all races, immigrants, women, and the unskilled.

Trade unions have sometimes been organized with the specific goal of challenging the existence of capitalism. At other times in history, they have been used to tame the working class and make it easier for capital to extract a profit without too much strife.

Around the turn of the last century, one in fourteen workers was in a union and 80 percent of those workers were in unions affiliated with the American Federation of Labor (AFL).[25] According to Howard Zinn, "The AFL was an exclusive union—almost all male, almost all white, almost all skilled workers. Although the number of women workers kept growing—it doubled from 4 million in 1890 to 8 million in 1910, and women were one-fifth of the labor force—only one in a hundred belonged to a union."[26]

One way to understand the strategy of the AFL was that it was trying to match the monopoly that owners had over the means of production with a monopoly on labor.[27] By being exclusive, the unions could keep wage levels high for an elite group of workers. This strategy of the AFL was challenged beginning in 1905 by the more radical approach of the Industrial Workers of the World (IWW, also called Wobblies). The original founders of the IWW were anarchists, socialists, and radical trade unionists.[28] They challenged the narrowness of the AFL's approach. They were interested in organizing everyone, including unskilled workers, women, immigrants, and people of color, into "one big union."

This, they hoped, would lead to real solidarity among members of the working class. And, unlike the AFL, they were interested in challenging capitalism at its foundation. Thus, IWW leader Big Bill Haywood argued in a speech,

> We are here to confederate the workers of this country into a working-class movement that shall have for its purpose the emancipation of the working class from the slave bondage of capitalism. . . . The aims and objects of this organization shall be to put the working class in possession of the economic power, the means of life, in control of the machinery of production and distribution, without regard to the capitalist masters.[29]

The working conditions that these people were challenging were horrendous. In 1914, thirty-five thousand US workers were killed on the job.[30] There were no legal limits on how many hours a day or how many days a week employees could be required to work, so eighteen-hour days and six-day weeks were common. There were no limits on the employment of children, so many children worked alongside their parents, under the same unhealthy conditions and for the same long hours.

In the early years of the twentieth century, there were thousands of strikes each year. Many were successful and resulted in better pay, shorter working hours, and healthier conditions. Still, according to Zinn, "Law and military force again and again took the side of the rich. It was a time when hundreds of thousands of Americans began to think of socialism."[31] The American Socialist Party was founded in 1901 and grew quickly.

With the coming of World War I, the rise of socialism in the United States was challenged dramatically. In 1917, Congress passed the Espionage Act, which threatened with twenty-year prison terms "whoever, when the United States is at war, shall wilfully cause or attempt to cause insubordination, disloyalty, mutiny, or refusal to do duty in the military or naval forces of the United States."[32] This law was used to imprison many IWW and socialist leaders. Under the cover of keeping the country united at a time of war, the government launched an all-out war on those who challenged the status quo.

Because the government wanted labor peace and unity within the country, important concessions around wages and working conditions were granted to labor during this period.

> Many unions won new contracts with employers and also won the eight-hour day, a goal since the Civil War. During the First World War, 49 percent of workers gained a forty-eight-hour workweek, partly through the efforts of the War Labor Board. . . . Wartime progressivism also had a repressive side. Union leaders pledged to cooperate with the pro-labor government by opposing strikes.[33]

With the IWW and the socialist movement virtually crushed, the AFL resumed its position of centrality in the trade union movement, and women, immigrants, people of color, and the unskilled began to lose their places in the movement. During the Great Depression in the 1930s, another wave of radical labor activity took off.

> In 1934 and 1935 hundreds of thousands of workers, left out of the tightly controlled, exclusive unions of the American Federation of Labor, began organizing in the new mass production

industries—auto, rubber, packinghouse. The AFL could not ignore them; it set up a committee to organize these workers outside of craft lines, by industry, all workers in a plant belonging to one union. This committee, headed by John Lewis, then broke away and became the CIO—the Congress of Industrial Organizations.[34]

In the early days of the CIO, the Communist Party influenced many of its unions. At that time, the Communist Party was committed to organizing black workers, and it brought that perspective to the CIO. As labor militancy rose again, the government responded again in a more conciliatory fashion. The Wagner Act, passed in 1935 largely as a result of this militancy, set up the National Labor Relations Board (NLRB) and

finally gave federal recognition to the rights workers had been asserting for more than a century: the right to engage in collective bargaining, the right to free speech in advocating unionism, the right to freely elect a representative union, the right to protest unfair labor practices and to seek redress of grievances.[35]

This was also the period that saw a massive increase in the number of people of color in trade unions. During this period, the Communist Party worked hard to fight racial exclusion in trade unions. As the country geared up for World War II, the March on Washington Movement, under the leadership of A. Phillip Randolph of the Brotherhood of Sleeping Car Porters, threatened a massive march of African Americans protesting their exclusion from defense industries. Wanting to avoid the international embarrassment of fronting for democracy abroad while being challenged on racism at home, the government responded. In 1941, President Roosevelt issued Executive Order 8802, which banned racial discrimination in the defense industry.[36]

During World War II, patriotism and the demands for national unity once again set a stage for the government to be able to challenge labor. The development of the Cold War, after World War II, led to a general anticommunism that was used to challenge the loyalty of the CIO unions. In 1947, Congress passed the Taft-Hartley Act, which largely brought an end to this long period of gains by the working class through labor organizing.

[Taft-Hartley] dramatically restricted the workers' right to strike. It permitted employers to sue unions for breach of contract in strikes taking place during the term of a collective-bargaining agreement. . . . The Act also outlawed secondary boycotts, thus restricting sympathy actions by unions. . . . It empowered the President to create a fact-finding board to inquire into any strike affecting the national health and safety and to act on the board's request to seek federal court injunctions and restraining orders that would make a strike "illegal" for a 90-day cooling-off period. . . . The NLRB could now be used against unions as well as against employers.[37]

Today, US labor activism remains profoundly constrained by Taft-Hartley. A very narrow labor agenda, often referred to as *business unionism*, predominates. Under business unionism, many unions forego organizing new workers in lieu of the less risky role of renegotiating and administering existing contracts with the simple goal of keeping wages relatively steady. Many of these unions have lost touch with their members. They do not put much of their resources into organizing, corruption and cronyism are problems, and larger issues, such as the power of workers to have some say over how work is organized, are ignored. Little is done to challenge employers, let alone the foundations of capitalism.

As a result of this, the relationship between the left and the trade union movement is often strained. Some social justice advocates see the labor movement as an important site for the struggle against capitalism. But for many, the exclusive nature of so much of the tradition has left them hostile to trade unionism.

This situation began to shift in the 1990s. Beginning in the early 1990s, there was a major shake-up in the AFL-CIO. Movements for democracy and a focus on organizing the unorganized developed within many unions. In recent years, there has been a dramatic rise in organizing by AFL-CIO unions, and that organizing has once again focused on people of color, women, and the unskilled.

One of the more exciting examples of this was the Justice for Janitors campaign, a project of the Service Employees International Union (SEIU). In this campaign, the union focused on building coalitions with community organizations in areas where a labor dispute was going on. SEIU developed materials in the diverse languages of their members and took a multi-issue approach. These coalitions then used a variety of tactics to bring attention to their cause, often engaging in civil disobedience. Organizers often went after the corporations that hired janitorial services, arguing that the strategy of subcontracting out to a janitorial company was just a way for a big company to avoid paying its janitors well. Workers in this field have largely been people of color and are often immigrants.

The Justice for Janitors campaign challenged some of the more insidious practices developing in the economy at that time. More and more companies began using subcontracting as a way to avoid labor law. Also, as the US economy shifts to being more service-based, more and more jobs are in those sectors that have never had strong unionization. Thus, unions have felt a push to branch out into areas that were never organized before.

More recently, a new phase of union activity is developing that does not focus on gaining contracts for workers in a particular industry. Instead it is focusing on things such as raising the minimum wage, and getting companies who hire low-wage workers to give them a better deal, without necessarily forming formal unions. This has largely happened because the labor law system makes it very difficult for a union to get recognized. Workers who attempt to unionize are often intimidated or fired, or if they are undocumented, threatened with deportation. And the laws against harassing people trying to form a union are rarely enforced.

Ai-jen Poo helped found the Domestic Workers Alliance in 2007, and in 2011 helped launch the Caring Across Generations, a project intended to address an intersecting set of problems. The first is that as our population ages the number of people needing personal assistance will grow dramatically. Right now working-class seniors and disabled people find it very difficult to afford the care they need. Yet the people who do that work are some of the lowest-paid workers in our economy, working with minimal legal protections. Many people are unemployed and would love to do those jobs if they could afford to do so.

These organizations are working to shift the equation so that more resources go to caring labor. Whereas in traditional labor organizing, the boss is the enemy of a campaign, with caregiving labor there are often strong bonds between caregiver and client, and the problem requires a more complex solution that just higher wages for the workers.

In 2010 they passed a Domestic Workers' Bill of Rights in the state of New York, which mandates basic rights, such as days off, minimum wages, and workers compensation.[38] They have also advocated for government policies to guarantee people the care they need, and to pay for this with progressive taxation.

Class consciousness

Many social justice advocates take the position that the way to unify the working class is to focus on the things that working people have in common. This view, usually taken by white males working on labor issues, has been criticized for not being sensitive to the different interests of members of subordinated social groups.

Since the 1960s, many social justice advocates, people of color, women, gays, lesbians, and immigrants have argued that it is crucial to focus on differences. Members of each group are interested in coming to some understanding of their specific situation and do not want to have to ignore the ways that their experiences of oppression are sometimes different from, and sometimes caused by their relationships with, members of other subordinated groups. This view is often criticized as leading to a fragmentation of movements for social change.

One lesson that can be learned from this debate is that we can only reach a deep form of unity when we are aware of our differences and take them into account. If we don't, then the unity we create will most likely reflect the interests of members of more privileged groups. Hopefully, we are learning ways to create unity out of difference, in order to be able to build a foundation for demands that are in the interest of all members of the working class.

In the past, the AFL-CIO had argued that undocumented immigrants take jobs from legal workers, and it supported several pieces of federal legislation in the 1980s and 1990s that punished the undocumented. The executive council of the AFL-CIO reversed this position in February 2000 and came out in favor of improved conditions for all workers, including immigrants—even the undocumented. It opposed employer sanctions against hiring the undocumented and instead argued for criminalizing employers who exploited immigrants. It argued for full workplace rights, such as the right to unionize for the undocumented and legalization of all undocumented workers in the country.

This new position broadens the scope of who gets to count as a legitimate member of the working class. While making the lines dividing workers blurrier, it makes the lines dividing the working class from the owning class more clear. With a clear sense of class solidarity, it is much easier for the working class to advocate for its needs.

CHAPTER 4

Transnational Capital and Anticapitalism

ACTIVISTS FROM ALL OVER THE WORLD CONVERGED ON SEATTLE, Washington, to stop the 1999 meeting of the World Trade Organization (WTO). Engaging in demonstrations and many forms of civil disobedience, while being relentlessly teargassed by the police, they succeeded.

At De Anza College, where I work, we had several educational forums to teach students about the goals of the WTO and why it was not good for workers or the environment. A group of students decided to travel to Seattle, and our student government helped pay the expenses. Staying on the floors of friends of friends of friends and eating at group houses, these students had a life-changing experience. For the students I know who participated, "the battle of Seattle" was like nothing they had ever experienced. They felt the power of collective action, and they saw how brutal the government can be when its policies are seriously opposed.

One chronicler of the protest tells this story:

> He was sitting across the pavement from me. . . . We assumed crisis formation because the police were gassing a few blocks away. A decision loomed before us (for the fifth time that day) to stay or go in the face of gas. We were exhausted and irritable and scared. He lifted his head up so that all of us could hear. I don't remember his exact words, but he talked about sacrifice. He talked from that place where rage is born and courage nurses it

to sustainability. He spoke with heart pounding, speaking words as they came.

"We must be willing to sacrifice. We must be willing to stay, for that was the only reason we have come." We consented to stay and poured more vinegar into our scarves to counter the fumes. The tactical team talked to the communication network and checked out the needs of the other intersections. Our position, though out of the center of confrontation, was pivotal to the success of the other blockades. We stayed.

I watched him rest his eyes and hold steady. I listened to his voice like seeing lines of blood for the first time connecting heart and brain and legs. Beginning to understand the meaning of true connection, feeling the heat of solidarity move through our veins to throat, tongue, mouth. Finding our voices. And holding on.[1]

Suddenly, throughout the country, newspapers were writing stories about this once obscure trade organization. Millions of people in the United States learned for the first time, as a result of the protests, that our government was entering into a legal arrangement that would put the needs of corporations above national laws.

The protests raised crucial questions about the roles played by procapitalist transnational organizations, multinational corporations, and national governments in controlling the world's economic and political realities. They also raised important questions for organizers about which of these forces to challenge, when to challenge which one, and how to challenge them, given their slippery and complex interrelationships.

Transnational organizations

One of the most important developments of the end of the twentieth century was the increased power of transnational organizations. More and more of the important decisions that impact people's lives were being made by transnational financial and trade organizations such as the WTO, World Bank, and International Monetary Fund (IMF), and by regional treaties such as the North American Free Trade Agreement (NAFTA). While proponents of the trade pacts negotiated in this period argued that the agreements were about allowing trade to operate more easily by removing barriers such as extra taxes on foreign imports, in fact the agreements did much more than this.

The North American Free Trade Agreement, negotiated between the United States, Canada, and Mexico and ratified in 1994, established the principle that when a country has laws that restrict a foreign company's profits, the country can be charged with unfairly "taking" private property and fined accordingly. Thus, for example, under NAFTA rules a US waste disposal company, Metalclad, was awarded $1.6 million in damages after the [Mexican] state of San Luis Potosí blocked its waste site in the village of Guadalcázar.[2]

One of the effects of NAFTA was to open the Mexican market to US corn, which is produced by highly subsidized agribusiness corporations. This undermined the rural economy in Mexico and made it very difficult for small producers to be able to raise corn economically there. That led to a decimation of the Mexican rural economy, which in turn sent thousands of Mexican farmers away from their rural homes, in search of better ways to make a living. Many of them ended up in the United States working as undocumented laborers.[3]

In 1998, the United States used the WTO to open European markets to meat produced with artificial hormones. The Europeans had opposed the use of the hormones as potentially harmful. The United States argued that there wasn't enough proof of harm. The European preference for greater precaution was undermined by the US preference for a higher risk strategy that favored agribusiness. The WTO agreed with the US claim that the Europeans were limiting trade without a good reason.

What these transnational bodies have in common is that they subordinate national decision-making processes to very undemocratic and unaccountable elite-controlled groups. Agreements on principles—and sanctions for those who violate the principles—are usually made in secret. This is a major step forward for those advocating for the rights of corporations and a major step backward for the rest of us and our ability to influence social policy.

The increasing role of transnational bodies in regulating the world's economies developed out of a change in the geography of capitalism. In the past, states gave charters for corporations, recognizing them as legal entities, allowing them to make profits and taxing those profits according to the policies of that country. States regulated the conditions under which these corporate charters could operate, and were often regulated and forced to do things to protect health and safety, to protect the environment, and for many other reasons. The nation-state was the most important geographic body impacting the conditions under which its own national capitalists operated. Nations set policies that fostered capital accumulation in their territories, and nations existed in a dynamic relationship to a body of people who were constituted as workers, consumers, and citizens, who could put pressure on those corporations.

Attempts to influence local corporations are made more difficult by the ways that larger corporations are increasingly transnational. They can move different parts of their businesses to the parts of the globe that will give them the best deals for any particular aspect of their business. And they can use transnational organizations to pressure nations to give them the best deals possible, on tax policy, labor laws, and environmental standards.

Transnational organizations such as the IMF and World Bank were set up to stabilize the world economy after World War II, but they only came to play a dominant role beginning in the 1970s. According to Jeremy Brecher and Tim Costello in *Global Village or Global Pillage*, in the previous period, transnational organizations "served as an adjunct rather than an alternative to nation-based capitalism. In the era of globalization, however, they were to become the nuclei around which a system of global economic governance would begin to form."[4]

Throughout the post–World War II period, many leading US corporations had been able to function as virtual oligopolies, dominating key sectors of the economy. They were able to pay fairly high wages and not worry too much about competition. With the economic downturn of the early 1970s and the rise of serious foreign incursions into the US market, especially from Japanese and German auto manufacturers, the postwar complacency was quickly undermined.[5]

According to Brecher and Costello,

> Faced with intensifying international competition, corporations began experimenting with strategies to increase their profits by reducing their labor and other costs. These strategies included moving their operations to lower-cost locations; transforming their own structures to operate in a highly competitive global economy; challenging national policies that increased their costs; and creating a new system of global economic governance which supported their other strategies. In short, they initiated the race to the bottom.[6]

In his book *The Network Society*, Manuel Castells sees the changes in the global economy as being spurred by the governments of the world's wealthiest nations and the institutions they control. And he argues that

> three interrelated policies created the foundations for globalization: deregulation of domestic economic activity (starting with financial markets); liberalization of international trade and investment; and privatization of publicly controlled companies (often sold to foreign investors). These policies began in the United States in the mid-1970s, and in Britain in the early 1980s . . . and became the dominant policy in most countries in the world, and the common standard in the international economic system, in the 1990s.[7]

Castells argues that this transformation required the development of advanced information technology.

> Advanced computer systems allowed new, powerful mathematical models to manage complex financial products, and to perform transactions at high speed. Sophisticated telecommunication systems linked up in real time financial centers around the globe. On-line management allowed firms to operate across the country, and across the world. Micro-electronics-based production made possible standardization of components, and customization of the final product in high volume, flexible production organized in an international assembly line.[8]

Where Castells focuses on the networks that form the basis of the economic transition and on the role played by advanced technology, David Harvey focuses more on what he calls "space-time compression." In *The Condition of Postmodernity*, Harvey argues that, with the rise of globalization, corporations are increasingly relying on "flexible accumulation" where production is coordinated over a vast network of suppliers and subcontractors. Companies can shift quickly to find the lowest prices for production, and what is produced can change quickly.[9]

This form of manufacturing is often called "just-in-time production." Instead of having factories produce large quantities of goods in relatively stable systems, the new manufacturing works by breaking the production process into small units that are done on the basis of individual contracts. The corporation orders only as much of each component as is thought to be needed in the short term. These elements are then delivered to the next point in the production process. This process relies heavily on outsourcing—the practice where businesses subcontract work out to other companies that specialize in doing only one step in the production process. Just-in-time production requires transportation over long distances and thus keeps the demand for cheap oil high.

For workers, this means ever worse working conditions and wages. In her book *No Logo: Taking Aim at the Brand Bullies*, Canadian journalist Naomi Klein uses factories in the Filipino "free-trade zone" of Cavite as an example of the kinds of conditions that are developing around the world.

> Manufacturing is concentrated and isolated inside the zone as if it were toxic waste: pure 100 percent production at low, low prices. . . . Inside it's obvious that the row of factories, each with its own gate and guard, had been carefully planned to squeeze the maximum amount of production out of this swath of land. Windowless workshops made of cheap plastic and aluminum siding are crammed in next to each other, only feet apart. Racks of time cards bake in the sun, making sure the maximum amount of work is extracted from each worker, the maximum number of working hours extracted from each day. . . .
>
> In Cavite you can't talk about overtime without the conversation turning to Carmelita Alonzo, who died, according to her co-workers, "of overwork." Alonzo, I was told again and again—by groups of workers gathered at the Workers' Assistance Center and by individual workers in one-to-one interviews—was a seamstress at the V.T. Fashions factory, stitching clothes for the Gap and Liz Claiborne, among many other labels. All of the workers I spoke with urgently wanted me to know how this tragedy happened so that I could explain it to "the people in Canada who buy these products."
>
> Carmelita Alonzo's death occurred following a long stretch of night shifts during a particularly heavy peak season. "There were a lot of products for ship-out and no one was allowed to go home," recalled Josie, whose denim factory is owned by the same firm as Carmelita's, and who also faced large orders at that time. "In

February, the line leader had overnights almost every night for one week." Not only had Alonzo been working those shifts, but she had a two-hour commute to get back to her family.

Suffering from pneumonia—a common illness in factories that are suffocatingly hot during the day but fill with condensation at night—she asked her manager for time off to recover. She was denied. Alonzo was eventually admitted to hospital, where she died on March 8, 1997—International Women's Day.[10]

The ability of multinational corporations to subcontract and move production quickly to the places where they can get the lowest wages and least amount of interference from labor unions puts these companies in an advantageous position with respect to workers throughout the world. James Mittelman in *Out from Underdevelopment* explains that the power of multinational corporations

> derives from the mobility of capital, but also from the relative immobility of labor. For as capital encircles the globe in search of cheap labor and other favorable conditions, Third World countries must vie with each other. If workers protest the conditions of capital or go on strike, multinational corporations either pull out and dip into another labor reservoir or simply threaten to pull up stakes. Either way the postcolonial state will crack down on its labor movement, for those in power and their allies would be hurt the most by the withdrawal of their patrons.[11]

This mobility of capitalism is not matched by a corresponding mobility in labor. As NAFTA caused more people to want to migrate from Mexico to the United States with the devastation of its rural economy, the United States did not open its borders. Instead it moved toward harsher penalties for those seen by many Americans as coming to take their jobs. And, thousands of people die every year trying to get across the Mediterranean Sea from Africa to Europe, looking for better life prospects. While the countries of the Global North have ravaged their economies, and put the high levels of greenhouse gasses into the atmosphere that make living at home hard to do, those arguing for the value of the "freedom" of capital to cross borders fluidly rarely argue for the value of freedom of movement for the people of the world.

Multinational corporations become less tied to nation-states as systems of production become more decentralized and more able to move over large distances with high speed. Along with this change has come a rise in the importance of what Saskia Sassen has called "global cities." Now, rather than having a country be the geographic locus of capital accumulation, with a legal system determined from within the nation's borders, capital can roam the globe more freely. Global cities are places where important parts of this process are coordinated. Increasingly, capitalist processes take place in large-scale networks, with global cities serving as nodes for their operation.[12] These cities then become places where transnational capital is vulnerable to being challenged.

In *Overdressed: The Shockingly High Cost of Cheap Fashion*, Elizabeth Cline writes about the ways that clothing has become a more recent sector of the US economy to be deeply globalized, with terrible results for labor, as well as for consumers. While 50 percent of the clothing consumed in the United States was manufactured in the United States in 1990, by 2014 it had dropped to 2 percent.[13] The results have been a loss of high-wage jobs, and a race to the bottom, leading to our clothing being made in places such as Bangladesh.

On April 24, 2013, the Rana Plaza garment factory collapsed in Dhaka Bangladesh. As a result, 1,129 people died and 2,515 were taken from the building alive. The day before the collapse workers saw cracks developing in the building and did not want to enter. They were told by managers that that they would lose a month's wages if they did not go to work. As a country that suppresses labor organizing, Bangladesh has become part of the bottom of the race to the bottom for global clothing manufacturing.

Cline points out that none of this has served US consumers well, as we begin to see clothing as disposable, and fashion as something we need to keep up with, constantly buying low-quality, cheap items to use and discard quickly. People in the United States buy an average of sixty-four pieces of clothing per year, yet as we move toward a fast-fashion approach to clothes, people are getting less pleasure from clothing than they did before. Following the slow food movement that is encouraging people to break the trend toward fast food, and move toward sustainable, socially just, as well as more deeply pleasurable approaches to eating, Cline asks us to break from fast fashion, and spend our clothing dollars in more conscious and sustainable ways.[14]

The World Trade Organization was for many years a primary agent for setting the terms under which governments and corporations interacted, and for making those terms as favorable as possible for the corporations. After the battle of Seattle the WTO was never able to negotiate a new trade pact. Every time they tried to reconvene, they were met with well-publicized protests. Transnational actors such as the IMF and World Bank began to meet in places such as Qatar, where there would be a high level of security and less local publicity. The World Bank and IMF began to talk much more about serving the poor, and the social implications of their work. This has largely been more a change of public relations than real practice, but the fact that they need to change what they say they are doing has been a step in the right direction.

In the years since that time there have been attempts to pass major transnational trade agreements and much resistance to them. There also has been a huge shift underway toward countries that were formerly colonized working together to form their own trade alliances and development banks. Brazil has formed a trading alliance, the Pacific Alliance, with other Latin America countries, especially with those having left-leaning governments.

China has begun to play a huge role investing in the rest of the world and developing trade relationships individually with other countries. In 2013, China launched the Asian Infrastructure Investment Bank, and as countries in Europe have joined, the United States has become increasingly concerned that its power, through its control of the IMF and World Bank, is being undermined.

All of these developments point in the direction of a movement from a world dominated by US-anchored transnational institutions to a multipolar world, where there are a few different powerful anchors for transnational activity. Thus, rather than there being one transnational ruling class based in the Global North, there are now several competing blocks of transnational ruling-class agents.

For now, much of the world's financial system is undergirded by the US dollar, which is the currency that oil is mostly traded in internationally. As the world moves away from fossil fuel dependence, dollars will not be as central as they have been, and along with a decline in US military hegemony, as well and a decentering of US-dominated transnational organizations, the world will become much more complex.

Capitalism and progress

Advocates of capitalism argue that as this system develops, production becomes more efficient, and people become more prosperous. It is true that this global system has led to incredible levels of material production. Throughout the twentieth century millions of people around the world moved out of poverty and into lives of more comfort and increased longevity. Yet that move happened in the Soviet Union as much as it happened in the Western capitalist countries. Life spans in the twentieth century increased largely as a result of basic public health policies that included use of sewers, clean water, and good nutrition.[15] Advocates of capitalism have argued that it is merely a matter of time before everyone in the world achieves access to a comfortable consumer lifestyle. Critics claim that capitalism relies on the existence of a poor working class.

Many theorists of capitalism, including Marx, have argued that capitalism is a part of a necessary path for human development. While Marx criticized capitalism and thought it should be abolished, he believed that it offered something positive to human development. Because capitalism is based on competition to produce goods in the most efficient way possible, it stimulates technical development. Marx believed that people lacking technology need to work so hard to achieve a basic standard to living that they have neither time nor energy to advance human relations or creativity.

Marx claimed that problems with capitalism could be overcome through a revolution in which the productive resources of society were taken away and administered for the good of all. In this case, Marx accepted an Enlightenment notion of progress that is fundamentally Eurocentric. Are people necessarily better off when they produce large numbers of goods in technically sophisticated ways?

In her book *Ancient Futures: Learning from Ladakh*, Helena Norberg-Hodge argues that in the cases of Bhutan and Ladakh, two small Himalayan societies,

> the standard of living is actually quite high when compared with most of the Third World. People provide their own basic needs, and still have beautiful art and music, and significantly more time for family, friends, and leisure activities than people in the West. Yet the World Bank describes Bhutan as one of the poorest countries in the world. Because its gross national product (GNP) is virtually zero, the country is ranked at the bottom of the international economic order. In effect this means that no distinction

is made between the homeless on the streets of New York and Bhutanese or Ladakhi farmers. In both cases there may be no income, but the reality behind the statistics is as different as night from day.[16]

There is a developing body of literature on happiness that shows that above a fairly low level of subsistence, there is no correlation between how much money people have and how happy they are. In a society with income stratification the rich are generally happier than the poor, because it turns out that one of the predictors of happiness is relative status. But countries with high levels of equality, and functioning social safety nets have generally higher levels of happiness than highly stratified countries, with high levels of wealth, with weak safety nets, such as the United States.[17]

While Marx criticized many of the dominant ideas of his time, he accepted others unquestioningly. The notion of progress was developed during the Enlightenment, at a time when Europe was engaging in colonialism and the slave trade. This period gave rise to contrasting sets of ideas that formed crucial parts of European consciousness. Europeans contrasted civilization to barbarism, modernity to tradition, the developed to the primitive. Unsurprisingly, Europeans came to believe that in terms of each of these pairs, Europe was better than the rest of the world. This Enlightenment idea of progress left us with the view that the more other societies become like Europe, the better off they are.

Proponents of capitalism have been even more single-minded than Marxists in their belief that the rest of the world must be made over in the image of the capitalist West. The key concept for that makeover has been "development."

Development

Many people believe that the spread of capitalism equals the spread of prosperity. It is true that capitalism often means technical development of the means of production. But whether or not this goes along with a rise in standards of living for the people of a society is related to the political context in which capitalist development takes place. In many situations, it has made life dramatically worse.

According to Norberg-Hodge,

> Development is all too often a euphemism for exploitation, a new colonialism. The forces of development and modernization have pulled most people away from a sure subsistence and got them to chase after an illusion, only to fall flat on their faces, materially impoverished and psychologically disoriented. A majority are turned into slum dwellers—having left the land and their local economy to end up in the shadow of an urban dream that can never be realized.[18]

Belief in unilinear progress led many Western thinkers, especially in the period after World War II, to believe that the economies of much of the world were stuck in primitive ways of doing things, and that as these societies modernized they would become more prosperous. "Modernization" was the name of a school of thought that argued that poor countries should be helped to move through the stages of capitalist development that characterized the wealthier nations.

This idea is misleading for two reasons. The first is that it assumes that non-Westernized societies have been stuck in the past. Western thinkers often think of these societies as if they were frozen in amber. Even the terms we sometimes use, such as "stone-age societies," implies that they are living as they had thousands of years in the past, as opposed to being dynamic parts of the present world.

While some societies change more than others, human societies are inherently dynamic. All of them go through changes over time. And, as Wolfgang Sachs puts it in the introduction to his anthology *The Development Dictionary*, the idea of development implies that

> all peoples of the planet are moving along one single track towards some state of maturity, exemplified by the nations "running in front." In this view, Tuaregs, Zapotecos or Rajasthanis are not seen as living diverse and non-comparable ways of human existence, but as somehow lacking in terms of what has been achieved by the advanced countries. Consequently, catching up was declared to be their historical task. From the start, development's hidden agenda was nothing else than the Westernization of the world.[19]

If we think of non-Western societies as backward, we are also likely to think of them as having a poor quality of life. Yet life has not always been so bad in many low-technology societies. Indigenous people all over the world are currently fighting to preserve their ways of life, which often are based on subsistence agriculture, low levels of consumption, and low levels of work. When looked at from the perspective of quality of life and environmental sustainability, it's not so clear that an industrialized, or developed, economy is an advantage.

As the climate crisis worsens, some of the most important activism happening globally to challenge it is coming from indigenous people. They are fighting to preserve traditional ways of life, and they are fighting against extractive industries that are destroying atmosphere we all rely on.[20]

The second reason the modernization view is misleading is that it often looks at the poor societies of the present and assumes that they have always been that way. Yet the extreme poverty of many societies in the modern world is not a holdover from a precapitalist past. Rather, much of this poverty is a direct result of colonial and capitalist exploitation.

In a period during which many people believed that Western banks were helping out the poor countries of the South by making massive loans, Walden Bello, the Filipino sociologist, wrote of the

> astounding net transfer of financial resources from the Third World to the commercial banks that amounted to US $178 billion between 1984 and 1990. So massive was the recapitalization of the South that a former director of the World Bank exclaimed, "Not since the conquistadores plundered Latin America has the world experienced a flow in the direction we see today."[21]

In *Capitalism's Achilles Heel: Dirty Money and How to Renew the Free Market System*, businessman Raymond Baker argues that as a result of complex ways of dodging taxation, $500 billion a year flows from the poor countries of the Global South to the wealthy countries of the Global North. For every $1 in aid $10 is taken through illegal financial flows.[22] So-called African backwardness is intimately connected to modern historical processes.

In *How Europe Underdeveloped Africa*, Walter Rodney argues that before the slave trade, Africa was a continent full of a variety of functioning societies—some more egalitarian, some less so—but virtually all able to meet the basic needs of their people. Through the successive stages of the transnational slave trade, colonialism, and then the current process of neo-colonialism, Europe and its allies have extracted wealth from, and destroyed the social fabric of, African societies. Modern poverty is a modern phenomenon that has its roots in slavery, colonialism, neocolonialism, and capitalist development.

Communism and anticommunism

The Russian Revolution of 1905 began a process of challenging the old czarist feudal regime and ushered in a period of increasing social reforms in the direction of bourgeois democracy. Many radicals who had been involved in that revolution felt that they wanted deeper changes than those that seemed possible in the new political situation. They fought for a more complete social transformation. The leaders of the Bolshevik party, including Lenin and Trotsky, wanted a society free from class exploitation. The work of those leaders, along with many other social movements in Russia at the time, led to the revolution of 1917 that attempted to set up a socialist society.

The leaders of the Russian Revolution adhered to Marx and his co-author Engels's theory that a workers' state needed to act in a dictatorial manner in the interests of the proletariat while the new government fought off anticipated challenges by the old ruling class. Engels had called this pre-communist stage "the dictatorship of the proletariat," when society could not yet be open and completely democratic. Only after the old ruling class was completely defeated could true communism develop.[23]

There are many reasons why the Soviet Union went from being an idealistic attempt to build a society based on democratic control over society's resources to being an authoritarian, imperialist state. At least part of the problem was that the West attacked this new revolutionary state, militarily and economically. While Lenin was still in power, the state became increasingly repressive and intolerant of dissent. Stalin, as leader of the Soviet Union after the death of Lenin, argued that in order to survive these assaults from the capitalist world, the country must be unified. This ended up being used to justify all kinds of undemocratic and brutal practices, from jailing artists and dissidents to the forced removal of peasants from their land and the mass starvation that followed.

As the Cold War developed and the Soviet Union became a major player in world affairs, the world began to be divided between countries allied with the United States and capitalism, and those aligned with the Soviet Union and what passed for communism. This process opened the way for many countries to become free from their former colonial powers as they used their alliance with the Soviet Union to overthrow their colonizers and neo-colonizers. It also led to the Soviet Union acting like an imperialist power, overthrowing governments and manipulating political situations in order to prop up its allies, which in many cases functioned as economic neocolonies.

The Soviet Union set up police-state regimes in much of eastern Europe. The governments of these eastern European countries were nominally socialist. They had national ownership of the means of production, the population enjoyed free medical care, a right to a means of making a living, old-age pensions, free childcare, access to education for all, and many other basic life support protections.

But these governments were politically repressive, not allowing independent trade unions, freedom of speech, religious freedom, political organization, or free travel. Reformers came to power in Hungary in 1954 and Czechoslovakia in 1968 and attempted to develop a more open and democratic form of socialism. The Soviet Union quickly put down these movements with military force.

In the former colonial world, the Soviet Union's record was also mixed. In many cases, the Soviet-aligned regimes in Africa and Asia were better at meeting the basic needs of their populations than their former colonizers had been. Still, these countries developed the same sort of dependent, export-based economies as did capitalist-aligned postcolonial countries.

Cuba

Cuba began its relationship with the Western world as one of the first Spanish colonies, and remained one until the first war of independence in the 1860s. At that time, nationalist leaders were fighting for an independent republic. The United States had major sugar interests in Cuba and wanted to annex the island. So the war for independence turned into a three-way battle between the nationalists, the Spanish, and the US government, with the United States supporting the nationalist struggle for independence from Spain, but then trying to take over Cuba for itself. This Spanish-American war involved many of Spain's former colonies. It ended in 1898 with the US annexation of Puerto Rico, Guam, and the Philippines. While Cuba gained its independence from Spain, it remained under US military control, with a US approved neocolonial government.

During that neocolonial period, the vast majority of Cuba's people were poor and without access to land. Havana, the capital, was a haven for Mafia leaders, gambling, and prostitution. President Batista was widely considered to be corrupt, brutal, and a puppet of the United States. A band of guerrillas led by Fidel Castro and Che Guevara overthrew the Batista regime in 1959.

Guevara has come to be an icon of the revolutionary struggles of that period. Born Ernesto Guevara to a middle-class family in Argentina, Guevara studied to be a doctor. As his political consciousness developed, he began to believe that medicine was not the answer to the problems of the poor. Without solving the basic political problems that kept people poor, a doctor would just be treating the symptoms of what made people's lives miserable. So he dedicated the rest of his life to working to transform Latin American societies.

He met Fidel Castro in Mexico, and the two of them worked together to lead the Cuban Revolution. Guevara became disenchanted with the bureaucratic direction of the Cuban government and was personally interested in being on the front lines of a new revolutionary movement. In 1967, he left Cuba for Bolivia, where he attempted to develop a revolutionary movement. There he was killed by the Bolivian government, probably with the help of the US government.

Because he was killed in battle, Guevara has become a major symbol of revolutionary struggle. His image on posters, T-shirts, and buttons reminds people of his emotional and spiritual commitment to the betterment of humanity, as well as his uncompromising determination to do the work necessary to realize that ideal. In his own words: "Let me say, with the risk of appearing ridiculous, that the true revolutionary is guided by strong feelings of love. It is impossible to think of an authentic revolutionary without this quality."[24] While Guevara has been criticized for his *foco* theory that argued that small groups of outsiders could make a revolution happen, as a symbol he stands for much more than that idea.[25]

The revolution that Castro and Guevara achieved in Cuba took place at the height of the Cold War, which put the Cubans in a difficult position. Originally, Castro was interested in setting up an independent, democratic government. The United States equated independence with communism. As if anxious to make this prophecy come true, the United States became increasingly hostile to the new Cuban government, forcing the Cubans toward an ever-closer relationship with the Soviet Union for trade, aid, and protection.

Over time, this relationship developed into one of extreme economic and political dependence on the Soviet Union. The Cuban economy became more and more oriented toward providing sugar to the Soviet Union. This led to real problems when the Soviet Union fell in 1989. Suddenly Cuba was without its major trading partner. This led to years of severe hardship, as the Cubans attempted to reorient their economy toward higher levels of self-sufficiency and other sources of foreign trade while enduring an intense economic blockade by the United States.

The Cubans began to develop a system of agriculture that was almost entirely organic, as they could not afford to buy chemical inputs. They also opened up the economy to some international investment. And they began to support the development of worker-owned cooperatives, as a way to add more dynamism to the economy, while not undermining its socialist character.

Throughout the period from the end of World War II to the fall of the Soviet Union in 1989, movements to overthrow colonial, neocolonial, and imperialist regimes were caught up in the dynamics of the Cold War. Many people fighting for independence were communists who wanted to set up noncapitalist societies. Others used a strategic relationship with the Soviet Union to gain space for more political and economic independence from the capitalist world. Still others attempted to find a place beyond the two Cold War positions and forge mixed economies based on relations with both superpowers. This was the strategy pursued in the early days of the Sandinista revolution in Nicaragua.

Alternative economic strategies

For much of the twentieth century, Nicaragua was ruled by a series of US-dominated regimes. In 1979, the Sandinistas came to power by overthrowing the government of US puppet Anastasio Somoza.

The Sandinistas wanted to end imperialist domination in Nicaragua, but they were also determined not to follow Cuba's footsteps into a dependent relationship with the Soviet Union. They were well aware of the dangers of bureaucratic and undemocratic forms of socialism. They tried to balance their trade between the capitalist world, the Soviet bloc, and those few countries that had forged a path of independence from either bloc. This third group came to be called the "nonaligned nations." The Nicaraguans hoped that, with this strategy, they would not be under the control of any outside force and they would be able to build a democratic society.

Their goals for the economy were to raise the standard of living of the poorest while avoiding the economic isolation and military hostilities that other socialist revolutions had experienced. Thus, they nationalized some land and redistributed it for subsistence farming but left undisturbed a large enough capitalist sector to keep foreign exchange coming into the country. They hoped that the United States would not invade, that the capitalist enterprises would be content to generate wealth without distorting the political process and that there would be enough of a noncapitalist sector to prevent the extreme poverty that can be generated by capitalism.

Like many such experiments, this one was never allowed to work freely enough to prove (or disprove) its economic viability. Almost as soon as the Sandinistas came to power, the United States began organizing, training, and funding an army made up of former supporters of the Somoza government: the contra army. The Reagan administration spent millions on the contra war, often against the will of the US Congress.

The contras were never able to overthrow the Sandinistas, but they largely achieved the goal that the US government had for them. Around thirty thousand Nicaraguan people, mostly civilians, were killed, and fighting the war cost the Sandinistas millions and had a big impact on their ability to carry out economic reforms. The last thing the United States and its capitalist allies wanted was a viable democratic socialist model for people living in poor countries to follow.

This aversion to successful models has led the capitalist powers to fight hard against democratic reform movements in many countries. This was true even when there was not much at stake in terms of profits. In the 1980s, the United States spent millions to suppress a leftist revolution in El Salvador and engaged in a full-scale invasion of the tiny Caribbean island of Grenada after a Marxist government came to power there.

In some situations, such as Chile in the 1970s, when governments came to power that were interested in democratizing the economy, the

US government, in addition to orchestrating a coup, used its influence to orchestrate a *capital strike*. When a country attempts to set up a mixed socialist and capitalist economy, the capitalist investors can be organized to withdraw their investment resources if the country does not operate in ways that are in the interests of capital. When capital goes on strike, a mixed economy can't function.

Since the dissolution of the Soviet Union, it has been very difficult for those interested in building economic systems that serve their nation's people to figure out how to proceed. For many years it did not seem possible for a country to pursue an economic strategy that is opposed by the United States, the European powers, or the transnational institutions. Many countries tried to build prosperity from within the capitalist model. The United States and Europe were able to do it, but they were also able to use slavery and colonialism to accumulate capital, and they got started on the race to capitalist dominance centuries before the rest of the world. While the United States and Europe were able to exploit the resources of the rest of the world, any country attempting to achieve capitalist development now faces very different conditions.

The ruling class in the world economic system is able to profit from efficiently produced goods made with high technology inputs and high wages in the core countries. The raw materials that are requisites for capitalist production are often available at low cost from poor countries because there is no one with the power to insist on higher prices for those raw materials. Increasingly, huge profits are made by using highly efficient forms of production in poor countries where the political situation allows elites to keep wages extremely low.

From the 1960s through the 1980s, there were attempts to bring prosperity to poor countries by using the state sector to invest in and protect certain industries when they were in their fragile early stages. The idea was that, eventually, the country would build up a higher level of efficiency in production by using local capital and keeping profits in the country.

This model worked to some extent in some Asian countries. Korea, Taiwan, Hong Kong, and Singapore built strong capitalist economies and raised living standards. These societies accomplished this with fairly repressive controls on labor organizing and political freedoms.[26]

It has also worked in many Latin American countries, as governments put up protectionist trade barriers to foster growth of industries each country saw as important. Millions of people have left poverty in South America in recent decades as a result of intentional government policies, most of them aimed at limiting free-market capitalism.[27]

This process of governments coming to power through elections and managing their economies more in the interests of their populations, and less in the interests of the transnational rulings class, is proliferating. Throughout the early part of the twentieth century, as the United States was focused on Middle East and did not pay much attention to Latin America, left-wing movements grew. They were able to win elections and develop governments that did a better job managing the relation of dependency, in many cases dramatically lowering level of poverty and building economies that better serve human needs.

Neoliberalism and TINA

When the Soviet Union fell, Britain's prime minister Margaret Thatcher triumphantly declared that "there is no alternative" to capitalism. This idea has come to be known by its acronym "TINA." Along with TINA came *neoliberalism*. The "liberal" in "neoliberal" isn't meant as a contrast to conservative. In economic theory, a liberal is one who believes that markets should be "liberated" or that government should be liberal in how it deals with corporations. So people who advocate for neoliberalism are often politically conservative, and in fact supporters of neoliberalism are often called neoconservatives. One of the basic premises of neoliberalism is that the government exists to promote the pursuit of profits.

In *A Brief History of Neoliberalism*, British social theorist David Harvey writes,

> The state has to guarantee, for example, the quality and integrity of money. It must also set up those military, defense, police, and legal structures and functions required to secure private property rights and to guarantee, by force if need be, the proper functioning of markets. Furthermore, if markets do not exist (in areas such as land, water, education, health care, social security, or environmental pollution) then they must be created, by state action if necessary. But beyond these tasks the state should not venture. State interventions in markets (once created) must be kept to a bare

minimum because, according to the theory, the state cannot possibly possess enough information to second guess market-signals (prices) and because powerful interest groups will inevitably distort and bias state interventions (particularly in democracies) for their own benefit.[28]

Neoliberalism is a new version of the old procapitalist idea that the best way for economic systems to develop is for governments to allow capital as much freedom as possible. The theory is that increased levels of capital investment lead to a stronger economy. *Free trade* has been touted as the path toward progress for the whole world, including the poor countries of the Global South. Transnational bodies such as the IMF and World Bank made plans to restructure the political and economic systems of poor countries through structural adjustment programs (SAPs). SAPs took the economic reins out of the hands of national governments that were dependent on foreign investment. As one organization fighting this trend put it, the "most powerful countries of the North have become a de facto board of management for the world economy, protecting their interests and imposing their will on the South."[29]

Neoliberalism does away with older ideas of government that developed during the New Deal, according to which the government had a positive role to protect people's livelihoods and create a safety new in which people could feel a sense of security that they would have access to the means of a decent living. It is replaced with the view of government as a force for maintaining the conditions for capitalism to flourish, and it deals with the poor by seeing them as threats to be managed. Thus, as Loïc Waquant argues in *Punishing the Poor: The Neoliberal Government of Social Insecurity*, rather than finding ways to care for the poor, or eliminate poverty, the neoliberal state focuses on punishing them. Incarceration becomes a preferred way of dealing with the problems of poverty associated with capitalist economic practices.

> The renewed utility of the penal apparatus in the post-Keynesian era of *insecure employment* is threefold: (1) it works to bend fractions of the working class recalcitrant to the discipline of the new fragmented service wage-labor by increasing the cost of strategies of exit into the informal economy of the street; (2) it neutralizes and warehouses its most disruptive elements, or those rendered

wholly superfluous by the composition of the demand for labor; and (3) it reaffirms the authority of the estate in daily life within the restricted domain henceforth assigned to it.[30]

The development of neoconservatism fostered support for neoliberalism in the wealthier countries. Ronald Reagan in the United States and Margaret Thatcher in Britain were pathbreakers in the neoconservative revolution. Neoconservatives, like all conservatives, challenge the idea that the population is entitled to a reasonable standard of living and that it is the government's responsibility to enable people to achieve that standard. Neoconservatives crushed unions, arguing that they slowed down capital accumulation. And they undermined popular support for taxation as a reasonable way to meet social needs. The political success of this neoconservative trend depended on appeals to popular ideals of individual achievement and responsibility, and on the belief that competition brings out the best in people and that things are done best when they are done for a profit.

Neoconservative leaders and their neoliberal transnational financial institutions promote privatization as key to keeping established economies competitive and new economies attractive to capital investment. Neoliberal economics means that practically everything, from national oil companies to drinking water, can be sold to the highest bidder, creating markets and profit incentives in more and more areas of life. Questions about what is good for whom, about who bears what costs, and about the environmental impacts of different policies are all left out of the equation. And neoliberalism assumes that the state does not play a positive role in managing the economy.

In the process of neoliberal development, many countries were forced to spend less on health care, clean drinking water, and education, as expenditures on these things were considered by transnational institutions to be wasteful. As conditions for receiving loans and credit, nation-states were pressured to be leaner and to spend more on building roads, hydroelectric dams, and militaries to crush insurgencies and labor organizing. As a report of the Inter-American Development Bank puts it:

> The long period in which the public sector has held the center
> of the economic stage has to be brought to an end, and a radical

remedy applied: the withdrawal of the producer State and assisted capitalism, the limiting of the State's responsibilities to its constitutional commitments, a return to the market for the supply of goods and services, and the removal of obstacles to the emergence of an independent entrepreneurial class.[31]

The IMF insists that countries carry out these "structural adjustments" before being given loans and credit. The impact on poor countries has been devastating. These programs always mean an immediate drop in the living conditions of the poorest members of society. And, contrary to capitalist propaganda, they have not led to the development of economic systems that might eventually make people's lives better.

In fact, the result has been the opposite. In terms of standard ways of measuring the success of economies, they have failed. Walden Bello writes that, in a sample of twenty-four countries that underwent IMF-sponsored SAPs, capital accumulation slowed in twenty, export volumes declined or grew negligibly across the board, and the percent of GDP that came from manufacturing stagnated or declined in eighteen countries.[37]

And impacts on the poor have been much worse than the overall effect on "the economy." Again, according to Bello,

> In Latin America, the force of the adjustment programs struck with special fury, "largely canceling out the progress of the 1960s and 1970s." The numbers of people living in poverty rose from 130 million in 1980 to 180 million at the beginning of the 1990s. . . . In a decade of negative growth, income inequalities—already among the worst in the world—worsened. As Enrique Iglesias, president of the Inter-American Development Bank, reports, "the bulk of the costs of adjustment fell disproportionately on the middle and low-income groups, while the top five percent of the population retained or, in some cases, even increased its standard of living."[32]

Structural adjustment has been one of the most successful mechanisms for maintaining imperialist relations in the postwar period. These policies have made it possible for international investors to make huge profits off the resources and cheap labor of developing countries, while doing nothing to improve standards of living or even overall economic growth.

While some authors have argued that neoliberalism and the rise of transnational organizations are making the nation-state obsolete, others, such as Philip McMichael, argue that its role is simply being transformed. Where nation-states used to be the primary site for mediating between the interests of capital and labor, now governments facilitate the needs of transnational capital. Nation-states now "convey the globalization project to their populations."[33]

In low-wage countries, governments need to discipline labor and make the population willing to work for low wages. In wealthier countries, governments must still do the work of getting people to support military spending and wars to keep client regimes in power which are important parts of the maintenance of the global system. Populations in the wealthier countries still need to be the consumer base for the products made throughout the world. And, at least for now, these populations need to be brought on board with the neoliberal program since they still have some ability to reverse its course through pressure on national governments. Poor countries ruled by governments that do not support neoliberalism have found that Thatcher's TINA accurately describes their own inability to shape their national economies. Running a large-scale, industrialized economy requires capital, and keeping capital in the country requires a certain amount of capitulation to the imperialist powers.

When Nelson Mandela came to power in South Africa, the African National Congress (ANC) almost immediately put in charge of its economy people who supported maintaining the relationship with the International Monetary Fund that had been the policy of the previous apartheid regime.[34]

Many radical observers have been disappointed by the ANC's performance, but it is hard to see what other options the South Africans had. Transnational financiers had South Africa in a vise and took advantage of that fact.

Fighting capitalism

While the forces pushing for neoliberalism have claimed that "there is no alternative" to neoliberal capitalism (TINA), a worldwide movement is growing and showing that, as Susan George argues, there are thousands of alternatives (TATA). For most of the twentieth century, those opposing capitalism believed in fostering national revolutions against capitalist domination. In the early days of the century, that meant advocacy for worldwide socialist revolution.

Through the 1980s, many socialists thought that one way to break the hold of capitalism was for nations to have revolutions and use a relationship with the Soviet Union to create small pockets of socialism or mixed economies. Many recently decolonized countries in the 1960s, '70s, and '80s attempted to develop ties with both superpowers without falling into dependent and subordinate relationships with either.

What happened in Nicaragua also happened in many other nonaligned nations that tried this strategy: procapitalist forces crushed their efforts. People in the rest of the world were left with a reaffirmation of the belief that it is impossible to break away from capitalism and have a functioning economy. And while this was because of military and economic threats rather than a result of any inherent impossibility of setting up an economic alternative to capitalism, it has nevertheless been very hard for nations to break away from the capitalist model.

Revolution, reform, and transformation

Social justice advocates often divide approaches to fighting capitalism into two types: reformist and revolutionary. A reformist is someone who believes that capitalism can be pressured into becoming more egalitarian and humane. Those supporting revolution have argued that capitalism cannot be reformed. They believe that capitalism is an exploitative economic system and must be overthrown. There is quite a bit of despair among anticapitalists, as many feel that they would like more than a reformed version of capitalism but cannot see the possibility of overthrowing the system.

J.K. Gibson-Graham has developed an interesting perspective on this strategic impasse. She argues that some of the despair we feel when we think about overthrowing capitalism comes from our ideas of overthrow and revolution. Gibson-Graham proposes that we stop thinking of capitalism as a system to be overthrown and start thinking of it as a set of practices to be challenged.

Feminists don't discount as reformist, and therefore insignificant, an individual heterosexual woman's struggle with her partner for equality; we understand that a movement that fosters these individual struggles on a broad scale is significant politically. Similarly, feminists see no problem going after specific practices they find problematic, such as forced sterilization, inadequate child support, or negative images in the media. There is a widespread belief that in challenging these practices, we are challenging male domination. We don't need to find the fulcrum point of patriarchy, or the key that holds the system together, to believe that these forms of struggle are politically transformative. Feminists can count as successes improvements in women's educational achievements, access to better paying jobs, and support for women who are victims of domestic abuse.

Yet when we turn to fighting capitalism, many radicals, especially those operating out of a Marxist perspective, feel that anything less than a demand for the total abolition of capitalism is reformist or not very politically significant. For them, these small struggles can never add up to the complete transformation of capitalism. Rather, a revolution is required.

Feminists believe that small struggles, if enough of them happen, will add up to a complete transformation of society.[35] If we analyze capitalism as a system that must be overthrown all at once or not at all, then it isn't clear how it is possible to struggle against it in the present period.

Getting past capitalism

Activist and theorist Grace Lee Boggs has supported a grassroots approach to fighting capitalism, that asks organizers to forge linkages between small-scale activities, and pull them together into an effective whole. Boggs was born in 1915 in New York to Chinese immigrant parents. She earned a PhD in philosophy from Bryn Mawr. For many years, she organized and wrote with her husband, James Boggs, an African American who had moved from Alabama to Detroit for a job in the auto industry. Both were followers of Leon Trotsky, a leader of the Russian Revolution who had been purged from the Soviet government and then murdered by Stalin. For many years, they worked with Trinidadian scholar and activist C.L.R. James and Raya Dunayevskaya, a Russian-born theorist and activist who had been Trotsky's secretary while he lived in exile in Mexico.

James and Grace Lee Boggs were deeply active in social justice movements from the 1940s on. In the 1980s, toward the end of James's life, the Boggses turned toward local politics and focused their anticapitalist work less on the industrial working class and more on the pervasive social damage caused by capitalist processes. This change was based, in part, on the fact that they were living in Detroit, a city devastated by deindustrialization. The African American youths with whom they worked were not moving into the industrial proletariat. Rather, they were kept on the margins of economic life, with little hope for decent jobs.

In this context, fighting capitalism was rooted in reweaving the patterns of economic relations at the local level. In 1982, they collaborated on a *Manifesto for an American Revolutionary Party*. In that document, written mostly by Grace, they observed,

> In its limitless quest for profits capitalism has defiled all our human relationships by turning them into money relationships: Health, Education, Sports, Art, and Culture, even Sex and Religion have all become Big Business. . . . Up to now most Americans have been able to evade facing the destructiveness of capitalist expansion because it was primarily other peoples, other cultures which were being destroyed. . . . But now the chickens have come home to roost. While we were collaborating with capitalism by accepting its dehumanizing values, capitalism itself was moving to a new stage, the stage of multinational capitalism. . . . Multinational corporations have no loyalty to the United States or any American community. . . . Whole cities have been turned into wastelands by corporate takeovers and runaway corporations.[36]

For the Boggses, this analysis led to a strategy that focuses on

> organizing committees to create communities out of our neighborhoods which today are little more than geographical areas where we live behind barred doors and windows, more afraid of one another than we used to be of wild beasts. . . . Grassroots organizations can become a force to confront the capitalist enemy only if those involved in their creation are also encouraged and assisted by the American revolutionary party to struggle against the capitalist values which have made us enemies to one another. For example, in order to isolate the criminals in our communities, we must also confront the individualism and self-centeredness which permits us to look the other way when a neighbor's house is being robbed.[37]

For Grace Lee Boggs, small-scale, grassroots, community-based organizing was important, but she believed that it should be linked to larger-scale work that weaves together a deep analysis of how the forces fighting one aspect of capitalist domination are connected to others. The Boggses' revolutionary reformism is becoming more popular, as we enter a period when people are seeing more linkages between a variety of anticapitalist tactics, and larger social transformations.

In my book *Getting Past Capitalism: History, Vision, Hope*, I follow the Boggses and J.K. Gibson-Graham and look at capitalism being constituted by a variety of forms of agency. Among these forms of agency are the transnational ruling class acting as an agent pushing for things such as free trade agreements. Another form of agency is related to the ways that capitalist forces capture states and get them to largely serve procapitalist interests.

In a world with a globalized commercial culture, many of us get swept up in an ideology that has us believe that the path to happiness is ever-increasing levels of consumption. In short, we become what Deleuze and Guattari call capitalist desiring subjects, and help to perpetuate capitalism through the ways we reproduce consumer culture and in the ways we buy things, without accounting for their costs to others and the environment.

Finally, when a society has a large enough capitalist sector, there develops an economic dependency trap of capitalism, through which our ability do well becomes dependent upon capitalist businesses being willing to employ us. It ends up becoming a reality that we only do well when capitalists do well, and so many people end up supporting policies that support capitalism.

In her book *Plentitude*, Juliet Schor argues that in order to deal with the climate crisis and to have more satisfying lives, we need to build economies that are based on consuming much less in terms of natural resources, and finding ways to make work more satisfying. People all over the world are engaged in building toward that society, which in most of the world is called a "solidarity economy" in the United States it is mostly called "the new economy." Advocates of sustainable solidarity economies argue that we need to focus on economic practices that improve human lives, rather than ones that stimulate economic growth.

Yet for as long as there has been capitalism, there have been noncapitalist aspects to all of those economies called capitalist. Most economies have sectors where governments provide goods and services, such as education, in ways that have nothing to do with profit making.

And there is a rapidly growing movement worldwide to develop solidarity economies alongside capitalist ones. These movement focus on building worker-owned cooperatives, sustainable agriculture, and finding ways to get credit for these projects.[38] Many economies have large sectors that are based on worker-owned cooperatives.

In his book *America Beyond Capitalism*, Gar Alperovitz highlights the thousands of projects in the United States that are noncapitalist.

> It is rarely realized that there are more than 48,000 co-ops operating in the United States—and that 20 million Americans are co-op members. Roughly 10,000 credit unions (with total assets supply financial services to 83 million members; 36 million Americans purchase their electricity from rural electric cooperatives; more than a thousand mutual insurance companies (with more than $80 billion in assets) are owned by their policyholders; approximately 30 percent of farm products are marketed through cooperatives.[39]

While the world's dominant banks are strangling southern Europe with pushes to undermine people' standard of living to serve the transnational bankers, there are movements in all of those countries to resist and the forms of resistance are increasingly challenging of the very idea of capitalism.

One of the problems of delinking from the imperative that our economies grow and create more jobs is the economic dependency trap of capitalism. While it is true that people in Bhutan, for example, are able to have healthy and satisfying lives with very little ecological throughput, and with almost no GDP, for those of us living in largely capitalist societies this is not true. We become dependent upon our work to provide money for old-age insurance, medical care, money to buy the things that provide the status that we come to believe is crucial to our social survival, as well as money for food that we must buy, and money for things such as transportation to get to work, and clothing to wear at work. Juliet Schor argues that as we become busier, we become more dependent upon buying to satisfy our needs.[40]

Once a society has a certain level of capitalist economic relations, our ability to live well comes to be dependent upon businesses doing well and wanting to hire us to work. Part of building a transition to a solidarity economy has to be finding ways to lessen the economic dependency trap of capitalism.

Freeing ourselves from the economic dependency trap

There are many important things we can do to fight capitalism. Few of them are easy, and indeed some of them are huge tasks, but all of them are things that many organizations are doing right now, that can be built upon to develop significant challenges to the reproduction of capitalism. Some of the things we can do to lessen the economic dependency trap, and so build a noncapitalist world, are to:

1. Promote the use of alternative economic indicators

If people are told every day in the news that the cause of their experience of poverty is a lack of economic growth, they will support progrowth policies. We need to help people distinguish what is good for social well-being from what is good for capitalist growth. One important way to wean people off growth is to promote the use of better economic indicators. Sometimes growth leads to more jobs, and sometimes it doesn't. But increases in well-being are always good. If we measure an economy based on quantitative measures of things associated with well-being, such as literacy, happiness, and longevity, then we will be able to figure out which policies are good for our economy, and distinguish them from policies that increase capitalist activity, which may or may not improve well-being.[41]

2. Develop social safety nets

In countries without strong national health care systems, and other systems of benefits, a full-time job in the formal economy becomes the required path to secure existence. In countries such as Bhutan, where there are strong social bonds that allow people to care for one another, full-time employment is not necessary to obtain this security. Similarly, in strongly social democratic countries, such as Sweden, or socialist countries such as Cuba, it isn't either, because the state takes care of those things. There are a variety of paths to a social safety net, but lessening the economic dependency trap of capitalism requires that they be developed in some way.

3. Reduce work time

Struggles for shorter workdays can have huge benefits. The move in the industrialized countries to the eight-hour day led to huge improvements in well-being. France's move in 2000 to a thirty-five-hour workweek, without a reduction in pay, was a major advance. Shorter accepted workdays have a variety of great benefits. The individual spends less time working in alienated labor, and so has a better life. Also, employers can hire someone else for the other hours, and so shortening the workday can lead to less unemployment. This is especially important in countries with high rates of youth unemployment, because older people have the "good jobs." And generally, the more hours people work, the larger their carbon footprint.[42]

4. Develop community capital

A community that is underresourced will go to great lengths to entice companies to locate there, even if the company offers very little to the community. The mere hope of jobs and maybe a small amount of tax revenue is often enough. But what if governments or local communities were to have their own capital to invest in socially useful projects? In contrast to finance capital that is always looking for a short-term return, or venture capital that is looking for the next big thing to generate profits, the more resources we have in patient capital, that comes from communities and from taxes, the more can be invested in the solidarity economy.

5. Wean ourselves from consumer culture

Given the billions of dollars spent on advertising and on commercial media that promotes a high consumption lifestyle, it isn't surprising that many people think that the path to happiness is in ever-higher levels of consumption. High levels of social solidarity and connection are far more important for happiness than high levels of consumption. Above a fairly low level of material culture, money does not contribute to happiness. People need a sense of security, access to food and other basic needs, and a sense of community. Some level of material wealth is needed for those things, but much of what we spend our time producing and consuming does not have any positive impact on our well-being.[43] Working to challenge the cultural forces that lead people to believe consumption is the path to happiness is an important part of a move beyond capitalism.

6. Promote equality

If the United States currently had completely equal levels of personal wealth, every family of four would make $200,000 per year. If that family were to work half time, they could have $100,000 per year.[44] Similarly, if worker productivity grows by 3 percent per year, then every twenty-five years, we could cut our work time in half, if the benefits of those productivity gains were to go to workers. That means full-time workers could all make their present salary while working twenty-hour weeks.[45] Policies that promote equality include progressive taxation as well as labor struggles to have a larger percentage of profits go to workers.

7. Challenge ruling-class actions

There is no way we can build a solidarity economy on a planet whose atmosphere has been destroyed by the fossil fuel industry. Similarly we cannot build a solidarity economy that is based on things such as worker-owned cooperatives, as long as procapitalist forces are able to manipulate governments to worldwide to support policies that favor transnational corporations and free trade agreements that make small-scale production uncompetitive. As we build the new we must to continue to challenge the old.

As long as growth and employment rates are the measures of a healthy economy, our environmental interests will be at war with our economic interests and what is good for capital will be seen to be the same as what is good for people. We need to wean ourselves off the belief that GDP and more work are crucial to improving people's well-being. But we must also transform society such that building solidarity projects can be a real way for people to meet their needs.

There are social movements working in all of the areas needed to lessen the economic dependency trap of capitalism. If we see the ways that our work is linked, we are more likely to build solidarity between our movements. And if we have a clear sense of a path forward, we can be more optimistic that our work can add up to real lasting change. If we attend to the context in which small-scale change takes place, and engage in large-scale struggles even as we build that small-scale change, we can build broad-based support for a real transition away from capitalism.

CHAPTER 5

Theorizing and Fighting Racism

ON FEBRUARY 26, 2012, SEVENTEEN-YEAR-OLD TRAYVON MARTIN WAS walking to his father's fiancée's home where he was staying, in Miami Gardens, Florida. He was on the way back from a convenience store where he had bought iced tea and candy. Martin was confronted by George Zimmerman, who was a neighborhood watch leader. Martin was African American and the neighborhood was largely white. Zimmerman called the police and was told to leave Martin alone. Zimmerman decided to follow Martin anyway. He challenged Martin's presence in the neighborhood, shot and killed him, and then claimed he had done it in self-defense. Police accepted Zimmerman's claim of self-defense and did not arrest him. Outrage around the injustice of the situation ignited protest and other forms of mobilization all around the country. Local officials were pressured to indict Zimmerman, and eventually Zimmerman was brought to trial. That trial resulted in a verdict of "not guilty," setting off another wave of protest.

In the following years, the country began to focus on what had been a largely silent epidemic of black men being murdered by police and their deaths not being taken seriously by the legal system. When Michael Brown was murdered by the police in Ferguson, Missouri, in 2014, that town's legal system came under federal scrutiny. It became clear that not only were the police able to murder black men with impunity, but the local government was engaged in systematic harassment of the local population by charging high fees for the smallest of infractions, so that the poor people of color were largely funding government services. A few months after Brown's death, Eric

Garner was put into a chokehold by New York City police. He died, shortly after saying "I can't breathe."

Responding to these and several other horrific high-profile cases, Alicia Garza used her Twitter account to communicate with friends. She started #BlackLivesMatter, which became a slogan for a movement to challenge police violence, and other injustices in the legal system, including mass incarceration.

Why was it that many whites could empathize with Zimmerman's concern that Martin was in the neighborhood? How did it come to be that almost one African American person a day was killed by police? How did the country move from having a very successful civil rights movement in the middle of the twentieth century, to a situation where the United States has the highest rate of incarceration in the world, with over 40 percent of those incarcerated being African American?[1]

Just before this time, many people in the United States had begun to claim that our nation was "postracial." Having elected an African American for president, and seeing many famous and powerful people in the public eye of all races, some had begun to think that racism was a problem on its way out, and that the best way to deal with it was by not talking about it.

For as long as racism has existed, there have been people working hard to challenge it, and many of those challenges have been successful. From the movement to abolish slavery to the movement to allow Chinese immigrants to become citizens, people of color have achieved major victories in this struggle. And, while people of color have usually been the ones leading these struggles, many whites have also dedicated their lives to challenging racism.

Mab Segrest is one such activist. In *Memoir of a Race Traitor*, Segrest tells the story of her work fighting the Ku Klux Klan and neo-Nazis in the 1980s. Born and raised in Tuskegee, Alabama, her antiracist politics were forged in family battles over the civil rights movement. In sharp contrast to the rest of her family, she empathized with the black kids who desegregated her high school just as she entered ninth grade, and with the four girls killed in a church basement by racist bombers that same month in Birmingham, Alabama. After moving to North Carolina for college, Segrest realized that she was a lesbian and recognized the way that this difference from the mainstream further estranged her from the oppressive politics she had been raised to uphold.

In 1984, Segrest helped found North Carolinians Against Racist and Religious Violence and became its first staff member. For many years, Segrest drove all over the state investigating acts of racist violence and organizing to challenge them. Looking back at that period in her life, Segrest writes, "What I uncovered in North Carolina in the 1980s will be our legacy into the next century, unless we intervene. The racism, the homophobia, the hatred of Jews and women, the greed accelerate, and they sicken us all. . . . There is a lot to be done, but how we go about it is also important. Because all we have ever had is each other."[2]

Reflecting on the title of her book, Segrest writes, "It is not my people, it's the *idea* of race I'm betraying."[3]

The idea of race

As we have seen in previous chapters, racism has been and continues to be an important part of the US political landscape. Yet race has not always been an important social category. People's consciousness of the distinctions between their group and others on the basis of physical differences has developed over time, and the values assigned to those differences have been determined more by politics than by science or common sense.

The concept of race has had such powerful effects on our social system that it is hard to imagine a world without racial categorization. The idea of the human species being divided into biologically distinct races goes back only about as far as the conquest of the Americas. Before that, people hated one another on the basis of all sorts of differences, but the nature of those dislikes was not centered on the idea of race.

We often think of race as the description of the natural differences that resulted from human beings evolving in different parts of the world, but biologists do not accept that popular concept of race. People who believe in race as biological fact have never come to agreement on how many races there are or how they are divided. Where on the globe do people stop being Asian and start being white? Are Arabs white or Asian or African? Aren't Native Americans from Asia, and what about Jews and biracial people? Which physical differences mark someone as white as opposed to black? Although we usually refer to race as being marked by skin color, many "white" people have darker skin than many "black" people do. Our racial designations are built upon a complex mixture of skin color, hair texture, eyelid shape, lip shape, noses, family histories, geographic accidents, and political ideology.

All of these complications lead Michael Omi and Howard Winant to assert that

> *race is a concept that signifies* and *symbolizes social conflicts and interests by referring to different types of human bodies.* Although the concept of race invokes seemingly biologically based human characteristics (so-called phenotypes), selection of these particular human features for purposes of racial signification is always and necessarily a social and historical process.[4]

To say that our popular ideas about race are not based in biological truths does not mean that race does not exist as a social reality. Race has become one of the most important axes of social power in the modern world.

Racial formation in the United States

The "discovery" of the Americas by English, Spanish, and other adventurers created such a cultural, economic, and physical dislocation as to produce the first "racial" formation in human history. Linked by their common goal of economic exploitation, the competitive English, Spanish, Dutch, and other explorers all began to see themselves as on the same side in one sense. Omi and Winant argue that at the time of Columbus's first voyage to the Americas,

> the "discovery" signaled a break from previous proto-racial awareness by which Europe contemplated its "others" in a relatively disorganized fashion. The "conquest of America" was not simply an epochal historical event—however unparalleled in importance. It was also the advent of a consolidated social structure of exploitation, appropriation, domination, and signification. Its representation, first in religious terms, later in scientific and political ones, initiated modern racial awareness. It was the inauguration of racialization on a world-historical scale.[4]

Although the eighteenth century in Europe saw the rise of ideas of natural rights, it also saw Europeans increasingly involved in practices of colonialism and slavery. The contradiction between belief in equality and their desire to treat others unequally necessitated the development of increasingly sophisticated systems of justification. The idea that human beings can be divided into fundamentally different types helped solve this problem. Thus, Thomas Jefferson, while arguing for equal rights for "all men" simultaneously argued that there were natural differences between people that should determine how we treat them. "Will not a lover of natural history, then, one who views the gradations in all the animals with the eye of philosophy, excuse an effort to keep those in the department of Man as distinct as nature has formed them?"[5] The gradations between European and Native American "man" was an essential distinction for those who wanted to expand their fortunes in the American colonies.

From its very beginning, the Anglo-Saxon occupation of North America was in the form of settler colonies. This distinguishes it from colonies in which the conquerors go to a place and set up a system of government with the sole purpose of extracting wealth from the indigenous population. The fundamental premise of a settler colony is that the indigenous people are to be eliminated, and a satellite of the original society is to be set up. The rationale of racial superiority was seen as an adequate excuse for the wholesale slaughter of any indigenous inhabitants.

The colors of white

The idea of race developed to help manage economic and political interactions between a variety of groups attempting to live and prosper in the colonies. The United States was founded on principles of economic hierarchy, and the wealthy acted to protect their privileges. As these privileges began to be challenged by European and African indentured servants and Indians, the ruling elite began to develop an ideology that allowed some privilege to poor Europeans in return for their allegiance against poor people from other backgrounds. Thus, according to Scott Malcomson, European colonial powers established "white" as a legal concept in 1676 after Bacon's Rebellion, during which indentured servants of European and African descent united against the colonial elite. The legal distinction of white divided the servant class on the basis of skin color and continental origin. In that period, the concept of "free person" shifted from being based on being a Christian to being white. Increasingly, legal rights became predicated upon race.[6]

At the time of the founding of the United States, "white" included English, German, and Dutch people. But it specifically excluded Irish, Italian, and Polish people. In his book *Whiteness of a Different Color*, Mathew Jacobson argues that, as large numbers of Irish, German, Polish, and Jewish people began to immigrate to the United States, members of the dominant Anglo-Saxon group engaged in a nativist backlash against immigration, questioning the whiteness of these groups, even those previously considered white in other contexts.

Jacobson argues that the Irish were welcomed in as whites during the Civil War by proslavery northerners and also by those whites who were agitating against Chinese immigration into the western territories. Both groups sought more whites, especially Celts, in order to develop a larger coalition of support for their policies.[7]

According to Omi and Winant, Congress's first citizenship law, the Naturalization Act of 1790, defined those eligible for citizenship as "free 'white' immigrants."

> Throughout the 19th century, many state and federal laws recognized only three racial categories: "white," "Negro," and "Indian." In California, the influx of Chinese and the debates surrounding the legal status of Mexicans provoked a brief judicial crisis of racial definition. California attempted to resolve this dilemma by assigning Mexicans and Chinese within the already existing framework of "legally defined" racial groups. In the wake of the Treaty of Guadalupe Hidalgo (1848), Mexicans were accorded the political-legal status of "free white persons," a fig leaf placed by the U.S. conquerors over the realities of Mexican *mestizaje* and slave emancipation. State racialization of Asians was even more baroque: In 1854 the newly established California Supreme Court ruled in *People v. Hall* (1854) that Chinese should be considered "Indian"[!] and denied the political rights accorded to whites.[8]

These racial categories have shifted over time, sometimes as a result of political movements on the part of people not defined as white and sometimes as a result of state action. According to Omi and Winant,

> The concept of "Asian-American," for example, arose as a political label in the 1960s. This reflected the similarity of treatment that various groups such as Chinese Americans, Japanese Americans, Korean Americans, etc. (groups which had not previously considered themselves as having a common agenda) received at the hands of state institutions.[9]

As the legal and cultural definitions of the different racial groups shifted over time, one thing remained central, though continuously challenged: the notion that the country is a fundamentally white nation. White supremacy has been the cornerstone of the development of US racial consciousness. While who exactly counts as white and how nonwhite people are categorized has changed significantly over time, what hasn't changed is the basic belief that the country fundamentally belongs to its white citizens.

In the United States, being legally white has meant having ancestors from exclusively European backgrounds. Since the beginning of slavery, blacks and whites have mixed, often as the result of white masters raping the black women they enslaved. In order to protect the lineage of the white family, the children from these liaisons were considered black. In this way, the legal system developed the famous "one-drop rule." One drop of blood from an African ancestor defined one as black. Similar rules applied for people of mixed heritage from liaisons between whites and indigenous peoples.

Even after slavery was abolished and people of African descent became eligible for citizenship, white supremacists still wanted to exclude other people of color from citizenship. From the 1870s all the way through the 1920s, there was a powerful movement to exclude Asians from US citizenship, with much of the battle taking place in the Supreme Court and Congress.[10]

Dalip Singh Saund was a Punjabi Sikh who immigrated to California's Imperial Valley in 1920. A successful farmer, he wanted to become a citizen. His desire was partly based on a desire for political rights, but even more crucial was the fact that without citizenship, under California's "Alien Land Law," Saund wasn't able to own land.

Saund formed an organization of South Asian immigrants who lobbied Congress and, after three years of fighting, eventually won the right to naturalized citizenship. In 1956, he was elected to the US House of Representatives.[11]

The government's responses to challenges from Asian immigrants affirmed the whiteness of all people from European backgrounds. Yet, at the same time, anti-immigrant rhetoric was heating up and challenging the whiteness of many immigrant groups. "Thus, in this period of volatile racial meanings, peoples such as Celts, Italians, Hebrews, and Slavs were becoming less and less white in debates over who should be allowed to disembark on American shores, and yet were becoming whiter and whiter in debates over who should be granted the full rights of citizenship."[12]

This conflict began a discussion of the meaning of ethnicity, which is how the differences between groups of Europeans came to be characterized. This discussion was split off from discussion of race. And the idea of the melting pot took off in popular consciousness. The melting pot was the idea that as European immigrants came to the United States they lost their ethnicities and became "American." This concept helped make sense of the position of whites from different backgrounds and facilitated their assimilation into one white group united against other nonwhite groups. Thus, the idea of the melting pot was used not to describe how all people in the country were to become part of one unified culture but, rather, how people from Europe would shed their ethnicities to become white.

In many important ways the United States has been a Protestant, Christian nation from the beginning. This religious category was used to exclude people who might otherwise be considered white, such as Catholics, Jews, Muslims, and Sikhs. The concept of white was stretched in the nineteenth century to include Catholics such as the Irish and Italians. Jews are the most recent group to go through this process of becoming "whiter." Most people in the white American mainstream consider Jews of European descent to be white. For their definition of whiteness, a European cultural background is more important than religious affiliation.

Middle Easterners are the most contested racial group in the United States at the present time. Many people consider Arabs and Persians to be people of color, yet legally they are classified as white. Members of these communities differ over whether they should lobby the US government for racial or ethnic minority status or whether they should continue to be classified as white. People from these groups are targeted with some of the most vicious racism in the present time, especially because they are associated with Islam. Earlier groups of immigrants from those areas were largely Christian, and members of those communities fought to be included in the category "white." Because they are not members of a group to which antidiscrimination laws apply, important forms of protection from discrimination are not available to them. The more assimilationist members of these groups see that lack of protection as worth the price, and hope that, over time, they will be considered just as white as Jews and the Irish.

What we can see from this brief look at history is that race is intrinsically linked to systems of economic domination. Yet, while racism originated as a justification for colonial and capitalist exploitation, it has developed a meaning of its own to the degree that even upper-class people of color cannot escape its confines. If we think racism is just a manifestation of class oppression, then we might believe that it is in the interest of white working-class people to oppose racism. While it is, in the sense that all oppression is ultimately not in our human interest, racism often offers benefits and privileges to whites that they are likely to want to hold on to. The biggest challenge in doing antiracist work is the resistance, sometimes passive and sometimes active, of white people and institutions controlled by them.

In talking about challenging racism, one of the important issues is figuring out the ways that racial formations are perpetuated. Racist patterns that we have inherited as a part of our history continually reproduce themselves in society as a whole. Racism shapes all our institutions—from schools to courts to churches to political parties—and forms a significant part of our culture and systems of meaning. Through these mechanisms it is then reproduced in the psychological structures of individuals.

Institutionalized racism

Sometimes when people talk about racism, they talk as if it were just a matter of attitudes. It is common for people to see racism as existing because some people believe that other people are inferior. While prejudiced attitudes do exist and are an important part of the picture, the way that racial differences have become woven into the fabric of society is far more important.

Racism is anchored and reproduced in people's psyches, but it is also embedded in our social institutions. Slavery and the extermination of Native Americans are two clear examples of institutionalized racism. They were not motivated by the psychic need of whites to feel superior. Rather, they were based on raw economic interests and sanctioned through Anglo-Saxon legal and religious institutions. The psychological dimension developed alongside the institutional to help rationalize the brutality in the eyes of the dominant group.

When we say that slavery was a form of institutionalized racism, what we mean is that it was not merely perpetuated by individual people on other individual people. Rather, it was built into the legal, political, and economic structures of society. It was enshrined in the Constitution. It was built into property law. Some people were considered property, and others had rights to control them as they would any other piece of property. Racism was institutionalized in the structures that determined who got a formal education and who was not allowed access to school, who was allowed to go to church and who was not allowed to read or study religion, and in legal strictures on who was and who wasn't allowed to marry whom.

When we say that racism continues to be institutionalized, we mean that there are structures in society that tend to privilege whites and disadvantage people of color. The "playing field" isn't level; the teams have not had access to the same training. One of the most important contributions of the theory of institutionalized racism is that it takes discussions of race outside of the arena of personal morality. Discussions of racism often bog down when one side sees an example of racism, and the other doesn't see that anyone is acting in an immoral way.

The theory of institutionalized racism says that whites are privileged by the system whether they like it or not, and that there can be racist outcomes even when no one is acting in a malicious way. Whites are privileged by having better access to good schools and housing, by being considered more intelligent and trustworthy, and by being held up as the social models of beauty. Those of us who are white receive this privilege even when we think it is a terrible thing.

While discussions of racism sometimes lead whites to feel guilty for their privilege, often the best way to deal with privilege is to acknowledge its existence and use it to dismantle the systems that perpetuate it. When white people challenge racism, they are more likely to be taken seriously than are people of color. And, often, simply having a white person acknowledge the racism in a given situation can be a powerful force for making others take it seriously.[13]

These patterns of privilege and disadvantage are structured into society in a variety of ways. We can fight racism more effectively if we understand the different ways that it works. Below, I'll describe five different mechanisms through which institutionalized racism works: overtly biased laws; the rules that organizations use; the legacies of racism that perpetuate unequal outcomes; institutional tolerance for racist actions by people in positions of power; and finally the ways that racism is embedded in culture.

To understand how each of these forms of institutional racism works, let's look at the example of housing. Housing segregation is one of the most obvious aspects of racial discrimination at the present time. Where we live has an incredible impact on the quality of the education we receive and the kinds of opportunities we will have later in life. The theory of institutionalized racism can help us understand why housing segregation remains so persistent.

For over one hundred years after slavery ended, much US housing was still segregated by law. Towns had laws that prevented people of color from moving into them. Many of these housing covenants excluded European Jews as well as people of color. In the 1960s, legal challenges began to put an end to this practice.

Although the dismantling of this first type of institutionalized racism—overtly racist laws—has been the law of the land for the recent decades, more subtle forms of institutional racism persist. The practices of banks have been some of the most powerful forces keeping housing segregated. At times, bank officers have literally taken maps and drawn a line around neighborhoods predominantly inhabited by people of color; they then refused to offer loans within the area marked by that line. "Redlining," as this practice is called, and restrictive covenants that don't allow people of color to move into certain neighborhoods are now both illegal. Although some financial institutions and housing developers continue these practices through covert rules—our second form of institutional racism—they can be sued when their practices are discovered.

Often, of course, it is hard to prove that an institution uses such discriminatory rules. And discriminatory outcomes—such as fewer or lower quality home loans for people of color—might be explained by our third category of institutional racism: the lack of a level playing field. Fewer people of color may get housing loans from a particular bank simply because they have less money than white people. People of color might not have enough income to get a bank loan because they are subject to job discrimination, which prevents them from getting promotions. Many people of color have little money for a down payment because their parents were not homeowners. And their parents may not have been homeowners because of overt racist laws from an earlier period. Many of the programs developed in the New Deal to promote home ownership among the lower-middle classes specifically excluded people of color.[14] This and other earlier forms of institutional racism have led to tremendous differences in levels of home ownership, and thus inherited wealth, between whites and people of color. These differences in wealth are much greater than the differences in income level that people usually focus on when talking about inequality. According to *Field Guide to the US Economy*, "In 2001 some 21% of white households reported having received an inheritance at some time, with an average value of $274,000. Only 8% of African Americans and 3% of Hispanic households had received inheritances, averaging $78,000 and $22,000 respectively."[15]

Finally, a person of color may not get a bank loan as a result of the fourth type of institutionalized racism: individual bank employees may be racist and can choose not to approve loans for people of color, or they can be offered loans with worse terms. The housing market crash of 2008 had dramatically disproportionate effects on communities of color. In that period, people of color were 30 percent more likely than whites with similar credit scores to get loans with bad terms.[16] While this was often a result of personal racism, it becomes institutionalized racism when an institution, the bank in this case, allows the person to act in racist ways. In this case, the institution is complicit in the racist behavior through its passivity. In analyzing this type of action, people often talk about gatekeepers: people in key positions within an institution who prevent the promotion of people of color or who use their institutional power to prevent structural and cultural changes from developing in the institution. We see this especially in professional settings, where there are less objective criteria for an employer's decision-making. Tenure committees at universities are a prime example.

The fifth form of institutionalized racism is the way that racist ideas come to be embedded in and perpetuated through cultural practices. In *Lies My Teacher Told Me: Everything Your American History Textbook Got Wrong*, James Loewen chronicles the numerous ways that children in our schools are taught a history that centers white experience as normative, and minimizes the challenges faced by, and accomplishments of people of color.[17] Attempts to shift the educational system to fair representation has been an important area of struggle, beginning with some huge victories in having ethnic studies programs at colleges. And most recently with a huge defeat with the passage of an Arizona law in 2012 that outlawed the teaching of ethnic studies in public schools. We will explore in more depth the ways that culture works as a political force in Chapter 9.

Psychology of racism

These institutionalized structures of racism could not persist if they were not also a part of the mental reality of people in a racist society. And in psychological terms, racism has deep roots. Deep within the consciousness of the Western worldview is the idea that reason is superior to emotion and the mind should rule over the body. Saint Augustine, a fourth-century philosopher for the Christian Church from North Africa, introduced this idea into Christianity. He was strongly influenced by the work of Plato, who in turn took much of his basic metaphysical philosophy from ancient Egypt. In a curious twist of history, one of the core ideas that has been used to keep white supremacy in place has its origins in a hierarchical, but nevertheless African, society.

According to this Egyptian-Platonic-Augustinian tradition, truth is something that exists in a world separate from the world of everyday experience. Truth is universal and absolute. We have access to truth through the mind, and only some people have cultivated their rational capabilities in such a way as to have access to this divine world of truth.

Other people need to be ruled over because they do not know what is good for them. These people are too embedded in the world of feelings and sensuality to be able to make good judgments. This paradigm has been central to the worldview of Western societies. It has been used to justify the oppression of people of color and women. People in these groups have been systematically denied training in the analytical traditions that are valued by our society. Then the society talks about them as beings ruled by their lower sides.

A dominant system of cultural meaning has developed in which whites and men are symbolized in positive ways and people of color and women are symbolized as subordinate. These symbols have tremendous impact on people's lives. When we think of ourselves, or when we think of other people, these symbolic structures act as lenses through which all material is filtered.

When bad things happen to white people, this lens encourages us to think of them as unfortunate victims. When bad things happen to people of color, the lens encourages us to think that they somehow did something to bring the problem on themselves. When a person of color walks into a store, this lens produces an image of that person as untrustworthy and likely to steal.

In his very influential book *Black Skin, White Masks*, first published in 1952, the Martiniquan social psychologist Frantz Fanon wrote about how the psychodynamics of this Western worldview construct racist consciousness. Fanon focuses on the black/white aspects of racism. In that dynamic, he argues, whites see themselves as rational agents and as regular people, operating according to universal values. Blacks, on the other hand, are constructed as "the other." They are seen as irrational and sensual. The idea of the primitive is a flipside of the positive self-image that whites have. They see themselves as on the side of progress, enlightenment, and morality, while blacks are seen as aligned with backwardness, amorality, and sensuality. As whites come to have a sense of themselves as good, sensible people, they anchor this self-concept by contrasting it with the negative things within themselves that they want to reject or deny.

Fanon argues that whites will often be fascinated with black culture precisely to give themselves back the sensuous, alive relationship to the world that they deny themselves the rest of the time. "The presence of the Negroes beside the whites is in a way an insurance policy on humanness. When the whites feel that they have become too mechanized, they turn to the men of color and ask them for a little human sustenance."[18]

Fanon describes dynamics that are an important undercurrent to the consciousness of white supremacy. While these dynamics most accurately characterize the ways that whites construct images of African Americans, they form a matrix of meaning that impacts the construction of any racialized other who is seen as "primitive." Indigenous, Latino, and African people are all built into the dominant racial consciousness as people with no history or civilization, as backward primitives.

Europeans had a harder time racializing their distrust of civilizations that had well known elaborate written records of their own histories before contact with merchants and adventurers from the West. This group of "others," including Asians, Arabs, Persians, and Jews, has been characterized as having decadent and hierarchical civilizations that were not compatible with the Enlightenment idea of progress. Where the mind/body split—and its correlative split between rational and emotional people—was central to basic beliefs about less literate peoples; these "decadent" civilizations were seen in terms of a different set of dynamics. They were defined in religious rather than psychological terms, that is, by the opposition between good Christians and immoral heathens.

In *White Racism: A Psychohistory*, Joel Kovel claims that there is a basic trauma associated with the legacy of slavery that lives on in the consciousness of white Americans.

> The slaver in effect said to his slave, "While I own much, much more than my body, you own not even your body: your body shall be detached from yourself and your self shall be thereby reduced to subhuman status. And being detached and kept alive, your body shall serve me in many ways: by work on my capitalist plantations to extract the most that can be taken from the land in the cheapest and therefore most rational manner; as a means to my bodily pleasure—both as a nurse to my children and as female body for sexual use (for my own women are somehow deficient in this regard); and as a medium of exchange, salable like any other commodity of exchange along with or separate from the bodies of your family.... Since I have a certain horror of what I am doing, and since you are a living reminder of this horror and are subhuman to boot, I am horrified by you, disgusted by you, and wish to have nothing to do with you, wish, in fact, to be rid of you. And since this set of ideas is inconsistent and will stand neither the test of reason nor of my better values, I am going to distort it, split it up, and otherwise defend myself against the realization."[19]

In this passage, Kovel describes both the benefits of racism for whites during the slave period and the ways that whites were invested in being confused about and in denying the situation.

James Baldwin was one of the most important writers about racism in the twentieth century. Born in Harlem in 1924, he wrote six novels, many short stories, and some of the most powerful essays ever written on race. Baldwin was gay and African American, and many of his novels involve gay as well as racial themes. He spent many years in Paris, choosing not to live under the racial and sexual structures he grew up with.

In his essay "White Terrors," Baldwin describes the dread that many whites experience on coming into contact with African Americans. The mere presence of an African American reminds whites of a terrible history they have yet to come to terms with. "This is the place in which it seems to me most white Americans find themselves. Impaled. They are dimly, or vividly, aware that the history they have fed themselves is mainly a lie, but they do not know how to release themselves from it, and they suffer enormously from the resulting personal incoherence."[20]

According to Baldwin, it is hard for whites to have a realistic and positive relationship to their position in the US racial formation. While the vast majority of whites believe that racism is wrong, they usually become very uncomfortable when racism is discussed.

Getting whites to take active antiracist positions usually requires some complex work untangling the knots these authors discuss. One of the biggest problems is white guilt. Whites often feel that when they look honestly at the history Baldwin describes, their only option is to feel guilty, and since they don't want to feel guilt and don't believe themselves to have done anything wrong, their only option is to avoid discussions of race. And when racial discussions are forced upon them, they are likely to feel all sorts of confusion and discomfort, in addition to feelings of guilt, and resentment at experiencing that guilt.

Antiracist organizers work hard to make a distinction between guilt and responsibility. White antiracists can be implicated in racism without being guilty of creating it. We can notice the privileges we have been given and still be good people. And we can work to undermine those privileges.

Doing that often puts us into very uncomfortable positions. It often takes a huge shift of consciousness for white people to accept the discomfort that comes along with talking about things that they don't really know much about and don't perceive very well on their own. Moving from a place of being the center of national consciousness and the ones who know, to being one people among many and often being the ones who know less, involves a deep shift of consciousness, and a humility most of us were not raised with.

Forms of racist consciousness

Racism is built into the institutional structure of society and is also perpetuated through deep psychological processes. Very few of the racist processes that exist today have to do with the direct and conscious hatred of people of color by whites. Instead, the racist attitudes that go along with institutionalized racism in the United States today are more subtle. In her essay "Something about the Subject Makes It Hard to Name," Gloria Yamato discusses four types of personal racism, as well as internalized racism. Yamato breaks her discussion of personal racism into the following categories: aware blatant racism, aware covert racism, unaware/unintentional racism, and unaware self-righteous racism.

Some people are consciously racist. They believe in the superiority of the "white race" and will let people of color know about it. They beat up Asian Americans because they believe that they are responsible for problems in the economy; they argue that all Middle Eastern people should be targeted with extra scrutiny at airports because they might be terrorists. They tell Latinos to go home because they don't belong in the country. They exclude Asians from their workplaces because they don't want to compete with them, and they throw a fit when their child dates someone from another race. That's aware blatant racism, Yamato's first type of racism.

Much more prevalent in the present day is her second type: intentional covert racism. According to this category, people will act out their racist beliefs in secret—by not renting an apartment to or not hiring someone, for example, but then coming up with some sort of an excuse to hide what they've done.

I have known several African Americans who found being in "liberal" Northern California to be very difficult because they were constantly subjected to all sorts of racist behavior that they only found out about after the fact. It makes it very hard to know who to trust and to feel safe among whites when you don't know who is going to treat you badly. At least with overt racism people know where they stand. Covert racism, while seeming to be more polite, can be more painful than overt racism.

Aware covert racism is very prevalent, but perhaps not as prevalent as Yamato's third form of personal racism: unaware/unintentional racism. As antiracist ideas become increasingly hegemonic, unaware unintentional racism becomes a larger part of the picture of racism. Whites often underestimate the intelligence and trustworthiness of African Americans and Latinos, without having an idea that they are doing so. Asian Americans are often asked where they come from, with the assumption being that they are foreigners, and not really American. Latinos who are native speakers of English are told that their English speaking abilities are impressive.

Yamato writes,

> Unaware/unintentional racism drives usually tranquil white liber-
> als wild when they get called on it, and confirms the suspicions
> of many people of color who feel that white folks are just plain
> crazy. . . . With the best of intentions, the best of educations, and
> the greatest generosity of heart, whites, operating on the misin-
> formation fed to them from day one, will behave in ways that are
> racist, will perpetuate racism by being "nice" the way we're taught
> to be "nice." . . . Then there's the guilt and the desire to end racism
> and how the two get all tangled up to the point that people, mor-
> bidly fascinated with their own guilt, are immobilized.[21]

Yamato's fourth category is unaware/self-righteous racism. Here, "The 'good white' racist attempts to shame Blacks into being blacker, scorns Japanese-Americans who don't speak Japanese, and knows more about the Chicano/a community than the folks who make up the community."[22] She classifies this as racism because it is based on a sense of entitlement and superiority. Rather than challenging racism, it asks people of color to live as if it didn't exist.

Another force that keeps racism in place is internalized racism. In cases of internalized oppression in general, the person in the group being targeted by oppression ends up believing many of the negative things that are said by the dominant culture. According to Yamato, "It influences the way I see or don't see myself, limits what I expect of myself or others like me. It results in my acceptance of mistreatment, leads me to believe that being treated with less than absolute respect, at least this once, is to be expected because I am Black, because I am not white."[23]

One way that internalized racism works is around beauty images. The dominant culture puts out images of what it means to be beautiful, and beauty is almost always built upon whiteness. People of color who are mod-els and movie stars often have light skin and features that are close to white ideals. The Black Barbie doll looks exactly like the white one except for her coloring. All of this makes it very difficult for people of color to see their own beauty and love themselves and each other.

Internalized racism often leads people of color to underestimate their own intelligence and competence and not go after educational opportunities or jobs that they might be able to get. It leads to accepting racism in its many forms.

Another form of internalized racism is when people of color accept the dominant negative images of people from other subordinate racial groups. In this case, they are internalizing the racist imagery of the dominant culture. People of all racial groups are working within a deeply racist dominant cultural system. Racism is then anchored in worldviews, in individual people's psyches, and in the structures of society. And people of color, along with whites, act it out.

Yamato is very clear that all of these forms of racism are related to the ways that racism is institutionalized in society. Racism is not just an attitude of prejudice against someone. This is why she argues that the concept of "reverse racism" doesn't make sense. "People of color can be prejudiced against one another and whites but do not have an ice-cube's chance in hell of passing laws that will get whites sent to relocation camps 'for their own protection and the security of the nation.'"[24]

Because Yamato sees racism as fundamentally about structures of power relations, she does not see the ways that people of color can be cruel to whites as constituting racism per se. Many theorists of racism see the ways some people of color mistreat whites as examples of prejudice and bigotry, but reserve the term "racism" for situations in which there is institutional power backing the prejudice.

The changing racial formation

As a result of the social movements of the 1960s, the racial and cultural system that had dominated the country since the end of the Civil War became deeply disrupted. What it means to be an American began to change, and many white people came to feel deeply uncomfortable about their identities. Well-funded conservative organizations swooped in to take advantage of that psychic discomfort, and a whole politics has emerged based on a backlash against the gains of those movements.

In the 1970s, think tanks such as the Heritage Foundation and politicians such as Richard Nixon began to form a new white consciousness that was not based on overt racism. It mastered the art of the use of code words and concepts to trigger people's insecurities without sounding racist. According to Omi and Winant, "Instead of defending segregation, institutionalized discrimination and white supremacy, the new right invoked the code words of "law and order."[25] This move was based on a well thought out approach to winning elections often referred to as "the Southern strategy." Omi and Winant write that as a young staff person working for Richard Nixon's campaign for president, Kevin Phillips,

> submitted a lengthy and rather scholarly analysis of U.S. voting trends to Nixon headquarters. Phillips argued that a Republican victory and long-term electoral realignment were possible on racial grounds. His subsequently published *The Emerging Republican Majority* suggested a turn to the right and the use of "coded" anti-black campaign rhetoric; he recognized quite accurately that a great majority of southern white voters had abandoned the Democratic Party and that Negrophobia was alive and well, not only in the South but nationally. In fact what was emerging had been there all along: a massive racist complex of white resentment, dread, and shame that went back to slavery, the "lost cause," and reactionary political resentment.[26]

One of the most tragic results of this coded use of latent racism to mobilize voters to vote Republican has been the way it fed the move to mass incarceration over the following thirty-year period, which led to the point in 2015 where more than 2.3 million people were incarcerated in the United States. In her book *The New Jim Crow*, Michelle Alexander argues that politicians found that if they raised the specter of the dangerous black criminal in the minds of whites, many of them would react with fear and support policies and politicians who incited those fears and calls for a "war on drugs" to keep their communities safe.

Beginning in the 1980s police began to use the "broken window theory of policing," which argued that communities can be made safe by going after small offenses, such as riding a bike on a sidewalk. People in low-income communities of color were stopped and frisked for little or no reason. As communities were constantly swept through, many people were caught possessing drugs. And while people of color are no more likely than whites to use drugs, they were much more likely to be caught as a result of being constantly searched. Given the racial disparities at all levels of the criminal justice system, the war on drugs has led to a deep devastation of low-income communities of color.[27]

This extreme over-incarceration has also led to another form of institutionalized racism, voter suppression. The Republican Party and allied organizations such as the American Legislative Exchange Council (ALEC) have been working to make it much more difficult for low-income people to vote by imposing burdensome identification requirements for voting, even though there are few cases in the United States of voter fraud that might require better identification at the polls. According to the Sentencing Project, "an estimated 5.85 million Americans are denied the right to vote because of laws that prohibit voting by people with felony convictions. Felony disenfranchisement is an obstacle to participation in democratic life which is exacerbated by racial disparities in the criminal justice system, resulting in 1 of every 13 African Americans unable to vote."[28]

That same sense of feeling displaced by a rising number of people of color in the country and a shift to a more inclusive culture has also led to an extreme backlash against immigrants, especially those who are undocumented. Rather than finding ways to integrate undocumented people more fully into society by granting amnesty, as Ronald Reagan did in 1986, the response by more conservative whites has been to militarize the border and advocate for increased deportation. The struggle over immigration reform can be seen as another part of the growing polarization in the country between those favoring an open and multicultural society that sees people from all races as full members, and one that wants to hold on to whiteness as a core condition to being accepted as a full member of society.

Nationalism

That sense of belonging that is being threatened for many white Americans has its roots in the dynamics of nationalism. One of the most important roles of the state in capitalism is to constitute a citizenry willing to work for a wage, be taxed for common projects, follow the law, and go to war to support national interests as defined by the government. A state needs citizens. One of the ways that it constitutes its citizens is through nationalism: the sense of belonging in a personally meaningful way to a larger community. Nationalism is one of the key foundations of this sense of belonging. It has been an important factor in the creation of subjects for capitalist modernity.

Older forms of nationalism in the United States have been focused on whiteness as a key part of belonging. In many ways, being American is synonymous with being white. We can see this in the way Japanese Americans were treated during World War II as opposed to German and Italian Americans. Japanese Americans were seen as fundamentally foreign—not really American—and were assumed to be more loyal to Japan than to the United States. German and Italian Americans, on the other hand, were seen at that time as true, red-blooded Americans, despite the actions of Germany and Italy in the war (although this had not been the case during World War I).

The state is able to target these populations as if they were outsiders—alien invaders—with impunity because they are not structured into the national consciousness as legitimate citizens, as members of the nation. This puts US people of color in a contradictory position, as many try to be patriotic Americans. Sometimes they are welcomed as members of the nation, and at other times they are not. After September 11, many people of color, particularly Arabs and South Asians, put flags on their houses and cars to make as strong a statement as they could that they wanted to be seen as members of the national community.

Imagined communities

In his book *Imagined Communities*, British historian Benedict Anderson argues that nationalism can be shallow in its historical roots and still be very emotionally intense. Nationalist leaders can refer to myths of national pride and humiliation that have the barest of historical truth to them and that few people are even aware of. In the right political context, these origin myths and stories become politically powerful.

In the former Yugoslavia, many people were amazed at how quickly the society was transformed by nationalist consciousness. Before the war began in 1991, many people from various ethnic groups, especially in the big cities such as Dubrovnik, intermarried without a second thought and barely knew which ethnic group they belonged to. Ethnic categories were not an important part of most people's consciousness. As the economic situation began to deteriorate, however, and people began looking for scapegoats and ways to protect what little they had, nationalism became appealing.

Soon opportunistic political leaders were able to mobilize people into groups by telling quasi-historical stories about ancient defeats and betrayals at the hands of other groups. Ancient heroes were dredged up from the past and old stories were given new meanings. While this was often seen as building on people's deeply held, hundred-year-old feelings, in fact, many people who became strongly nationalist had no prior sense of connection to their supposed ethnic roots.

Nations and utopia

The Western press often reports on nationalism as if it were an irrational traditionalism adhered to by people in backward cultures. The framework of intertribal warfare is one of the major lenses that Western reporters use for trying to make sense of conflict in other countries, especially in the Global South.

Usually, these struggles can better be understood as political struggles over resources; tribal or religious conflict is more often a secondary rather than a primary motivation. The Western press is attracted to ideas of tribalism, religious conflict, and nationalism, which tend to keep the legacies of colonialism and internal class struggles out of the picture.

Concomitantly dominant cultural groups often use their position of centrality in society to favor their own over members of other groups. This means that material political struggles often take place under the guise of cultural politics. The roots of the contemporary struggle over Northern Ireland are related to British imperialism and the imposition of a colonial social and political system over the Irish, which began hundreds of years before the English left the Catholic Church. Over time, a shorthand description of this political reality became focused on the difference between Protestants and Catholics. But the bloodshed in Ireland wasn't caused by the fact that some people believe in the infallibility of the pope while others do not. Rather, the people who happened to believe in Catholicism were disenfranchised by the people who didn't. The English were interested in control over land and wealth, not in religion. The Irish nationalists, similarly, have been fighting for civil rights and economic opportunity rather than specifically for religious freedom.

The Western press's tendency to misrepresent political conflicts as tribal, ethnic, or religious reached an extreme of absurdity in the coverage of the movement for national liberation in South Africa. In the 1950s, white South African elites followed the divide-and-conquer strategy by setting up Bantustans where some South African blacks were allowed some form of self-rule under white authority. More radical blacks always opposed this as a poor substitute for equality.

During the movement for liberation in South Africa, there were many struggles between the radical African National Congress (ANC), which wanted democratic rule, and the forces of Inkatha, whose members fought to uphold their power as privileged representatives of the status quo in the Bantustans. These struggles were regularly reported in the Western press as tribal in nature. And those who did not understand the situation well were led to believe that African tribalism is particularly violent, making peaceful coexistence impossible. Absent from this analysis was the heavy hand of the white supremacist apartheid government, which funded Inkatha attacks on the ANC and which set these groups against one another.

Reactionary forms of nationalism have been a very powerful ideology during the last few centuries, but it may be that we are moving into a period in which nation-states, and hence nationalism, have less meaning. It is also possible that, as capitalist elites transfer political power away from nation-states and toward transnational bodies such as the World Bank, World Trade Organization, and United Nations, people may become more nationalistic as a way of trying to hold on to what little power they have.

As the nation-state becomes less powerful in the world, advocates for social justice have some new questions to look at when asking what their ideals are. Many have advocated for the end of the nation-state, or the end of states or governments altogether. Others have wanted to fight for democratic national governments that can act as a counterbalance to undemocratic transnational phenomena.

Challenging racism

We can see from the discussion of institutionalized racism that racism is embedded in the practices of our society and tends to reproduce itself. Racism can keep reproducing itself in society without anyone having a desire to oppress or mistreat anyone. This situation has important implications for antiracist practice. If racism were only a matter of personal prejudice, then the solution would be simply consciousness-raising.

Because racism is built into the structures of society, abolishing it requires challenges to power structures and institutions. People in historical movements to abolish racist practices have faced a number of difficulties that are still significant for contemporary antiracist struggles. The next section looks at some of these historical struggles, in order to understand some of the persistent issues in antiracism.[29]

Agents of social transformation

Frantz Fanon argues that in racist Western societies, people of color are seen as objects and whites are seen as subjects. The stories of grand achievements usually focus on whites: the presidents, white explorers, white authors, and white women suffragists. Things happen to people of color, but they are rarely represented in popular culture as people who make things happen. One consequence of this is that stories of liberation from racism often cast people of color as recipients of liberation rather than as its agents. Nowhere is this story more persistently believed than in the fight against slavery. Liberation from slavery is often portrayed as something that "just happened" as a side effect of the Civil War. The great dramatic actions that were part of the abolition of slavery are minimized, and the role that African Americans played in their own liberation is ignored.

While many people are taught in school that African Americans did not resist slavery, the fact is that, for as long as there was slavery, there was resistance to it. Slaves escaped, they resisted by not working hard when they could, they helped others escape, and they engaged in organized rebellions. One of the most famous of these rebellions was the one led by Nat Turner, who had been born into slavery in Virginia in 1800. In 1831, Turner led a group of seventy enslaved people from plantation to plantation, killing those who got in their way, gathering supporters as they went. Eventually they were captured. Many, including Turner, were executed.[30]

While white abolitionists generally tended to focus more on moral suasion as a tactic, one of the most famous white abolitionists was John Brown, who led a dramatic antislavery insurrection. With support from Harriet Tubman and Frederick Douglass, Brown gathered a group of black and white supporters to launch an assault on the federal arsenal at Harper's Ferry in Virginia. The idea was to seize and distribute arms, setting off a general insurrection throughout the slave states. The insurgents were captured, however, and subdued before the plan got very far.[31]

As the movement for the abolition of slavery developed, there were real differences of opinion over the role played by rebellions such as these. Many of the more mainstream white abolitionists, such as William Lloyd Garrison, argued that insurrections set the cause back by discrediting the abolition movement in the minds of moderates. Garrison and his followers tended to believe that the most important tool on their side was moral righteousness. Others, such as Frederick Douglass, who grew up enslaved, believed that the battle should be fought using whatever means were possible, whether this meant moral discourse, political maneuvering, or violent insurrection. Many of the more radical forces among the abolitionists argued that mere words would never overthrow the system. People were making too much money from it, and the interests supporting it were too entrenched. The combination of insurrections, resistance, and oral arguments combined to lead to the abolition of slavery.

An important theorist of the African American contribution to the abolition of slavery, and one of the great American intellectuals of the twentieth century, was W.E.B. Du Bois. Born in Massachusetts in 1868, eighty-five years after that state had outlawed slavery, Du Bois was the first African American to get a PhD from Harvard. He wrote the influential *Souls of Black Folk* and many other sociological, historical, autobiographical, and fictional books. He lived for ninety-five years and remained deeply involved in antiracist work until the end of his life. Du Bois founded the National Association for the Advancement of Colored People (NAACP) in 1910. He was involved with the Communist Party for many years. At the end of his life, he grew frustrated with the slow pace of change in the United States and went into self-imposed exile in the newly liberated West African nation of Ghana, where he was a close associate of African revolutionary leaders.

In his analysis of the Civil War, *Black Reconstruction in America*, Du Bois wrote that while Lincoln and most people in the North were not abolitionists, abolitionism played an important role in the war. Challenging the historians who argued that African Americans gained their freedom without any effort of their own, Du Bois points out that the abolition movement played an important role in developing an ideology that was then used by the North to justify its use of black soldiers. He quotes Lincoln as saying, "Without the military help of black freedmen, the war against the South would not have been won."[32] Du Bois goes on to write that blacks, "Far from being inert recipients of freedom, at the hands of philanthropists, furnished some 200,000 soldiers in the Civil War [approximately 10 percent of the

Union armed forces] who took part in nearly 200 battles and skirmishes, and in addition perhaps 300,000 others as effective laborers and helpers."[33]

Du Bois argues that the debate over the humanity of African Americans was at the core of the North's ability to win the war. In addition to the military need for soldiers, the moral high ground of emancipation was important as well: "Unless the North faced the world with the moral strength of declaring openly that they were fighting for the emancipation of slaves, they would probably find that the world would recognize the South as a separate nation."[34] Du Bois claims that, as those defending the union in the name of democracy

> gained in prestige and in power, they appeared as prophets, and led by statesmen, they began to guide the nation out of the morass into which it had fallen. They and their black friends and the new freedmen became gradually the leaders of a Reconstruction of Democracy in the United States, while marching millions sang the noblest war-song of the ages to the tune of "John Brown's Body."[35]

Whatever influence the abolitionists exercised during the battle against slavery, they were unable to sustain their momentum long enough to ensure the dignity of the newly freed. With the end of the war, the federal government remained in control of the South, providing physical and financial resources for Reconstruction. During this time, African Americans voted in large numbers, electing blacks to state and federal offices, and many believed that equality between the races was an achievable goal. But African American progress during this period was constantly contested by white supremacists. Within fourteen years, federal support for Reconstruction was withdrawn as a result of an incredible racist backlash that included: the creation of the Ku Klux Klan; lynching as a regular practice supported by government authorities and ignored in the North; and a systematic disenfranchisement of black voters. Blacks were relegated to near slavery conditions that remained largely intact until the civil rights movement of the 1960s.

Assimilation versus social transformation

A common theme in discussions of antiracism is the debate between assimilationists and those advocating for holding on to cultural differences.

Some want to make a place for themselves in society without challenging the status quo, while others think it is necessary to radically transform the social order. This debate appears in different forms over and over again in the history of antiracist and other activism.

In an early attempt at assimilation, the Cherokees established in 1820 a government modeled after the US system, with a president and two houses. They developed a public school system and newspapers. They hoped that this appropriation of white social structures would enable them to survive alongside the whites.

While the US government claimed that Native Americans would need to adapt to survive, as it turned out, there really was no option leading to survival. In 1828, the government of Georgia expropriated Cherokee lands to give to whites. The reality was that white supremacy was a much more important principle to those in power than the goal of freedom and equality for all who would adapt.[36]

Booker T. Washington was an important proponent of the strategy of accommodation among African Americans in the post-Reconstruction period. He argued that African Americans needed to get basic technical training in order to fit into society in a way that was not threatening to whites. He was bitterly opposed by Du Bois, who argued that the demand for equality contained within it a deeper demand for radical changes in society; a society founded on white supremacy would need to go through some deep transformations to grant real equality to people of color. Thus, while Washington wanted African Americans to find a place in the social order without making any waves, Du Bois wanted that order to be upset.

More recently, ideas about assimilation and transformation have been central to discussions about the place of Asian Americans in US racial hierarchy. In the 1980s, many political commentators began to notice that quite a few Asian Americans were doing fairly well in society and, most noticeably, that they were disproportionately represented in institutions of higher learning, such as the University of California.

To explain this phenomenon, social conservatives proclaimed their *model minority* theory, which argued that Asians should serve as a model to other minority groups of how to succeed in US society. Asian success was attributed to hard work, a high value on education, and a propensity not to engage in political movements that challenged racism. Asian Americans were portrayed as politically passive and economically successful.

Almost immediately, Asian American activists and intellectuals began to challenge this concept as "the myth of the model minority." They argued that the data used to indicate high levels of Asian American wealth were skewed in important ways. One is that they were based on measures of mean family income, without taking into consideration that most Asian American households contain more wage-earners than do white ones, because of a tendency toward extended families living together. Another is that many of the wealthier Asians were already wealthy when they entered this country. Asians who enter the country poor, such as Vietnamese refugees, tend to remain poor for as long as members of other immigrant groups.[37]

The myth of the model minority implies that while members of other minority groups have agitated for their liberation, Asians are doing fine simply by keeping their noses to the grindstone and not complaining. This ignores both the extent to which Asian Americans have agitated for their rights and against discrimination, and the extent to which they have benefited from the agitation of other groups.

The idea that members of other groups of people of color should act like Asian Americans in order to succeed in the United States ends up working to divide people of color and pit them against one another.

Nationalist liberation movements

Nationalism can serve progressive as well as reactionary political interests. Many movements for liberation use nationalism to build a sense of common identity among people fighting for more political power.

Radical forms of nationalism have been at the core of the liberation movements of US people of color. The black liberation movement of the 1960s focused on the unity of African Americans as a people and conceptualized them as a nation in need of liberation. In this context, nationalism meant challenging internalized oppression, working together for common economic interests, and fighting against the ideology and practices of white supremacy.

The nationalisms of people of color in contemporary liberation movements have their roots in older anticolonial struggles. Simón Bolívar used the rhetoric of racial unity to help build a sense of outrage against Spanish domination as Latin Americans fought for independence from Spain in the early 1800s. In later years, Nicaraguans, Cubans, Chileans, and others used the idea of national identity to argue for independence from the foreign powers that dominated them.

Mohandas Gandhi was one of the greatest nationalist leaders of the twentieth century. He directed his nonviolent struggle toward the goal of getting the British out of India. Born in 1869, Gandhi went to South Africa as a young man to work as a lawyer for the Indian community there. He was appalled by the mistreatment of Indians in South Africa, and there began his politicization.

Gandhi was committed to Hindu spiritual principles and was influenced by the ideas of Leo Tolstoy of Russia and Henry David Thoreau of the United States. He developed a philosophy of social change based on the idea that we should try to make the world over according to our image of an ethical life. After working to develop a movement for basic rights in South Africa, Gandhi returned to India, where he focused most of his energies on the fight against British colonial occupation.

As a radical nationalist, Gandhi was exemplary in his attempt to free India for all Indians. While the leaders of many national liberation movements have focused on the unity of the nation—ignoring issues of ethnic, religious, class, and gender differences within the nation—Gandhi insisted on keeping his ideals for independence from Britain consistent with the goal of justice for all.

Gandhi's ideal of religious pluralism was challenged at every step of the way, and he was eventually killed in 1948 by a Hindu nationalist who believed that India should be governed by and for Hindus alone. National liberation movements have often been made up of uneasy alliances between people like Gandhi and his killer.

Both reactionary and progressive nationalism were apparent in Indonesia in 1999, when a broad popular movement developed to overthrow the repressive pro-Western government of Suharto. This movement was mostly progressive and against neocolonialism. But the nationalistic aspects of the movement also led to scapegoating Indonesia's ethnic Chinese minority population. In the struggle, the stores of Chinese merchants were burned, and many Chinese Indonesians were killed.

Radical political Islam is another contradictory form of nationalism. Even though it is based on a religion, Islamic fundamentalism is often called nationalism because it involves the forging of a common identity for political reasons. In the present situation, radical political Islam has been fueled by the deep resentments of people in areas of the world that continue to endure neocolonial relations with the West. Millions of people have turned to a particular understanding of their religion, one that claims the need for a government based on religious law and that opposes foreign influences.

Which foreign influences are considered "anti-Islamic" has more to do with the political realities in which these movements form than with actual religious doctrine. So movements such as the Taliban in Afghanistan can argue for the complete seclusion of women, even though the Koran has very mixed things to say about women's roles in society. And they can reject women's liberation as "Western," while accepting Western military hardware as authentic revolutionaries.

In many cases, corrupt, militaristic, pro-Western regimes have suppressed local populations and crushed oppositional movements. In some, such as Saudi Arabia, religious movements have been allowed to flourish as outlets for people's frustrations and oppositional consciousness. These movements tend to be anticolonial and deeply reactionary at the same time.

Colonial powers are very much aware of the dual political potential of nationalism. In Africa, the colonial powers worked deliberately to set up states that were made up of people from different ethnic groups, and they worked hard to make sure these ethnic groups played different roles in the societies and were in conflict with one another. This facilitated European control, as the colonial powers gave privileges to one group and set up resentments and divisions among groups. This became known as the policy of "divide and conquer."

As these countries decolonized, the divisions remained as powerful wounds and impediments to national unity. One of the worst examples of this in recent times was the Rwandan genocide of 1994. Members of the Hutu ethnic group slaughtered between five hundred thousand and one million ethnic Tutsis. What the Western press omitted from most stories on the situation was that the Tutsi minority had been favored by the Belgian colonists, leaving a legacy of bitter resentment that played itself out in a horrible way after the Belgians left.

Another political danger of nationalism is that it can be used opportunistically by ruling elites. While a nation can be united by its ethnic identity, class divisions remain potential sources of conflict. Ruling elites in poor countries often use the rhetoric of nationalism to build consensus and deflect attention from their own privileges. Regardless of their rhetoric, elite class groups often have more in common with ruling elites in the West than with their own people.

A nationalist response to racism involves building a sense of unity among members of an oppressed group or nation, and trying to build an alternative worldview and set of values based on this group identity. One example of a nationalist movement in the United States was Marcus Garvey's Universal Negro Improvement Association founded in 1914. Garvey argued that the best hope for American blacks was to return to Africa and to develop pride in their African heritage.

More recent examples of nationalism include the Nation of Islam, which focuses on independence and black self-help, often promoting black capitalist enterprise. And there were powerful nationalist tendencies in the Chicano movement of the 1970s.

What all of these movements have in common is an ideology that focuses on group unity. Thus, nationalist leaders will develop a story of the group that focuses on heroism and historical achievements. There is usually a strong element of pride-building in nationalist movements. And they attempt to foster group solidarity by emphasizing the inherent hostility of oppressive forces.

Nationalism can play a crucial role in helping members of oppressed groups develop an alternative worldview to the dominant hegemonic one, overcoming the internalized oppression we looked at earlier. Because the dominant worldview positions them in subordinate ways, it is important for members of oppressed groups to form their own cultural systems. These alternative cultural systems value their members and reflect back to them a sense of pride in their accomplishments while rejecting dominant stereotypes and negative images. They also build political and financial resources and train people to work together for common goals of social transformation.

While much of this has been very positive, nationalism has a less positive side, as differences within the group are often suppressed in the attempt to build unity and insights from other communities are not taken into consideration. Nationalism often leads to an inattention to class differences, such that wealthy nationalists can use the notion of group unity as the basis for economic exploitation of other members of the group. And it can lead to an explicit suppression of feminist and queer issues, which get painted as divisive. Women of color who advocate for feminism and queer people of color who attempt to fight homophobia within their own communities, or who simply try to exist within their communities, are often criticized as bringing foreign elements from the dominant white society into the community.

Starting in the 1970s, feminists of color resisted this charge by claiming that they were not causing rifts in the community, they were merely pointing out divisions that already existed. By advocating for the needs of women within their communities, they were also advocating for the needs of the community. If sexism no longer hobbled women's ability to contribute, the community would be much stronger.

Intersectional approaches to antiracism

Women are often used as political currency in nationalist discourses around crime, war, and protection. These discourses often focus on women from the dominant group as the mothers of the nation and as frail and in need of protection. The nation, in turn, is often seen as a mother who needs the protection of her loyal sons.

The lynching campaigns that took place in the United States after the end of slavery relied on the gendered idea that protecting vulnerable white women was crucial to safeguarding the sanctity of the nation. When African Americans gained some rights after the end of slavery, an intense reactionary movement developed to try to put blacks back into subordinate roles. Racist consciousness, which had previously characterized African Americans as happy-go-lucky people who didn't really mind slavery, suddenly shifted. The dominant images in the media were of wildly violent, overly sexual men, intent upon raping white women. Many whites accepted patriotic and nationalist views that claimed that "our" women needed to be protected from "them." White women became social currency in the struggle of white men to maintain their dominance.

In many nationalist movements, in which a subordinate group is demanding national liberation, women are also used as a token of national pride. Men are encouraged to fight for national liberation so that women will be safe from an aggressive outside force.

This puts feminists who advocate for national liberation into tough situations. While men in many groups romanticize the virtues of the nation in demanding liberation, this romanticizing makes it hard to look at unequal gender relations. Thus, feminists are often accused of fostering disunity when they fight for gender equality within a national liberation movement.

Many feminists of color are hesitant to criticize their own cultural groups because they know how this can play into the dominant society's interest in perpetuating negative images of subordinate cultural groups. As a part of their colonial propaganda in India, the British focused on the "backward" practices of the Indians and the need to protect Indian women from Indian men.

Intersectionality grew in part as a response to the nationalist tendencies of many of the movements of the 1960s and 1970s. Its first major impulses came from women of color who were trying to find a way to be both feminist and committed to the survival of their racial and ethnic communities. Many were lesbian. People such as Audre Lorde and Gloria Anzaldúa argued that feminism must be transformed to take race, class, and sexuality into account, and that antiracism must consider gender, sexuality, and class. The '70s taught both the power of overcoming internalized oppression and the importance of learning about the variety of oppressive social structures. Coalition-building became the watchword for many formerly single-issue activists. The right's aggregation of power under Reagan and Bush, and the terrible devastation of AIDS and the drug war, encouraged people to go into the trenches together. This work of understanding how systems of oppression are interrelated and turning that understanding into coherent political projects is an unfinished task. But what we are finding in the present period is a real step forward in people's ability to balance the competing demands of multiple and intersecting systems of oppression.

Civil rights

One of the most effective strategies of antiracism has been the demand for civil rights. While human rights are the protections we believe we deserve simply on the basis of being human, civil rights are the protections we ought to have as members of a society. They are usually thought of as the right to equal protection under the law and the right to freedom from discrimination. The demand for civil rights has been at the core of movements for racial justice since at least the end of slavery.

Much of the power of the concept of civil rights is that it uses dominant ideas of "equality and justice for all," which resonate with large numbers of people in the United States. Martin Luther King Jr. was an expert at using the dominant values of the majority society to build support for radical change. As with demands for equality, demands for civil rights can sound moderate but end up being very radical. By pushing these ideas into new areas, by insisting that they apply to everyone, they end up having deeply transformative implications.

The civil rights movement, which began in the 1940s, was probably the single most important movement of the twentieth century. It was enormously effective at achieving its goals. Before the movement, African Americans, especially in the South, were second-class citizens by law. They were not allowed to use facilities, such as local municipal swimming pools, water fountains, and bathrooms that were reserved for whites. They were prevented from voting and were refused housing in white neighborhoods. They were sent to second-rate schools and barred from state universities. And they were required by law to defer to the needs and desires of whites in many arenas of life, such as seating on buses and space on sidewalks. The situation was not very different from apartheid in South Africa.

Thousands of African Americans and their white allies engaged in sit-ins, boycotts, and other forms of protest to challenge segregation. They used the media effectively, appealing to the better aspects of the dominant ideology.

After the civil rights movement, it was no longer legal for states to discriminate. This change led to the elections of African American government officials, from city councilors to senators. It also led to an ongoing struggle for better schools, jobs, and housing. And probably most significantly, it led to a major cultural change, through which African Americans no longer were forced by law to defer to whites.

In addition to its impact on the lives of African Americans, the civil rights movement inspired major changes in US society as a whole. It inspired movements among other groups that were not given their full civil rights as equal citizens. Beginning in the early 1960s, movements for cultural and political equality developed among Latinos, Native Americans, and Asian Americans.

On college campuses, these movements led to demands for ethnic studies and women's studies programs, and, in general, a less biased curriculum. They led to the development of the idea of student empowerment, the demand for free speech on campuses, and the abolition of the principle that colleges were to act like they were the parents of students. This was the beginning of the student movement that would eventually develop into a full-scale movement to oppose the war in Vietnam.

Many women who were involved in the civil rights movement began to notice how, even within the movement, the rhetoric of equality for all wasn't extended to them. Women in the movement, as in the rest of society, were treated as second-class citizens, expected to support the leadership of men, but not expected to take leadership themselves. As we shall see in the next chapter, that beginning led to a whole movement to challenge the gender structure of society.

Conclusion

After many years of dormancy a new civil rights movement is developing to challenge the new Jim Crow of mass incarceration and to fight for the rights of undocumented people. Those movements focus on the demand for fair and equal justice. And the powerful cry that "black lives matter" also resonates with the deeper challenge to a society that does not respect the full humanity of people of color, and especially of black people.

As we move toward the middle of the twenty-first century, when whites will no longer be a numerical majority in the United States, the "Southern strategy" is likely to decline in effectiveness. Yet as we move toward that point we are seeing increasingly frantic moves toward voter disenfranchisement, punitive restrictions on immigration, and increased backlash among whites who cling to an older, less inclusive, notion of American identity. In the coming period it is an open question whether or not the United States will be able to make progress to becoming a truly multicultural society, where everyone's humanity is valued and everyone's needs matter.

CHAPTER 6

Theorizing and Fighting Gender-Based Oppressions

I GREW UP WITH UNCLES WHO WERE BASEBALL PLAYERS AND HAD MY OWN left-handed glove since before I can remember. When I was in the fifth grade, I wanted to play baseball at school. At my school, there was only one girl who would hang out around the baseball diamond. She was there because she was the girlfriend of one of the boys. The rest of us were not allowed there. Something important was happening on the baseball diamond that required that girls not be there, except as admiring onlookers.

Since we weren't allowed to play in the game that was using the real diamond and the school's equipment, I brought equipment from home and my friends and I played by ourselves. Our teacher didn't make the boys let us play. The most we could get out of her was to let us store our gear in the classroom and not tell us we couldn't play in our own game. At the time, I thought the teacher and the boys were being mean to us. It was only much later that I came to understand that our exclusion from the game was part of a much larger picture.

At that time, girls were not supposed to be athletes; we were encouraged to use our bodies as objects of admiration rather than authors of action. And we certainly weren't supposed to compete with boys. Having girls in on the game would have interrupted the rituals the boys were engaged in, such as bonding around common goals and ranking themselves according to skill. And at that time, if a girl played sports, calling her a lesbian was part of the teasing to get her to conform.

Since that time, the relationship between women and sports has changed dramatically. Now girls are expected to play soccer, colleges fund women's sports, and a few women's professional sports leagues have even had some successes. Women who play sports are less likely to be called lesbians as a form of harassment, as more high-profile gay, lesbian, and transgender people have become accepted for who they are. What caused these changes in the world of sports—and in the world's expectations for girls and women in all life spheres? One of the main forces forging this change was feminism, the other was the queer liberation movement.

At least since the late 1800s, women and men have organized to demand a better life for girls and women. Women's rights activists worked hard to get the population as a whole to see women as more than mothers, low-paid workers, and sex objects. They pushed for a change in consciousness, for women to be recognized as full human beings—active participants in the game of life, players and not just observers of someone else's sport. Along with early demands for suffrage and other civil rights, feminists critiqued corsets and invented bloomers to make physical activities possible for more girls and women. Among many other strategies developed over decades of organizing, the women's movement worked hard to pass Title IX in 1972, the federal law that outlaws discrimination on the basis of gender in educational institutions that receive federal funding. Ever since Title IX, schools have been under pressure to equalize the way they fund male and female sports.

But feminism has not just been about women finding a way into male games. Many feminists have had a deeper critique of society and have argued for more far-reaching changes, such as an end to hierarchy, competition, and war. Feminist movements have always included a range of perspectives.

For much of the twentieth century, gay men and lesbians worked for equal rights in the system as well as for deeper transformations of the gender system. Many activists, in what John D'Emilio has called the homophile movement of the 1950s, were intent on arguing that gays and lesbians are just like everyone else, except in terms of what they did in their bedrooms and in social places such as bars and clubs. And what they did in these places should be no one else's business. An important exception to this tendency was the Mattachine Foundation in Southern California, which theorized in 1950 that gay men and lesbians offered fundamentally distinct and valuable diversity to the culture as a whole. The next flourishing of radical queer organizing coincided with the broader social uprisings of the late 1960s.

Many people date the beginnings of the current more radical gender liberation movement to the riot that took place at the Stonewall Inn in New York on June 27, 1969. That night, police engaged in what they thought was a routine sweep of a bar where transgender people, gay men, and lesbians, many of them people of color, found community and freedom. The difference that night was that the patrons resisted. According to an article that appeared in the *Village Voice* at the time,

> Suddenly, the paddywagon arrived and the mood of the crowd changed. Three of the more blatant queens—in full drag—were loaded inside, along with the bartender and doorman, to a chorus of catcalls and boos from the crowd. A cry went up to push the paddywagon over, but it drove away before anything could happen. . . . The next person to come out was a dyke, and she put up a struggle—from car to door to car again. It was at that moment that the scene became explosive. Limp wrists were forgotten. Beer cans and bottles were heaved at the windows, and a rain of coins descended on the cops.[1]

Marsha P. Johnson and Sylvia Rivera were two of the transgender women of color who were instrumental in starting the riot. Stonewall was not the first or the last high-profile attack on a gathering of queer people.[2] But shortly after it the Eastern Regional Conference of Homophile Organizations decided to commemorate the attack in annual pride marches to be held in June. Those annual pride marches have been an important part of the movement since that time, and have spread to be celebrated all around the world.

Stonewall marked a major phase of radicalization in the movement. As Dennis Altman put it, "No longer is the claim made that gay people can fit into American society, that they are as decent, as patriotic, as clean-living as anyone else. Rather, it is argued, it is American society itself that needs to change."[3] As gay men and lesbians became more radical, they began to look at the ways that sexuality is organized in society and how important a part of the social structure sexuality is. As these movements developed and became more radical, gay men and lesbians went in very different directions for a number of years, with gay men moving toward more open and unrestricted sexuality, and lesbians becoming more involved in the women's movement and interested in overthrowing patriarchy.

One of the challenges to changing the gender structures of society is that unequal gender roles seem natural and normal to most people. When I think back to my early example of sexism on the playground, I am struck by its everydayness. The roles society sets up for boys and girls are learned through routine interactions. I remember my own childhood experience with some anger, but also with a bit of doubt—it can't have been so bad; these things happen to girls every day. Part of the problem lies precisely in the fact that there was nothing brutal or outrageous in what I experienced. I accidentally bumped up against the walls the society had constructed for gender roles. I pushed against them a bit. But, in the end, my friends and I learned how we were supposed to behave, and eventually we gave up on playing sports.

Our sense of self develops by learning these expectations and taking them into account as we make our life choices. For some of us staying in these boundaries happens with only a small loss to our personal integrity and happiness. And we can resist with only small amounts of personal risk. For others the loss involved in conforming is huge, and many people have pushed hard against those expectations. And that harder push leads to reactions, often violent ones, from those trying to maintain the gender system. People who don't conform to the gender systems encounter tremendous levels of ostracism and violence.

Nature and nurture, sex and gender

The acceptance of oppression as natural and normal by oppressed and oppressor alike is especially striking in the gender-based forms of oppression: sexism and homophobia. One of the important theoretical innovations of the feminist movement in the 1970s was the claim that there is an important difference between sex and gender. Sex, they claimed, is a biological difference; gender is a social one. While nature was seen as giving us men and women, masculinity and femininity were seen as social constructs that differ from society to society and are subject to change.

In analyzing the way contemporary Western societies construct gender, Judith Butler has argued that the push toward heterosexuality is deeply ingrained in the social order. Underlying the whole cultural system is what she calls the "heterosexual matrix." Challenging the feminist idea that sex is a biological given while gender is a social construct, Butler argues in her book *Gender Trouble* that, in fact, even the biological categories of male and female are social constructs.

Biological sex is determined by a combination of external genitalia, chromosomes, hormones, and secondary sex characteristics. There are quite a few cases of human beings born with ambiguous biological genders.[4] These babies are most often surgically treated, regardless of actual health concerns, so that they can be assigned to one or the other category. Butler's point is intended to open up our perception of the possibilities for humans to go beyond male and female.

This is particularly important for a politics of queer liberation. Here Butler argues that the duality of male and female that is at the heart of our cultural system implies an understanding of sexuality that is based on two opposing types. This leads to our trouble in conceptualizing love outside of the heterosexual matrix. When we release our perspective from this dualistic frame, we are more open to a multiplicity of understandings of human ways of being.

Reproduction is the aspect of biological difference most people focus on when discussing gender differences. After men and women's equally short-lived contribution of sperm and egg, it is only the female who must endure the appropriation of her body for nine months, and then, barring the aid of modern food substitutes, spend several months nursing the baby around the clock before it can survive without her milk. But the social meanings attached to this and other differences are not the same from one human society to the next.

Most anthropologists believe that all human societies have systems of gender, that is, some way of assigning roles based on sexual differences. But the nature of these roles varies widely. According to the anthropologist Margaret Mead, who did groundbreaking work in the 1930s in this area, many of these gender systems contrast with what we in the United States now take for granted.

> No culture has failed to seize upon the conspicuous facts of age and sex in some way. Whether it be the convention of one Philippine tribe that no man can keep a secret, the Manus assumption that only men enjoy playing with babies, the Toda prescription of almost all domestic work as too sacred for women, or the Arapesh insistence that women's heads are stronger than men's.[5]

In most large-scale modern societies, masculinity or maleness is associated with strength and power, rational and logical thinking, and aggressive emotions such as anger rather than the more empathic emotions associated with vulnerability. Femininity, on the other hand, is associated with weakness and deference, intuitive reasoning, and with emotions related to vulnerability rather than anger.

Many people believe that there are biological causes for these differences. Some point to the nurturing character required for rearing children. Others point to the aggressive personality supposedly caused by testosterone. Some say that these emotive or behavioral differences developed in early human societies in which men were aggressive, individualistic hunters and women were peaceful, communal gatherers. Feminists have addressed these claims by challenging the biology and history behind them and by looking to other societies that have different gender systems.

To the argument that women are nurturers because such characteristics are necessary for raising children, feminists have responded that the argument is circular: Isn't nurturing a learned response to the social demands of parenting rather than a biological capability that only comes with a womb? Don't men also learn to be nurturing when they are responsible for infants and children? People often claim to be able to see masculine and feminine characteristics in small children and thus argue for the biological naturalness of gender roles. In response to this, researchers have found that people treat children of different sexes very differently from a very young age.

In a well-known study, called the "Baby X Study," researchers gave three-month-old babies to a group of adults and lied to them about the babies' sexes. In describing the babies' characters, the adults described them in sex-stereotyped ways according to each baby's assigned sex.[6] The supposedly male babies were "rambunctious." The female babies were "sweet." Gendered expectations thoroughly pervade our society, and of course babies respond to the expectations of those around them. When they are encouraged at rough and tumble play and scolded for expressing fear, as male babies disproportionately are, they become more active and emotionally guarded; when they are warned against risk-taking and cooed over for how cute they look, as female babies disproportionately are, they become more passive and responsive.

Because we never see a baby who hasn't been socialized in some way, we have no way of knowing if there might be some personality characteristics that are determined by biology. In discussing the debate between nature and nurture, biologist Anne Fausto-Sterling writes that many researchers reject the idea that either nature or nurture alone causes gender differences. Instead, they argue for

> a more complex analysis in which an individual's capacities emerge from a web of interactions between the biological being and the social environment. . . . Biology may in some manner condition behavior, but behavior in turn can alter one's physiology. Furthermore, any particular behavior can have many different causes.[7]

Feminist scientists and philosophers of science have challenged the idea that hormones determine behavior in any simple way. Fausto-Sterling points out that studies of the relationship between testosterone and aggression have been very inconclusive. And, she argues, popular discussions of the relationship between hormones and behavior, and their impacts on gender roles, are overly simplistic.

> Mired in the morass of arguments about testosterone and aggressive behavior, it is easy to forget that our bodies have a number of different hormone systems, all of which interact with one another. . . . Thus, to attribute a change in behavior to a change in a single hormone, when many different hormones rise and fall simultaneously, misrepresents actual physiological events.[8]

Another way feminists have challenged the naturalness of gender systems is by highlighting the variety of ways in which different societies structure sexual relations, such as hetero- and homosexuality. The dominant worldview links sexuality closely with reproduction. Most strains of Christianity have claimed that any sexuality that is not for reproduction is sinful. As scientific ideology eclipsed the power of religion, it inherited many older beliefs; nonreproductive sexuality was now seen as unnatural rather than sinful. And even though scientists know that many animals engage in "homosexual" behavior, most of us are taught about biology in a way that claims homosexual activity to be "unnatural."[9]

Homophobic ideology has not always been dominant, neither in the West, nor in many other societies. In ancient Greece, same-sex practices among upper-class men were seen as the highest form of love. In the

Symposium, Plato argues that erotic love between men could inspire the lovers to the deepest forms of spiritual practice.

In *Changing Ones*, Will Roscoe discusses the Native American practices that are often called *two-spirit*.

> In this land, the original America, men who wore women's clothes and did women's work became artists, innovators, ambassadors, and religious leaders, and women sometimes became warriors, hunters, and chiefs. Same-sex marriages flourished, and no tribe was the worse for it—until the Europeans arrived. In this "strange country," people who were different in terms of gender identity or sexuality were respected, integrated, and sometimes revered.[10]

Just as there are a variety of ways that sexual orientation is expressed in different societies, many small-scale societies do not have the same expectations of male and female behavior as do large-scale urban ones. Sherry Ortner writes about the balanced gender roles of the people of the Andaman Islands of India:

> [Men] hunted or fished, women gathered; everyone seems to have done a lot of child tending. It also appears relatively flexible, such that women might go on collective hunts, men might do a lot of gathering in certain seasons, and both men and women might jointly gather honey (which is highly valued). Both men and women worked on hut building, men cutting and erecting posts, women collecting leaves and weaving the mats for roofs. Men and women made their own respective tools and artifacts.[11]

But if male domination is not determined by our biology, why is it that so many societies have been largely male-dominant? Since the 1970s, many feminist theorists, historians, and anthropologists have researched the question of the origin of male domination. In her book *Making Gender*, Ortner writes that there are two general approaches to answering the question of why male domination has been prevalent in a wide variety of societies. Echoing the nature/nurture split on gender development, on the social level, male dominance is attributed either to social structures or biological propensities—or an interface of the two.

One of the most influential exponents of the social theory of male domination is Michelle Rosaldo. Along with Louise Lamphere, Rosaldo published one of the first books in feminist anthropology and helped to create that field. In her essay "Women, Culture, and Society: A Theoretical Overview," Rosaldo argues that being primarily responsible for raising children put women at a political disadvantage.[12] Many feminists agree that there is something about the lack of mobility that comes from bearing children and breastfeeding that encourages male domination.

Ortner, who teaches anthropology at Columbia University, is another influential feminist anthropologist. She writes, "Men as it were lucked out: their domestic responsibilities can be constructed as more episodic than women's, and they are more free to travel, congregate, hang out, etc., and thus do the work of 'Culture.'"[13]

This social construction theory has been criticized for projecting the modern Western situation of a separation between public and private spheres onto societies that are much more integrated. Most small-scale societies do not have a sharp division between public and private. That split only becomes pronounced in large-scale, state-level societies, especially capitalist ones, where wage labor and formal government are separated from the home.

Evolutionary biologist Barbara Smuts has argued that

> the *ultimate goal* of male control over females is reproduction: men coerce, constrain, and dominate women in order to maintain control over female sexuality and the offspring women produce.... Although human systems of gender inequality differ from those of animals in numerous important ways, the *ultimate sanction* underlying male control over females is often the same in humans as it is in nonhuman animals: the use of physical force, or violence, to inflict costs on females who resist male control. *So the ultimate goal is control over female reproduction, and the ultimate sanction to achieve this goal is violence.*[14]

She argues that men's ability to control female sexuality increases as human societies become more hierarchical. Many anthropologists have pointed out that for most of our history human beings have lived in relatively egalitarian societies. They have noted that it was around the time of the beginning of the development of agriculture that human beings began to live in more stratified societies, and as societies stratify, the subordination of women, and mechanisms to control female sexuality become more intense.

According to the biological approach, there is something in men that naturally inclines them to domination. According to this view, "issues of greater male physical size and strength, and perhaps greater male 'aggressiveness' in some form, do matter in many cases, although in a wide variety of not entirely predictable ways."[15]

The argument that there are natural ways for men and women to be is often used to support the claim that we shouldn't change our society. The argument is that egalitarian gender systems aren't natural, and perhaps any attempts to institute such a system will ultimately fail because human nature—here meaning male dominance and female submissiveness—will always reassert itself. Feminists have argued that the range of possibilities for how human beings can be is very wide, and it is up to us to decide how we want to live. Our biology or our "nature" can't tell us that.

Gender formation in the United States

We really don't need to know the causes of male domination to look at the ways that it is structured into society. We can take an approach similar to that taken by Omi and Winant in their analysis of the racial formation of the United States, and look at the ways that gender has become woven into the social fabric. As we do this, it is important to keep in mind that there are very different gender roles for people of different races and classes.

As the English became the dominant settler group in the eastern parts of what was to become the United States, their form of social life came to dominate the social organization and cultural ideology of white society. As we saw in Chapter 4, the early English settlers brought with them a male-dominant social order. Men had more political power and were the heads of families. Women worked hard in household and farm labor but were not allowed to play a strong role in public decision-making. As systems of wage labor developed, increasing numbers of men were expected to work in wage labor, while the women in those households did the majority of the work associated with the home.

Eventually this division developed into what feminists call the separation of spheres. While many older societies, such as ancient Athens. have had public/private splits, we also see this split develop in European influenced societies as they became more capitalist. John Locke, the great theorist of capitalism, helped to justify the split in his book *Two Treatises of Government*. In that book, Locke explains that men are fundamentally individualistic and competitive. Government and the economy are structured according to principles of agreement between these competing individuals. This public world of competition and negotiation is supported by a private world of the family. That world is run on principles of mutual support and care. This is the world of home and women.

Locke believed that he was describing the natural state of humanity. Feminists have argued that he both explains and justifies the roles men and women from dominant groups are supposed to play in a largely capitalist society. This division of labor into public and private spheres for the white middle and ruling classes developed and deepened in time, and the ideology around it became one of the cornerstones of US patriarchal culture. White men are supposed to work aggressively for money, and white women are supposed to care lovingly for their families. Of course, this ideal has never been realized by more than a minority of families, even for that brief period of time in the 1950s when the nuclear family reached the goal to which everyone was supposed to aspire.[16]

The model of the separation of spheres set the pattern for today's dominant conceptions of masculinity and femininity. It is a template used to keep women, working class and poor men, and all people of color in subordinate places in society. Working-class white men and men of color are deemed failures in their roles as men when they are not able to provide for their families. And all working women are seen as failing in their roles as women because they can't provide round-the-clock attention to their families and homes.

Being a homemaker was never an option for enslaved African women in the United States. Instead, they were integrated into society as laborers, doing both hard farm labor and household labor. Unlike the supposedly delicate, sexually pure white ladies, white supremacists portrayed enslaved women as sexually available and all Africans as licentious. Slave masters and overseers frequently raped their female slaves. Enslaved men were considered further debased from ideal masculinity for their failure to protect enslaved women from this violence.

Throughout colonial America, as people formed sexual relationships across racial lines, preventing white women from involvement with men of color was important for the ideology of racial purity. The common practice of white men raping black women, on the other hand, did not upset the social order. The children of these liaisons were considered black. But because maternity is much harder to hide than paternity, there was intense social anxiety about white women's sexual choices.

As we saw in Chapter 5, many of the human characteristics that whites repressed in themselves they projected onto African Americans. Thus, where dominant whites wanted to see themselves as pure and rational, they saw African people as highly sexual, physical, and expressive.

In the post–Civil War period, the extreme social anxiety of defeated white supremacists was partially expressed through concerns about the white race maintaining its "purity." This period saw an incredible explosion of lynching, as blacks were murdered by vigilante mobs, usually with the support of local law enforcement. One of the most important fighters in the crusade against lynching was Ida B. Wells.

Wells was born into slavery in 1862. She became one of the most prominent women of her time. As a young woman, she was the plaintiff in a case in the Tennessee Supreme Court against segregation in railroad cars. She was actively involved in fighting for women's rights. But what she has become known for is her work in exposing the horrors of lynchings.

Most middle-class blacks had shied away from addressing the problem of lynching. Usually a lynching involved a black man who was accused of raping a white woman. Wealthier blacks tended to believe that lynching victims were lower class and while they didn't deserve to be lynched, they had probably been involved in unsavory activities.

After some friends of hers were lynched, Wells began to research the problem. She found that very few of these cases involved rape. Consensual relationships between black men and white women were implicated in some lynchings; in others, there was no evidence of sexual involvement at all. Wells found that in the case of her friends, whites simply wanted to assert their power over blacks who were competing with them in business. She found that many lynchings had this sort of economic competition at their base, or they involved a black person who had broken some rule of interracial etiquette, such as looking a white person in the eyes.

While few lynching cases involved actual rapes, the vast majority included some element of sexual panic on the part of whites. Thousands of whites could be mobilized into a passionate mob at the mere accusation of sexual improprieties, and lynchings often involved brutal mutilations of the victim's genitals. This was more than vengeance; it was the acting out of deeply rooted sexual anxieties. These psychosexual issues still underlie much of the dynamics of racism today.

Stereotypes and role expectations for Latinos are similar in some ways to those of blacks. In the early years of immigration or, in the case of Mexicans, of annexation, women from these groups were often engaged in farm labor and hired to do domestic labor. Latino men and women are often seen as more fit for physical than mental work than are whites, and the men are perceived as violent and overly sexualized, while the women are seen as sexually available. These stereotypes have deep impacts on the social possibilities of people from these groups, as their intelligence and fitness for being responsible members of society are constantly in question.

Early Asian communities in the United States were almost entirely male due to restrictive immigration rules that favored men coming under short-term labor contracts. Many white men had come to the West in the nineteenth century without their families, and Asian men were pushed into the sorts of work usually done by women, such as in laundries and restaurants. Because they performed what was deemed women's work, Asian men were characterized by white supremacists as effeminate. A large percentage of the first groups of Asian women who were allowed into the United States were recruited as prostitutes, leading to stereotypes of Asian women as sex objects. As Helen Zia writes,

> Geishas, gooks, and geeks have been the staples of the main characters of mass culture's Asian universe: the subservient, passive female; the untrustworthy evil male; the ineffectual, emasculated nerd. As each stereotype gained a foothold in the popular culture, it brought on new prejudices that real-life Asian Americans would have to contend with.[17]

These stereotypes helped foster a climate in which Asian and Asian American women are targeted with tremendous levels of sexual harassment and sexual violence, Asian men are rendered almost socially invisible, and the whole group is seen as passive and effeminate. The rise of Hong Kong action films have somewhat softened these images, as some Asian American men get seen as fighters.

Native Americans also had to conform to the dominant public/private gender arrangement. Reformers always saw the key to civilization in the family, a family in which the man held the land. Individualism, private ownership, the nuclear family—all were marshaled to defend the breakup of reservation life. Tribal government meant socialism to many and thus had to be destroyed.[18] In most preconquest societies, women engaged in hard labor as much as men did, and in many they had important roles in social decision-making structures. In her article "Native American Women and Agriculture," Joan M. Jensen analyzes the gender structure of the Senecas. The Senecas, one of the tribes of the League of the Iroquois, had a complex decision-making structure in which men and women shared power. One of the cornerstones of women's power in Seneca society was their control over economic resources.

In their attempts to break the Seneca society, the US government supported missionary work that attempted to make "ladies" out of Seneca women. The missionaries taught that it was proper for women to spin, knit, and tend children, but not to engage in agricultural labor. Girls were forced to go to government-run schools, taught "household sciences," and trained for their proper roles as ladies. In forcing these transformations, the US government encouraged the development of a Native American social structure that was compatible with the dominant capitalist economic system.

The goal of helping indigenous women to be more ladylike was used to justify the destruction of Native American societies to the white public. Jensen claims that many whites thought they were helping indigenous women and believed that "coeducation would lift the Indian women out of servility and degradation." One reformer argued that it would force indigenous men to "treat them with the same gallantry and respect which is accorded their more favored white sisters."[19]

The claim that a society needs to be destroyed in order to help women is a surprisingly persistent idea. In recent times, claims to be favoring women's liberation has been used to support assaults on non-Western societies. We saw this with the war in Afghanistan in 2001. While Afghanistan's Taliban government had oppressed women for many years without too much complaint from the rest of the world, when the United States wanted to bomb Afghanistan, the plight of Afghan women became a popular cause. In a curious twist, antisexist rhetoric is often used to support such crusades, where "our" men need to be brought in to save "their" women.

In the nineteenth century, while the US government was trying to turn Seneca women into proper ladies, white women and some African American women met at Seneca Falls, in the heart of what had been Seneca territory, to work for women's right to vote. Some of the men present at the Seneca Falls meeting argued that women shouldn't be able to vote because they were too weak, physically and emotionally. This is when Sojourner Truth, the ex-slave, made her famous speech in which she challenged the idea of women as weak and in need of protection. "Nobody ever helps me into carriages, or over mud-puddles, or gives me any best place! And ain't I a woman? Look at me! Look at my arm! I have ploughed and planted, and gathered into barns, and no man could head me! And ain't I a woman?"[20]

The meeting at Seneca Falls was an instance when alliances of women across races were helpful for breaking through sexist ideology. The fact that the dominant ideology of white femininity was denied to African American women meant that these women were able to construct a different notion of what it meant to be a woman. If African American women were strong and independent, then it was hard to accept weakness as a necessary condition of being female.

Feminist theory

The variety of ways that the European gender template was used to denigrate all the different ethnicities and genders in the Americas produced a variety of responses to combat that oppression. Men, in general, accepted the limitations on their emotional and relational potential for the prerogatives of power. Women, in general, strained to gain access to better lives. White women, who had been put down as weak and deferential, often chose to fight sexism by claiming that women are just as strong and competitive as men. On the other hand, black women's clubs in the nineteenth century often focused on developing an image of black women as respectable ladies, in opposition to the sexual and physical brutality they had been forced to endure. While some feminists asserted the need for society to incorporate the nurturing values of traditional femininity, others challenged the very idea that women were more nurturing than men.

Different schools of feminist thought have grown up around each of these ways of thinking about the problem of sexism. When I first became interested in feminism in the 1980s, I was baffled by the contradictory images of feminists that I saw in the media. Feminists were either antiwoman because they were critical of "femininity" and wanted women to be just like men, or they were man-haters who wanted all men to be eliminated from society. They were Amazon warriors, loving earth-mothers, or corporate climbers.

For myself, I knew that I didn't want to be just like a man—I didn't like competitive and aggressive ways of being. But I also knew that I wasn't a very feminine young woman, and I didn't like the weakness and deference that seemed to be expected of me. I also knew that I wanted a form of feminism that allowed men to be a part of the solution. As I got closer to the women's movement, I began to see these stereotypes for what they were. But I also began to see that the contradictions in the images were in part related to some real differences in different schools of feminist thought.

One helpful way of understanding the main schools of feminist thought is to look at the ways they relate to dominant ideas of the public/private split. Liberal feminists have argued that women should be able to be just like men and have access to the public sphere. Their primary focus has been civil rights for women. Radical feminists have argued that the values of the private sphere—the cooperation and nurturance traditionally associated with women—should come to rule society. Radical feminists have also been called cultural feminists, and they have given more attention to the psychosocial elements of gender oppression. Socialist feminists have argued that the whole setup of public and private spheres is a political operation that must be challenged. They have most frequently identified the economic impediments to women's liberation, and the lack of resources devoted to care giving labor.

All three of these theoretical frameworks have been criticized as doing more to explain the sexism experienced by white women than by women of color, and a fourth type of feminism, intersectionality, developed to make sense of the racial differences in women's experiences. Thinkers in this school have looked at the specific ways that the public/private split sets up false expectations for women and men of color and for working-class people. They have insisted that feminist theory focus on the complex interrelations between race, class, and gender.

Liberal feminism

Liberal feminism has been the most prominent and widely known school of feminist thought and much of the early work of feminists at the turn of the nineteenth century falls into this category. According to liberal feminism, women should be allowed to do what men have done. Thus, liberal feminists have argued for the importance of women being able to vote and have other basic civil rights. They have argued for equal rights in the workplace, for equal pay, and for freedom from sexual harassment.

Liberal feminists have argued for women's equal access to the public sphere. They have tended not to question the structure of society or the values that structure it. Rather, they have simply demanded that women have access to the places in society where power and privilege lie. Liberal feminists largely accept Lockean individualism, and in a society in which individualism is the most acceptable way to package one's demands, this approach to feminism has had a strong resonance. Liberal feminism has been responsible for dramatic changes in society, as more and more women gain access to the worlds of government and economic power.

Liberal feminism was an important part of the second wave of the women's movements that flourished in the 1970s. The abortion rights movement was and continues to be largely based in the liberal feminist tendency, as women argue that they should be able to do what they want with their individual bodies. Women in that part of the movement challenged the traditional association of women with children. Why should women, as individuals, be any more responsible for taking care of the needs of children than men? While correctly challenging the unfairness of the current division of labor, liberal feminists rarely had an answer to the questions of who should take care of children and how society could be organized to take their interests into consideration.

One of the most important liberal feminists in the second wave of feminism was Gloria Steinem, one of the founders of *Ms.* magazine. Steinem was born in Ohio in 1934 and grew up with a chronically depressed mother. Steinem came to believe that a large part of her mother's problem was that she gave up her career for her family and felt trapped in the domestic life she was leading.[21]

Wanting to avoid the same trap, Steinem had an abortion when she discovered she was pregnant in college. She became a journalist and joined the movement of women in the 1970s that fought for abortion rights. She powerfully spoke out about her own experiences as a part of that struggle. Steinem has become a major symbol for feminism and has continued to write books and give lectures, in addition to her work with *Ms.* She remains deeply involved in feminist politics, having dedicated her life to activism.

Conservatives have reacted to the relative success of liberal feminists such as Steinem by trying to blame the women's movement for some complex social problems, usually under the rubric of the breakdown of the nuclear family. They argue that, as a result of feminism, women increasingly work in wage labor and don't have time to devote to their children. They also claim that liberal divorce laws advocated by feminists have harmed children.

Behind these criticisms are assumptions that women are naturally responsible for raising children, that the interests of women and children are the same, and that conflict-filled two-parent families are better for children than resolved divorces. As women have tried to escape from the confines of the heterosexual nuclear family and the ways that motherhood limits their access to money, prestige, and a sense of accomplishment, they have been blamed for not doing what these same conservatives don't expect men to do.

One consequence of the success of liberal feminism is that, as women have less time to spend taking care of household needs, more and more of those tasks are being taken care of by the market. Thus, people without time to spend with their children pay others to care for them; people without time to cook eat out more often and buy more prepared foods; and housework is increasingly something that is paid for. Thus, the very real gains that liberal feminism achieved for women were accompanied by the increasing dependence of wealthier people on poor women—often women of color—for domestic service.

The domestic sphere of labor is especially important for understanding the ways that sexism has impacted the lives of women of color. Much of the labor these women have done and continue to do is underpaid and often done "under the table" to avoid taxes. There is no job security, and their labor is not recorded in the nation's official economic figures. Feminists have argued that women's disproportionate labor in their own homes is economically invisible—in the sense that it doesn't count in economic calculations. Professional domestic labor is doubly invisible when it is paid for under the table.

Many feminists have criticized liberal feminism for not asking deeper questions about the nature of society. Are women really liberated when some women rely on the exploited labor of others to take care of the domestic sphere? Do we want a society based on increased levels of alienation and competition? Are women really liberated when they begin to act according to the value structure propagated by men in the dominant groups of society?

Radical feminism

The second major school of feminist theory, radical feminism, poses a deeper set of challenges to society by arguing that the structure and values underlying modern societies are patriarchal. For them, patriarchy—literally "rule by fathers"—is the dominant organizing principle underlying the present social order. Many radical feminists argue that because patriarchal society is inherently based on aggression, violence, and competition, all other forms of oppression, such as racism and class-based oppression, are effects of patriarchy. Overthrowing patriarchy would lead to the elimination of oppression in all its forms.

When asked why a male-dominant society is based on hierarchy and violence, most radical feminists, such as Marilyn Frye, argue that it has something to do with masculinity, that is, the social definition of maleness, as opposed to men's biological capabilities. Other radical feminists, such as Mary Daly and Susan Griffin, have argued that women are inherently more loving and caring than men. This view is often called *essentialism*, since it supposes ways of being that are in our nature or essence.

One of the most common arguments made by radical feminists is that women's relationship to childbearing makes them into nurturers. Men, on the other hand, are alienated from the deep human connections that childbearing gives to women. Various arguments have been posed for how men's alienation leads to aggression, but the main idea is that men lack the deep connectedness that mothering gives to women.

Essentialist radical feminists have argued that if we want a society based on care and mutual support, we would need to take men out of positions of power. This might mean having separate societies for women, or it might mean setting up a society in which men were subordinate to women. For nonessentialist radical feminists, it means that people would need to work hard to develop alternative cultural institutions in order to socialize males as well as females according to a feminist value system.

Radical feminists are often called cultural feminists. This is because many of them have argued that the development of a nonsexist world requires a radical reorientation of patriarchal culture. In the present culture, women's and men's minds are both so colonized by patriarchy that we won't really know what we want or what is in our interests until we find a way to develop our own consciousness.

One of the powerful tools developed in the early days of the second wave that was especially popular among radical feminists was consciousness-raising. This technique was developed in the women's movement by Kathie Sarachild, who claimed that she and her colleagues were "applying to women and to ourselves as women's liberation organizers the practice a number of us had learned in the civil rights movement in the South in the early 1960s." According to Alice Echols in her history of radical feminism, *Daring to Be Bad*, "Sarachild declared that all previous theorizing about women was inadequate and maintained that women were the only genuine experts on women. . . . Sarachild and others argued that consciousness-raising would bring the group 'closer to the truth' from which theory could be developed and appropriate action taken."[22]

The experience of talking with other women about what bothered them was powerfully transformative, especially as many women found that others shared experiences similar to their own. Through the process of consciousness-raising, they came to see that there were deep social patterns behind their own insecurities and frustrations. Their negative feelings were transformed from being personal failings into political causes. Being "overweight" was no longer a reason to feel ugly and like a failure, instead, it became clear there were social forces making almost all women feel insecure and ashamed about their appearance.

Many feminists have challenged the ways in which women have been socially constructed as objects rather than as subjects. Men, especially those from the dominant racial and class groups, are encouraged to develop a sense of themselves as agents of their own will. Those of us who are women, on the other hand, are often encouraged to see ourselves as supporting actors in someone else's play. Our job is to help others, and we often see ourselves in terms of how we impact others. We see ourselves as good people when we are helpful to others, while men are more likely to see themselves as good people when they achieve something on their own. Men often experience their bodies as extensions of the self, as vehicles for self-expression and action. Women often experience their bodies from the outside, as if looking in a mirror. We are constantly trying to see ourselves as others see us to and improve our looks based on that external perspective.

Radical feminists have worked to get women to experience their bodies from the inside out, to trust their emotions, and value their experiences. For many years they created alternative women's spaces, such as bookstores, political organizations, collective farms, and women's music festivals. Radical feminism has encouraged separation as a way of helping women to decolonize their minds.

Radical feminists have pushed society to value emotion, care, interdependence, and the other characteristics that have often been associated in advanced capitalist societies with the private sphere. Where the dominant culture values the public sphere and the personality traits that go along with it, radical feminists revalue the work of the private sphere and the characteristics linked to that labor.

Socialist feminism

Members of the third school of feminist thought, socialist feminism, are similar to the radical feminists in their attention to the values of the private sphere and in their critique of liberals as not doing enough to challenge the structure of society. They also argue for a deep analysis of the structures of society and claim that overcoming sexism needs to involve a radical restructuring of the social order. Unlike essentialist radical feminists, however, they are not comfortable with valorizing "women's ways" as biologically determined. Socialist feminists argue that the personality types we associate with masculine and feminine are the results of social conditioning.

Socialist feminists criticize radical feminists for making a virtue of the roles assigned by a sexist society. One example of this is seen in the radical feminist response to the claim often made in the dominant society that men are more rational and women are more emotional. Where a liberal feminist might be compelled to argue that women can be just as logical as men, radical feminists are more likely to challenge a value structure that puts reason above emotion. They would revalue the terms and argue for the importance of the female side.

Socialist feminists pay more attention to the social structures that force women and men to play their assigned roles. They would support liberal feminists' argument that women can be as rational as men, as well as radical feminists' claim that emotion is something important that needs to be valued. Going beyond these, socialist feminists would also look at the content of the terms and wonder what we mean by rationality and how it has come to mean something cold and calculating. This insight was the basis for a whole field of feminist philosophy of science that challenges the dispassionate approach to knowledge that is at the core of Western thought.[23]

Socialist feminists are interested in the political history that creates these roles and differences. They have done most of the work on analyzing the separation of spheres and how this historically based structure influences the roles and expectations put on men and women.

They have shown that the separation of spheres maintains women as the primary caregivers of children while at the same time making that labor socially invisible as labor. They also argue that the ideology of privacy has meant that the forms of abuse that take place in the home have not been, until recently, taken seriously as social problems.

Two of the more important demands of feminist movements have been for seeing the family as a social institution and for seeing violence against women as a political issue. Prior to the women's movement, political issues were those that had to do with participation in the public sphere. Feminists began to see that how these spheres were constituted was a political issue. It is a political issue—meaning an issue having to do with power relations—that many of the concerns of women were, by definition, seen as unimportant. One of the early slogans of the women's movement was "the personal is political." This meant that the ways women are kept in the private world, and the ways that the work done in the private world is ignored and degraded, are political in the sense of being based on operations of power.

Heidi Hartmann wrote an influential article in 1981 called "The Unhappy Marriage of Marxism and Feminism: Toward a More Progressive Union."[24] That article prompted many feminists to look more seriously at how male domination is structured into our predominantly capitalist society. Hartmann went on to found the Institute for Women's Policy Research in 1987, which focuses on economic issues such as better access to childcare, flexible work schedules, and health care for all.

Socialist feminists such as Hartmann are interested in challenging the gendered implications of the labor structure of capitalist societies. Where the dominant order was built upon the ideology of separate spheres, socialist feminists have worked hard to get society to acknowledge the activities of the private sphere as work. One of most influential books on this subject was Arlie Hochschild's *The Second Shift*. In that book, Hochschild argues that, while many heterosexual families have an ideology of equality, time-use studies show that women still work many more hours a week on the average than men, when wage labor and household labor are both counted. Who does the housework is seen by many as a trivial concern, but authors such as Hochschild show that it matters tremendously. Her work shows that a married woman with children works an average of one month a year more than her male partner.[25]

If we think of productive labor as the things that we do to meet our needs, then there is no good reason not to count household labor as labor. Ann Ferguson labels this category of work "sex/affective production." She argues that people must engage in three sets of activities that are largely outside of the sphere of wage labor to meet their basic survival needs.[26] One set of activities is related to our basic personal maintenance. These activities include cleaning up after ourselves, getting and preparing food, and taking care of children's physical needs. Another set involves taking care of our psychic needs. We all need to be listened to and receive emotional support. The third set is related to sexuality, which is a basic human need.

One commonality of these forms of labor in Western industrial societies is that women are disproportionately responsible for them, and because they are performed outside the sphere of wage labor, they are not considered part of the economy in standard economic calculations. Using a Marxist theory of exploitation, Ferguson argues that there are social structures in place that make it such that women tend to do more of this sort of work than they have done for them. They tend to pick up after others more than they are picked up after. They tend to do more supportive listening than they are listened to. And in the sexual arena, they do more to satisfy the sexual needs of others than they have their own sexual needs satisfied. In referring to all of these things as labor, Ferguson is following Marx in arguing that labor is not necessarily a bad thing, it is merely the name given to the things that we do to meet our needs. Things become work when the social relations around them are exploitative. For example, sexuality is a pleasurable human activity unless relations of domination structure it in exploitative ways.

One of the exciting things about the work of socialist feminists is that they are asking radical questions about the concept of work. The issue of how we define labor also has a real impact on women in the Global South. Many development strategies are aimed at increasing productivity. If productivity is defined as engagement in wage labor, then development programs will be aimed at getting more men involved in capitalist processes. Since many people living in poverty in the Global South are mostly engaged in subsistence lifestyles, these policies have tended not to decrease poverty and have often led to the breakup of the family, as men move to areas where wage work is more available. Women are then left with the even greater burden of managing the subsistence economy at home. Poverty reduction plans that focus on women as managers of the household economy have been much more successful at improving the lives of the world's poor.[27]

The gender systems in modern capitalist societies are built upon the myth of the nuclear family: the myth that a two-generation private family with a male wage earner and a female stay-at-home parent is the optimal form for human intimacy and childrearing. According to the dominant ideology, this family structure is natural and timeless. In her book *The Way We Never Were*, Stephanie Coontz shows that this family was never very widespread in society. It has been presented as a social ideal in order to keep women in place, and there is nothing natural about it.

Children's rights

In looking at the critique made against liberal feminists that they have abandoned the family, socialist feminists have pointed out that it is not their fault that there are fewer resources going to support home life. Concurrent with the second wave of feminism has been a marked decline in average wages. Whether they sought liberation or just money for the rent, many women had no choice but to go to work. The fact that fewer children have stay-at-home mothers has not been matched by increases in the availability of childcare or after-school care. The problem is one that the society as a whole needs to be responsible for. We need to find ways to make the needs of children a priority for everyone in society, not just for women.

Advocates for the needs of children have created their own movement in conjunction with, but separate from, the rise of the women's movement. Some in this movement work to give children as many rights as possible. Others see their role as advocating for adequate resources to be given to children. Children are disproportionately represented among the poor, and they don't have their own voices in public policy.

Penelope Leach has been an important member of this movement, and her ideas are in line with socialist feminism. She is most well known as the author of "how to" books for new parents. She also wrote an important book called *Children First: What Society Must Do—and Is Not Doing—for Children Today.* In that book, Leach argues that modern industrial societies are organized in ways that do not take the needs of children into consideration.

She describes the trap that our societies put mothers in:

> Babies and young children have to be cared for by committed adults in suitable environments for twenty-four hours of every day. Society expects all able-bodied citizens of working age to earn the money they need and the satisfaction they crave at specialized all-day jobs in special, distant and unsuitable places. People cannot be in two places at once, ergo one person cannot be simultaneously a solvent, self-respecting citizen and an actively caring parent.[28]

Leach believes that we should think of children as having some basic rights.

> Human rights must include children, because they are human. Children's rights must therefore, by definition, be the same as everyone else's. That phrase "children's rights" is only needed because children have been excluded. A new respect for children's rights will only upset the balance of power between the generations to the extent that it corrects accumulated inequities that arise from past disrespect and are lost in the mists of family histories that start "When I was a child . . ." and end ". . . it didn't do me any harm." The harm done has been so great that many individuals cannot even identify with the children they used to be. No wonder they see children in general as an out-group.[29]

Her solution to the problem of how to make the needs of children come first in society is consistent with the demands made for years by socialist feminists: we need to change the structure of our labor markets to make part-time jobs with benefits a reality. We need to have social resources given to generous forms of parental leave so that people can devote the time necessary to raise their children well. Many of the social democratic governments of Scandinavia have done well in these areas; the governments of the United States and the United Kingdom are two of the worst when it comes to taking care of children.

The United States is also moving toward a complex demographic problem, where children are disproportionately born in families of color, and the elderly are disproportionately white. Many states see a decrease in support for public programs, such as public school, as older, voting white majorities, do not see the children in public school as their children.

Intersectional feminism

While socialist feminists have done an excellent job analyzing the political and historical roots of much of the sexist structure of society, their analysis has often focused too much on the experiences of white women in the United States. Many women of color, and some white women, have worked to develop analyses that help us to understand the ways that sexism operates in the lives of women of color and how those insights will change the ways we understand sexism in general.

In her book *The Color of Privilege*, Aída Hurtado argues that the public/private split impacts women from different groups in different ways. Whereas white women are expected to occupy the private world, women of color are not allowed to have privacy.

Women of color have never needed to fight for their inclusion in wage labor. For as long as there has been wage labor in the United States, they have participated in it. They never were part of a domestic sphere that was romanticized and degraded. As Hurtado puts it,

> Women of color have not had the benefit of economic conditions that underlie the public/private distinction. Instead the political consciousness of women of color stems from awareness that the public is *personally* political. Welfare programs and policies have discouraged family life, sterilization programs have restricted reproduction rights, government has drafted and armed disproportionate numbers of people of Color to fight its wars overseas, and locally, police forces and the criminal justice system arrest and incarcerate disproportionate numbers of people of Color. There is no such

thing as a private sphere for people of Color except that which they manage to create and protect in an otherwise hostile environment.[30]

Where whites, especially those from the middle class, have often experienced the family structure as if it were natural, people of color have always had to fight for the right to have their family relations respected by society. This experience has also led to a stronger tendency to understand the role that the state plays in creating and maintaining aspects of the gender structure. Women of color have also done some of the most important work in feminist theory of looking at the ways that different systems of domination intersect with one another.

We can see this difference in issues such as domestic abuse. White feminists have demanded that violence in the home be taken as seriously as violence outside the home. This was a challenge to the dominant order because, according to the Lockean scheme of things, what happens in the home is not supposed to be the business of the state. Instead, each (white) man is the king of his household. Changing this situation has been very powerful for many women, and the government is getting better at taking domestic violence seriously.

But for people of color, this has been an ambivalent change. Many women of color have been helped by the fact that police departments and the judicial system are taking domestic abuse more seriously. But there is a downside for people of color and poor whites. Traditionally, the state has not been hesitant to intervene in the family lives of people of color and the poor. The private lives of people of color have always been seen as places where the state could intervene if it wanted to, for example, in targeting men of color with trumped up criminal charges.[31] Thus, the demand for freedom from intrusive state policies was as important for communities of color as was the need for a more active state.

Hurtado is working in the tradition of many women of color and antiracist white women by focusing on the ways that systems of domination are interrelated. Intersectional theory argues that it is impossible to understand sexism as a system on its own, without understanding how it is interrelated with racism, classism, and homophobia.

One of the most important books that challenged the limitations of a single-issue approach to sexism was bell hooks's *Feminist Theory: From Margin to Center*. Published in 1984, it argues:

> Privileged feminists have largely been unable to speak to, with, and for diverse groups of women because they either do not understand fully the inter-relatedness of sex, race, and class oppression or refuse to take this inter-relatedness seriously. . . . They reflect the dominant tendency in Western patriarchal minds to mystify women's reality by insisting that gender is the sole determinant of woman's fate.[32]

Because hooks sees forms of oppressions as interrelated, feminist struggle can never simply be about gender.

By repudiating the popular notion that the focus of feminist movement should be social equality of the sexes and emphasizing eradicating the cultural bases of group oppression, an intersectional multisystem analysis requires an exploration of all aspects of women's political reality. This means that race and class oppression are recognized as feminist issues with as much relevance as sexism.[33]

Hooks was born into a large working-class family in Kentucky in 1952. From an early age she began to question the world around her, especially the abuse her father perpetrated on her mother and the children. She began writing her first book at age nineteen and went on to write many influential and popular books. Her writing and lecturing have had a strong influence on feminist theory and helped many young women of color find a way to feminism that felt right for them.

The works of hooks and many other feminist theorists such as Audre Lorde, Gloria Anzaldúa, Angela Davis, and Elizabeth Spelman has been crucial for the development of intersectional theory that is the foundation of this book. Women of color working in a feminist context have done some of the most important work of analyzing society in ways that help us see the intersections of multiple forms of oppression.

Engendering sexuality

One of the main axes of power that is analyzed using intersectional theory is sexuality. The relative newness and accessibility of reliable birth control accompanied a "sexual revolution" in the 1960s. The increase in premarital sex unfortunately preceded an increased understanding of women's sexuality. Feminist critiques of the "myth of the vaginal orgasm" and other norms of hetero-sex were countered by male supremacist attacks on feminists as man-haters and lesbians.[34]

Lesbianism, and people's opinions about its political significance, was at the core of many discussions during the second wave of feminism in the late 1960s and 1970s. As feminists worked to understand the theoretical and strategic importance of lesbianism, many different approaches were taken.

Radical feminists tended to argue that having intimate relations with men was a bit like sleeping with the enemy. They argued that for women to truly decolonize their minds from patriarchy, it would be necessary for women to separate themselves from men. Some, such as Adrienne Rich in her very influential essay "Compulsory Heterosexuality and Lesbian Existence," argue that all women have a natural orientation to love and be close to other women.[35] She sees women's closeness as existing on a continuum from friendships to sexual relationships, and argues that this woman-to-woman bond is inherently revolutionary and that patriarchy works hard to suppress it. One of the early slogans of second-wave feminism was "feminism is the theory, lesbianism is the practice."[36]

The centrality of lesbianism to the movement provided rich ground for exploring the nature of sexuality and questioning the naturalness of the relations people found themselves in. As time went on, and more mainstream and less radical forms of feminism came to dominate, lesbians, and a radical critique of the patriarchal nature of many heterosexual relationships, became marginalized. Liberal feminists often went to great lengths to separate themselves from the more radical parts of the movement. Homophobia was used very successfully to scare many of these women into line.

Homophobic harassment is one of the most powerful tools for keeping rigid gender structures in place. Many straight feminists have discovered this as they have decided to play sports, to express their opinions publicly, and to refuse to defer to men's wishes. The most common reaction to these steps outside the boundaries of acceptable femininity is a charge of homosexuality.

As the women's movement developed, separatism became an increasingly important part of lesbian politics: separatism from straight men, from straight women, and from gay men. Looking back from the perspective of the current queer liberation movement, it is hard to imagine how separate lesbian and gay struggles have been. For much of the 1960s and 1970s gay men and lesbians largely worked in different organizations. It wasn't until the late 1980s that gay men and lesbians began to be deeply involved in the same organizations in any major way again. The decline in lesbian separatism began in the mid-1970s, as working-class women, women of color, bisexual women, and lesbian mothers of sons argued that separation from men was counterproductive to their struggles. In lesbians' rapprochement with gay men, the role of AIDS cannot be underestimated.

Lesbians and gay men shared outrage at the government's lack of interest in solving the AIDS crisis and at the vicious antigay rhetoric that many straight people expressed about AIDS. Many lesbians nursed brothers and coworkers through their terrifying illnesses.

The early 1990s saw an exciting new wave of gay and lesbian activism. This time, gay men and lesbians were working closely together. The movement engaged in intense debates about bisexuality. The word "queer" became the sign of a new political coalition that would include sex and gender outlaws of many stripes.

Queer politics was reminiscent of the early days of the women's movement, in which the goal was to challenge the constraints and hypocrisies of bourgeois family life. A large part of queer activism was cultural. By producing and wearing stickers with slogans such as "What causes heterosexuality?" and "Queer," by going en masse to straight bars and kissing and holding hands, and by being whoever they wanted to be wherever they were, queer activists were more focused on challenging the status quo than joining it.

And, whether it was a cause or an effect, the rise of a queer identity was an important part of the transformation that began to take place in the early 1990s. By taking the insult "queer" and turning it into a positive identity, groups such as Queer Nation instigated a whole new politics of visibility and radicalism.

In this process, queer politics revitalized discussions about the nature of sexuality and family and revitalized the cultural feel of a radical politics that was in many ways culturally empty. I remember going to demonstrations in San Francisco at this time and being so happy to see young militant people who looked like they were remaking the world around them. Just before the rise of queer politics, radicals had gone through a long period of being so marginalized that very few radicals expressed their politics in the ways they dressed and lived their lives. There was little going on in the cultural sphere that distinguished radicals from everyone else. So when we got together in demonstrations, there was little that was new in how we acted together. Demonstrations full of queer youth had a different quality. There people were forming a culture and making a new world by coming together. Demonstrations became colorful, outrageous, and full of life.

That more political movement was very important for pushing the larger society to see queer people as members of our society who were not going to be discreet or secretive about who they were. This increased level of visibility opened the doors to greater acceptance. During this period the larger more mainstream gay rights organizations began to push for the legalization of gay marriage and for equal treatment in the military. Those movements were often based on an assimilationist desire for equal rights more than for a deep transformation of the social order. The military has changed its rules to allow for full participation of gay and lesbian soldiers, and as "gay" marriage becomes legalized in more and more places, it is becoming clear that a fight for equal rights has radical implications. Overcoming legal discrimination means a deep transformation in the ways that we see gender in our society, and a deeper acceptance of people who do not conform to dominant gender expectations.

There has also been a strong push for recognition of the full humanity of people with a variety of gendered ways of being. There is a movement to allow babies with ambiguous genitalia to remain ambiguous until they are of an age to choose if they want surgery to make them conform to one particular side of the biological sex binary; there are movements for access to hormone treatment and surgery among transgender people; and there are movements among those who don't have sexuality as a large part of their world to be accepted. The wide variety of gender identities, and biological realities, as well as ways of connecting sexually has led many to in the movement use a string of letters to recognize the amazing variety of gendered ways of being. At this point some call this movement LGBTQQIA (lesbian, gay, bisexual, transgender, queer, questioning, intersex, and asexual).

Men and masculinity

Like femininity, masculinity is a tight box that people are often pressured to stay in, and any straying outside the box is met with fierce reactions that help scare people into playing their assigned roles. Dominant forms of masculinity set men up to be both the perpetrators and the major victims of violence. Seventy-five percent of murder victims in the United States are male.[37]

In recent years, the United States has experienced an epidemic of mass shootings at schools, with more than one happening each week. Almost all of the perpetrators of those shootings have been young white men. In his book *Angry White Men: American Masculinity at the End of an Era*, sociologist Michael Kimmel explains that there is a sense of "aggrieved entitlement" happening as a backlash to the cultural changes of the last fifty years. As whites and men have had to share a sense of status with women and people of color, and as the middle class has become squeezed economically, so that most of us have fewer economic opportunities and a more bleak sense of our future, many white men perceive their loss of a sense of security as being caused by the government favoring people of color and women, over white men.

> American white men bought the promise of self-made masculinity, but its foundation has all but eroded. The game has changed, but instead of questioning the rules, they want to eliminate the other players. Instead of questioning those ideals, they fall back upon those same traditional notions of manhood—physical strength, self-control, power—that defined their fathers' and their grandfathers' eras, as if the solution to their problem were simply "more" masculinity. [38]

And he argues, those same white men who feel intimidated by the changes society has gone through are vulnerable to having their fears preyed upon by organizations, such as the Tea Party, and media, such as hate radio, that whip that insecurity into anger and help focus its target against government spending for a social safety net.

In his book *Masculinities*, Robert Connell argues that there are a variety of dominant images that different men are expected to live up to. There is hegemonic masculinity, the white man of power who is in charge and powerful and always knows what's best, and there are different stereotypes of men of color, gay men, and working-class men. Connell argues that all men need to navigate these stereotypical expectations as they come to have a positive sense of themselves.

Approaches to organizing

In both the women's and queer movements there have been powerful organizations that have taken a mainstream lobbying and lawsuits approach to social change. Two of the biggest organizations at the present time are the National Organization for Women (NOW) and the Human Rights Campaign (HRC). These groups use the ideology of civil rights to demand an end to discrimination on the basis of gender or sexual orientation. Radicals often criticize these organizations for being assimilationist and for not putting up enough of a challenge to the status quo.

For much of the later part of the twentieth century, radicals in both the women's and queer liberation movements challenged the institution of marriage, arguing that marriage supports male domination and allows the state to regulate and domesticate sexuality. So, the focus on "gay marriage" was hotly contested in radical queer circles. Those supporting gay marriage have argued that activists should be against state-sponsored discrimination, which is what the prohibition against gay marriage constitutes. A similar argument is made around the question of gays in the military. You don't have to support the military to be against the state being able to keep you out of it.

In both of these gender-based movements, there has been a general acceptance among radicals of the goals of the liberals, while at the same time demanding deeper changes that the liberals often do not talk about and sometimes want to distance themselves from. While NOW has worked hard to challenge workplace discrimination, radicals have also challenged the structure of a labor market that was built around the needs of a male breadwinner. And while early second-wave feminism demanded access to abortion, radicals worked to redefine a reproductive rights movement to include opposing forced sterilization.

Many people have noticed the extent to which feminism has been able to accomplish significant changes from within the network of present social relations. Some social justice advocates have taken this success to mean that feminism is not really a radical movement—it is merely a superficial change from within the basic oppressive structure of society. This idea is often at the heart of claims that feminism, queer politics, and antiracist politics are "identity politics." What this expression means is that these are movements about personal identity, and only class-based politics is about transforming the structure of society.

Yet feminist theorists have shown how intertwined the structural and the cultural are. As women begin to feel that they matter and that their role in life should be as more than support people for men and children, they bring complex perspectives into the political mix. When they advocate for pay equality, they often also advocate for workplaces that are less based on competition. Fighting for equal pleasure in the bedroom often leads to a confidence that manifests itself at work. Women of color have argued strongly that for women to be free, society needs to be rid of racism, sexism, and homophobia. Socialist feminists have worked through trade unions and other forums to advocate for more flexible work schedules and for better access to childcare and better pay and working conditions for childcare workers. This change in childcare institutions is linked to women's desires to develop parts of themselves that are not related to the home. Identity and personal desires are intricately connected to the web of structural oppression.

There is a broad world of feminist and queer politics that exists in-between liberal demands for inclusion without radical change and radical demands for total social transformation. Within this broad range there is a general belief that change happens from within the network of social relations; and cultural, personal, and economic demands are interrelated, and can be won through consciousness-raising, direct action, and the power of many people refusing to settle for less than justice.

Radical social change happens when many heterosexual women fight with their partners about who does the housework; it happens when feminists or queers develop styles of dress that challenge dominant expectations; it happens when women insist on wearing comfortable clothes and not shaving their legs.

But these personal struggles only have significant social impact when they exist as parts of a movement that links these acts and gives them social meaning. Feminists and queer activists have been at the forefront of theoretical developments that help us to understand the psychological and cultural aspects of movements toward social change. Much of the social change work done by feminists and queer activists takes place in the cultural and personal spheres. Changes of consciousness are important for transforming the social fabric. The relationship between changes in consciousness and culture and changes in the structure of society is a complex one that will be dealt with in more depth in Chapter 9.

CHAPTER 7

People, Nature, and Other Animals

WHEN AL GORE'S FILM *AN INCONVENIENT TRUTH* CAME OUT IN 2006, IT got a lot of people to take climate change seriously. In the popular imagination, it became clear that on the horizon of our existence horrific things were going to happen. The polar ice caps would melt, coral reefs would die, hurricanes and droughts would become more severe, and the oceans would rise. Gore ended his film with a list of things one could do to address this catastrophic problem: change the kind of light bulbs you use, drive less, write your congressperson. There was something deeply disturbing to many of us who do social justice work about the end of the film. Were those solutions really enough to deal with a problem of such apocalyptic proportions?

Many people in the environmental movement feel that their job is to ring the alarm bells and get everyone to see the depth of the problems. The hope is that people will be shocked into action. It turns out that the opposite is the case. Most people know climate change is a serious problem, and the more they get a sense that the things they can do are tiny compared to the scope of the problem, the more disempowered they feel. This all leads to a sense of paralysis that looks like apathy and denial.

I shared in that general sense of paralysis that followed that film, until I read George Monbiot's book *Heat: How to Stop the Planet from Burning.*[1] In the book, Monbiot shows that the kinds of changes needed to solve the climate crisis are challenging, but within reach. He argues that we need policies to push a shift toward massive investments in public transportation, policies that invest in new energy infrastructure, policies that get people

185

to make their houses more energy efficient, and serious investments in renewable energy. The main takeaway I got from the book was that there are
enough resources for everyone to live well on this planet in sustainable ways,
and that the actions needed were more political than individual.

Many people are working on cheaper and better sources of renewable
energy, more sustainable processes for making things, and better ways of
organizing our cities. Even with existing technical knowledge we could build
a world in which everyone has a comfortable life and we stay within our
ecological limits. But we won't be able to get there simply by each of us
being green consumers. Rather what needs to happen is the development
of policies that promote the use of renewable energy and efficient ways of
doing things. That is a political problem. Once I realized all of that, I became
a climate change activist.

Currently, I am working to get institutions to divest from fossil fuels.
The idea behind the fossil fuel divestment movement is that the main thing
blocking a move to the kind of things that are needed to make this massive
shift is the power that the fossil fuel industry has over our political systems.
And there are reasons for them to push for things to stay the same. If we
are to stay within safe levels of greenhouse gasses in the atmosphere, then
more than 75 percent of the assets of fossil fuel companies will need to remain unburned.[2] Those companies have a lot to lose, and they are some of
the most powerful entities in the world, with economies larger than most
countries.

In her book *This Changes Everything: Capitalism vs. the Climate*,
Canadian journalist Naomi Klein writes that dealing with the climate crisis
is in alignment with a set of practices necessary for building a more socially
just world. She argues that as she came to understand the things needed to
solve the problem of climate change, she

> began to see all kinds of ways that climate change could become
> a catalyzing force for positive change—how it could be the best
> argument progressives have ever had to demand the rebuilding of
> local economies: to reclaim our democracies from corrosive cor-
> porate influence; to block harmful new free trade deals and rewrite
> old ones; to invest in starving public infrastructure like mass tran-
> sit and affordable housing; to take back ownership of essential ser-
> vices like energy and water; to remake our sick agricultural system

into something much healthier; to open borders to migrants whose displacement is linked to climate impacts; to finally respect indigenous land rights—all of which would help to end grotesque levels if inequality within our nations and between them.[3]

For much of the twentieth century, environmental politics were on a different path from the rest of the world of social justice. Many environmentalists had argued that people were the problem, and that nature was something to be kept pristine and separate from people who were seen as a scourge. Others were convinced that if we each changed our personal consumption habits the problem would go away. Klein is part of a growing environmental justice movement that sees the deep connections between environmental problems and other problems in the social world.

Within the environmental movement, there are different approaches to the most basic question of what is causing the problems the movement is trying to solve. Are environmental problems caused by ignorance? By individual irresponsibility? By too many humans? By a separation of people from nature? By racism and capitalism? Each of these has been given as an answer by major sectors of the environmental movement. And each rests on a different theory of the nature of the environmental crisis. Understanding these differences can help us understand more fully the implications of what people say when they talk about environmental problems and it can help us see what kinds of action are likely to lead to a better world.

Liberal environmentalism

Liberal environmentalists tend to frame the issue as one in which all people are hurt by irrational policies. They believe that these bad policies can be changed by informing people about them, by individuals choosing to act more responsibly, and by asking the government to develop and enforce protective regulations. Liberalism as a philosophy tends to focus on the individual as a rational person who can be persuaded to do good. This leads many liberals to focus on education as one of the most important strategies to create change. They believe that if everyone knew about the problems, they would be easily solvable. Beyond education, liberal environmentalists often engage in lobbying government officials and in lawsuits against companies that break environmental laws. People taking this approach have been very effective at gaining support for many important environmental laws that constrain polluters.

Liberal environmentalists have been able to pass groundbreaking legislation, such as the Clean Air and Water Acts. These pieces of legislation have made a huge difference in the quality of life, especially in urban areas. Before the Clean Water Act of 1977, many lakes and rivers were used like sewers, expected to drain pollutants from factories. In 1969, the Cuyahoga River in Ohio was so polluted it actually ignited into flames. As a child in Southern California, I remember having to stay indoors during recess at school because the air was so polluted that it was dangerous for us to play outside.

While the lakes are still not very clean, and urban children still breathe polluted air, each of these environmental problems has improved significantly. Liberal environmentalists were also able to lobby for the protection of much of the nation's parklands; for the Endangered Species Act, which has had a significant impact on slowing down development and other practices that cause species extinction; for outlawing some pesticides; and for setting limits on the emissions of other pollutants, such as dioxin.

Deep ecology

Deep ecologists argue that these approaches have not been enough to solve the problems facing us. Deep ecologists see human beings as inherently destructive and argue that, if we want to have a good environment, we need to limit the impact of human beings as much as possible. One of the founding documents of this movement was "Deep Ecology Eight Point Platform," written by Arne Naess and George Sessions. Its authors claim that nonhuman life has value in itself, independent of its usefulness for human purposes. Naess and Sessions argue that human beings could live in harmony with nature, but that this would require drastic changes in how we live our lives and, most significantly, in how many people there are. "The flourishing of human life and cultures is compatible with a substantially smaller human population. The flourishing of non-human life *requires* a smaller human population."[4]

Like the liberals, deep ecologists don't make distinctions between different sorts of human society and like liberal environmentalists they rarely talk about power and how it impacts human practices. Dave Foreman, one of the cofounders of the deep ecology organization Earth First!, has written that human impacts should be limited by any means necessary. In his book *A Field Guide to Monkeywrenching*, he argues for the use of militant tactics, such as property destruction and putting spikes in trees so that they cannot be cut down without endangering loggers.

Foreman brought a lot of controversy to the movement with his advocacy of tree spiking. He also generated animosity toward deep ecologists when, in the 1980s, he argued that AIDS was not such a bad thing. He claimed that there were too many people on the planet and that famine and disease were the earth's way of limiting the scourge that is humanity.

In more recent years, people who have this perspective often argue that we have entered the age of the Anthropocene. Among scientists the term is gaining ground as a description of a new geological period, where human impacts are so large that *anthros*, or humans, are a defining factor of the physical processes of the planet. Among environmentalists, it is often used to mark humans as the cause of environmental problems, without marking what kinds of human practices are the ones that are destructive, and which human practices are to blame.

Ecofeminism

Sharing somewhat the nature-centered view of the deep ecologist, ecofeminists argue that people need to develop more healthy relationships with the rest of nature. Susan Griffin's *Women and Nature* was one of the most influential texts in this school of thought. In it she argues that, because of their relationship to childbearing, women tend to be closer than men to the processes of life, and are therefore more attuned to nature and its needs than are men.[5] For her, as long as men dominate, society will have a dominating relationship to nature. To solve this problem, we must shift away from an instrumental relationship to nature, whereby we see nature as insensate matter to be used for human gain. Instead, we must see ourselves as a part of the biological world and strive to bring that world into harmony. Thus, solving the problems of how people deal with the rest of nature is part of solving the problem of domination more generally. The most central task for saving the natural world is to abolish male domination.

Many people have objected to the essentialism in Griffin's approach. Are women really more attuned to nature? If women do experience the world more in terms of relationships than in terms of individuality, is this difference biological, or is it something we are socialized into? If men are inherently disconnected from nature, what will their role be in a nonoppressive society? All of these questions have been raised with respect to Griffin's work and to ecofeminism in general.

There is another strain in ecofeminist thought that argues that there is nothing inherently nature-centered about women, but that there is something deeply antagonistic to nature about masculinity as it is constructed in Western society.

Val Plumwood makes this argument in her essay "Nature, Self, and Gender: Feminism, Environmental Philosophy and the Critique of Rationalism."[6] Plumwood develops a theory of relationships between people and nature. Her work helps us conceptualize what healthy relationships would look like and to distinguish them from unhealthy ones. She is critical of strains in ecological thought that start from the claim that people are one with nature. The problem with seeing people as part of the cosmic whole of nature is that "the view of humans as metaphysically unified with the cosmic whole will be equally true whatever relations humans stand in with nature— the situation of exploitation of nature exemplifies such unity equally well as a conservation situation and the human self is just as indistinguishable from the bulldozer and Coca-Cola bottle as the rocks or rainforest."[7]

In other words, if humans are simply part of nature, then everything we create is also natural. So saying humans should be one with nature doesn't help us learn how we should relate to the rest of the natural world.

But Plumwood also rejects the view that we should see nature as something fundamentally separate from people, and as something to be used instrumentally. The seventeenth-century French philosopher René Descartes did much to develop this view. He saw nature as dead material working according to mechanical rules. For him, people are rational creatures who can use their reason to control the material world. Plumwood sees this dualistic and instrumental view of nature as a template for our destructive attitude toward other people as well as nature. Instrumental reason encourages us to understand the world in terms of hierarchies, to see ourselves as meaningful and important and other beings as mere tools to accomplish our desires.

Plumwood wants us to develop ways of understanding human relations and relations between people and nature that are built upon a view of human beings as deeply interrelated with one another and with the rest of nature. Unlike the cosmic unity view that she criticizes, she does not see people as indistinguishable from each other or from nature. But neither is it the case that nature is merely a passive thing to be used. Rather, people and the rest of nature have concrete and specific needs in relation to one another, and it is the task of human beings to figure out ways to make this set of relationships work.

Vandana Shiva develops a similar idea in her book *Staying Alive: Women, Ecology, and Development.*[8] Shiva is Indian and was trained as a physicist. She is one of the leading theorists and organizers of the transnational environmental movements growing out of the Global South.

Shiva argues that the industrial societies of the West have turned complex relationships between people and their natural world into simple relationships between people and "natural resources," understood only in terms of their profit-generating capabilities.

> The scientific revolution in Europe transformed nature from *terra mater* into a machine and a source of raw material; with this transformation it removed all ethical and cognitive constraints on its violation and exploitation. The industrial revolution converted economics from the prudent management of resources for sustenance and basic needs satisfaction into a process of commodity production for profit maximization. Industrialism created a limitless appetite for resource exploitation, and modern science provided the ethical and cognitive license to make such exploitation possible, acceptable—and desirable. The new relationship of man's domination and mastery over nature was thus also associated with new patterns of domination and mastery over women, and their exclusions from participation *as partners* in both science and development.[9]

Shiva draws on the experience of rural women in India who extract resources from the forest while also working to maintain the forest's health. She contrasts those who see a forest as "timber" from those who see it as a complex living organism, capable of providing many things for human needs.

Animal rights

Another movement, very different from and sometimes in conflict with the environmental movement, also developed out of a critique of the relationship between people and nature in Western societies: the animal rights or animal welfare movement. In the 1980s, many people began to question the ways animals were treated in laboratory experiments and in factory farming. They began to question the instrumental uses animals were being put to. As in the environmental movement, many people saw the problem as one of people's alienation from nature. If people were to stop seeing themselves as a species chosen by God for domination over other species, and were to begin to see all of life as interconnected and as valuable, then many of the practices currently engaged in with respect to animals would be seen as intolerable.

The use of animals in laboratories was almost completely unregulated in the 1980s. It was easy for activists to find horror stories of labs in which animals were tortured for amusement and experiments in which animals were subjected to much more pain than was necessary for scientists to achieve their goals.

Many people in this movement were not radicals in any broad sense. They were compassionate people who wanted to stop what they saw as unnecessary suffering. Some were not particularly concerned about human suffering, either.

Others have linked their opposition to animal suffering to an opposition to human oppression. Like ecofeminists, they see the way nonhuman animals are treated as part of a more general alienated and instrumentalist approach to life that is related to systems of human oppression. Some, especially those in the movement to fight factory farming, have anticapitalist leanings. They see capitalist agriculture, in which animals are used as "inputs," as part of a system in which profit comes first and human needs and compassion don't count.

Many used this analysis in the fight against Monsanto's push in the 1990s to have dairy farmers inject their cows with bovine growth hormones in the early 1990s. Activists pointed out that the practice would put small family farms out of business, do nothing good for consumers and possibly put their health at risk, while turning the cow into even more of a milk machine than she was already forced to be. Cows are already bred to produce so much milk that their udders are dangerously large. Some are so large that they drag on the ground and cause back problems for the cows, leaving them barely able to stand. Making them produce more milk would only make these problems worse.

More recently the movement has focused on the conditions in pig farming, where massive farms have cruel conditions for pigs, their waste destroys local ecosystems, especially rivers, and the pigs must be fed huge quantities of antibiotics and hormones to keep them alive under such unhealthy circumstances.

When the animal rights movement puts its demands into a perspective that focuses on the need for compassionate relationships with all beings, there is a real continuity of interests between it and other social justice movements. But sometimes people in the animal welfare movement, like deep ecologists, see the problems they are trying to solve as being caused by people in general, and are not always sensitive to the ways that systems of social power lead people to treat animals or the environment badly.

If we think of our social problems as caused by people in general, then the solution is getting rid of people or arguing that there should be fewer of us, which leads to a self-hating paralysis, or a racist desire to get rid of other people, usually defined as overpopulating people of the Global South. If, on the other hand, we are able to see the social mechanisms that cause our problems, then we are in a much better position to work toward changing them.

Environmental justice

The environmental justice movement shares the attention paid by ecofeminists to the relationships between systems of human oppression and nature. This tendency focuses on ways that the destruction of nature is related to oppressive political and economic relations, and people in this tendency have worked hard to create a broad environmental movement with ties to other progressive movements.

Many people see Warren County, North Carolina, as the birthplace of the environmental justice movement. It was there, in 1982, that the first demonstrations took place that explicitly linked issues of race to the environment. The state of North Carolina had decided to place a toxic landfill in Warren County, which was overwhelmingly populated by people of low income and people of color.

Over five hundred protesters were arrested in demonstrations led by some of the nation's leading civil rights organizations. The Congressional Black Caucus, United Church of Christ Commission for Racial Justice, the Southern Christian Leadership Conference, and others came together to raise the issues of race, class, and the environment.[10]

While the demonstrations were not able to stop the landfill, the protests had a few successes. They resulted in the Government Accounting Office doing a nationwide study on race, income, and environmental destruction. Residents were able to force the county to monitor the leaching of PCBs out of the landfill and into their drinking water. And they forged a powerful coalition that has since been working nationwide to fight against racial and economic discrimination in the impact of environmental destruction.[11]

The environmental justice movement focuses on race and the ways that environmental destruction has disproportionate impacts on people of color. It also focuses on class and the ways that the poor are disproportionately impacted, and on capitalism as an important force in generating poverty and unaccountable corporate behavior.

There is a tradition in the environmental movement of seeing environmental problems as fundamentally about wilderness. This part of the movement was developed by people who liked to visit wilderness and were concerned that it be protected. Thus, they tend to focus on the development of national parks and the protection of endangered species.

Since its beginning in the early part of the twentieth century, the mainstream environmental movement also focused on issues such as urban air pollution, clean water, and occupational health and safety. Still the image of the movement, and the cultural politics of many in it, led to an impression that environmentalism was something for middle-class white people to pursue. And many of the white and middle-class people in the movement carried their racial and class blind spots into the work they did, often not valuing the different perspectives brought by people of color or their leadership.

Like ecofeminists people in the environmental justice movement define the environment as the whole set of relations between people and the rest of nature. The environment includes the air we breathe, the water we drink, the ways our cities are designed, the ways food is grown and marketed, etc. By looking at environmental destruction through the lens of the experiences of people of color, the environmental justice movement has forced a major shift of perspective in other parts of the environmental movement.

The environmental justice movement started out in communities of color wanting to challenge the racial politics of the movement as a whole. The organization Urban Habitat, based in San Francisco, is a leader in this movement. It started the journal *Race, Poverty and the Environment*, which links environmental issues with movements to protect farm workers, immigrant rights organizations, those concerned with the quality of life in urban areas, and struggles against neocolonialism and for the sovereignty of indigenous people in the United States and throughout the world.

The disproportionate impact of environmental destruction can be seen in the following facts, outlined by Mark Dowie in *Losing Ground*:

> More than 200 million tons of radioactive waste lie in tailings piles on Indian reservations The rate of cancers affecting the sex organs among Navajo teenagers is 17 times the national rate. . . . Every year 300,000 farm laborers (mostly Hispanic) suffer pesticide-related illnesses and disorders. . . . Black urban male children are almost three times more likely to die of asthma than their white counterparts.[12]

People in the movement have found that when whites complain about environmental problems they are much more likely to be taken seriously and have their problems addressed than when problems are raised by people of color.

In 1994, the Sierra Club had a bitter internal fight over these issues. At that time, voters in the state of California were considering a ballot initiative, Proposition 187, aimed at limiting the civil rights of undocumented immigrants. Many members of the Sierra Club supported this move because they believed that as the population of the state increased, there would be an increase in stressors on the environment. One way to protect the environment was to limit population by making immigration less attractive.

Many other people inside the Sierra Club supported the politics of the environmental justice movement and promoted the view that the mainstream environmental movement needed to be more hospitable to the interests of people of color. They argued that the population increase caused by immigration was not a significant cause of environmental destruction, and that the proposition amounted to nothing more than scapegoating. The internal fight was intense, and in the end those advocating for the rights of immigrants won.

In addition to the focus on race, and the importance of voices of people from low-income communities of color, environmental justice advocates point to capitalism's drive for profit as an impulse toward environmental destruction. Capitalism allows producers to externalize many of their costs so that the producers don't need to pay for the costs associated with what they produce.[13] This means, for example, that even though cars clearly create smog, and smog significantly increases the rate of asthma, car manufacturers are not taxed for the cost of caring for people who develop asthma. Cars remain relatively cheap and health care remains a separate, and for many people impossible to afford, expense.

Because of this externalization, the pressures to limit automobile use or lessen the pollution they generate must come from social movements. To some extent, government has represented the interests of those negatively affected by cars, but it often capitulates to the power of the automobile manufacturers and the ideology that they are not responsible for the pollution created by their products. And capitalism has led to a situation where corporations have a disproportionate amount of influence on government policy.

In his book *Divided Planet: The Ecology of Rich and Poor*, Tom Athanasiou focuses on the drive for profit among transnational corporations (TNCs) as the main engine of environmental destruction. These corporations "play country against country, ecosystem against ecosystem, simply because it is good business sense to do so. Low wages and safety standards, environmental pillage, ever-expanding desires—are all symptoms of economic forces that, embodied in TNCs, are so powerful they threaten to overcome all constraint by the society they nominally serve."[14]

Solving the climate crisis involves deep challenges to entrenched power. Given the power that fossil fuel companies have over our political system, solving our environmental problem will not be easy. It will require an end to subsidies that make fossil fuel so cheap, strong regulations and planning for improved building and transit practices, massive investment in better energy grids, and massive incentives for renewable energy. But as

Naomi Klein argues, dealing with climate crisis "could become a galvanizing force for humanity, leaving us all not just safer from extreme weather, but with societies that are safer and fairer in all kinds of other ways as well."[15]

As we move to a greener economy, many environmental justice activists are working hard to make sure that the solutions chosen are ones that benefit everyone. Organizations such as Green for All and the Emerald Cities Project are working to get resources to low-income communities of color to get jobs in the emerging areas of solar installation and weatherization of older homes. All of these authors see a transition to a new sustainable and socially just economy as growing from our work to solve the climate crisis.

Population versus consumption

The relative significance of the rate of population growth versus the rate of consumption is one of the key dividing lines within environmentalist camps. Because liberal environmentalists and deep ecologists do not look at the ways society places people into different social positions, they tend to see the problems related to nature in generic terms: people cause environmental problems, so fewer people would cause fewer problems. This leads many in each of these camps to focus on population as a major cause of environmental destruction. Since population generally grows more slowly in more affluent societies, strategies to limit population inevitably target poorer parts of the world. When liberal environmentalists and deep ecologists address issues of consumption, they point out the looming problem of fast-growing populations in the Global South becoming wealthy enough to consume on par with the industrialized nations.

This view is often called neo-Malthusianism after Thomas Malthus, a nineteenth-century English writer who argued that population growth inevitably leads to poverty, as too many people fight over a finite amount of resources. It is one of the most common views of the cause of environmental destruction but is strongly opposed by environmentalists in the Global South, by ecofeminists, and by those involved in the environmental justice movement. These forces argue that how society is organized and how resources are used is far more important than how many people there are.

In his book *How Much Is Enough?*, Alan Durning argues that consumer society is a major cause of environmental destruction.

> In industrial countries, the fuels burned release perhaps three fourths of the sulfur and nitrogen oxides that cause acid rain. Industrial countries' factories generate most of the world's hazardous chemical wastes. Their military facilities have built more than 99 percent of the world's nuclear warheads. Their atomic power plants have generated more than 96 percent of the world's radioactive waste. And their air conditioners, aerosol sprays, and factories release almost 90 percent of the chlorofluorocarbons that destroy the earth's protective ozone layer.[16]

What this means is that a focus on reducing population as a way of solving the environmental problem targets the wrong people and targets them with the wrong remedy. The problem isn't too many people, it is too much consumption. A whole village of people in some poor countries consumes less than one person from the United States, a country that houses only 5 percent of the world's population but consumes 18 percent of the world's energy.[17] On a worldwide scale, the world's wealthiest 20 percent of people consume 86 percent of the goods and services produced from the earth's resources.

On the question of consumption, environmental justice advocates argue that capitalism structures society in such a way that decisions about resource use are largely controlled by capitalist interests. When we look at the consumption patterns of people in the United States, we see that they are not determined by individual choice alone. Rather, large-scale social forces determine the consumption choices we have before us.

In her book *Asphalt Nation: How the Automobile Took Over the Nation and How We Can Take It Back*, journalist Jane Holtz Kay explains that during the period when automobiles were becoming more popular, car manufacturers worked hard to get government subsidies for the infrastructure needed for the expansion of car use. Trolley owners, on the other hand, took a different strategy and tended to try to make it on their own. Where many US cities once had well-developed systems of mass transportation, the largest being in Los Angeles, those systems were dismantled as people switched from public transportation to private cars.

The auto manufacturers were interested in promoting buses as an alternative to trolleys and trains because buses required the same road development as cars.

> In 1932, General Motors, the manufacturer of buses and owner of the largest share of Greyhound [Bus Company], formed a consortium of tire, oil, and highway men to buy and shut down America's streetcar systems. Attacking the trolley mile by mile, the syndicate of General Motors, Firestone, Standard Oil, and Mack Truck, allied as National City Lines, cajoled and bought off local officials. . . . By 1940 total public transportation ridership had shrunk by 2 billion. The magnificent rail lines fell, taking with them the private rights-of-way, the street corridors, that had insured their fast passage.[18]

As car use became more popular, cities were organized to be compatible with car use. "With the trolleys would go the cities they served. In their stead the motor suburb demanded even more cars. Housed in places ill equipped to provide public transportation, some 13 million suburban Americans were now devoid of rail service altogether."[19]

In 1949, the federal government passed a housing act that was supposed to replace old dilapidated housing in the cities with new, higher quality housing. This policy, along with a push to build highways, led to the development of the contemporary situation of "white flight" suburbs and cities with disproportionate numbers of poor people of color.

> For cities the combination of building highways and taking homes was a disaster; for if urban renewal sounded fine in theory, it was mayhem in practice. "Negro removal" was the epithet of opponents. Beset by road building, the continuing arrival of the rural poor from the South and from Caribbean nations, and the exodus of the rich, cities flared into that expletive, "inner cities." Costing more than $10 billion, the urban renewal program leveled 300,000 more homes than it raised in the next quarter century. Combined with the magnet of single-family housing policies—FHA [Fair Housing Administration] and VA [Veterans Administration] postwar programs that excluded urban and minority populations and income tax deductions for property taxes and mortgage

interest—the 1949 act had monumental consequences. The out-
ward drift seemed like an act of nature. Its hurricane force swept
through urban centers and blew the brick house down.[20]

Carlos Davidson writes that while many neo-Malthusians see urban
sprawl as caused by too many people, they ignore more important factors
such as "economic incentives for developers to build large houses at low
density, real estate interests' dominance of zoning and land-use planning
decisions, and government funding for sprawl-inducing freeways instead
of urban mass transit."[21] Thus, much more important than the number of
people in a city is how that city is organized. And city organization is as
much related to broad social policies and the actions of government and
financial interests as it is to the individual choices of consumers.

Some cities have attempted to solve the problem of urban sprawl and
poor transit systems through careful planning. One planning technique
called "urban growth boundaries" has been used successfully by the state
of Oregon. Jane Holtz Kay, author of *Asphalt Nation*, writes that Portland,
Oregon, "was revived to become a transit-friendly pedestrian place. The
downtown plan, based on light-rail, has become the symbol of success.
Fare-free zones bring walkers striding a dozen abreast along city streets in
the center. In the outskirts, mass transit, not the freeways, has become the
armature of growth."[22]

Urban growth boundaries make it difficult to build on the outskirts of
cities and relatively easy to build within the urban core. This leads to denser
cities and less suburban sprawl. A city with less sprawl is one that is much
more energy efficient and easier to get around in by foot, bicycle, rail, and
bus.

The wealthy people of the world consume more resources than do the
poor. This is true in wealthy countries and in poor ones. But our consumption is determined by many factors beyond the control of individuals, such
as how our cities are organized, the availability of mass transit, where our
jobs and homes are located, and the systems of production used to produce
the things we need to survive.

There are exciting moves in cities all around the world to move toward
sustainable practices, such as bus rapid transit, where buses are given pref-
erential treatment over cars; smart growth; and opening up cement sur-
faces to allow water to soak into the ground. More than half of the world's

population currently lives in cities, and people are figuring out ways to make city life work for people as well as for the environment. While many environmentalists romanticize life in the country, in the United States, the carbon footprint of people who live in cities is significantly lower than it is for people who rural areas. Homes are smaller and people travel shorter distances. Many people are working to reengineer cities so that they are environmentally and socially sustainable.

These projects are much more likely to move us toward our goals than ones that focus on population as the cause of environmental problems. Feminists have pointed out another problem with the neo-Malthusian approach to solving environmental problems. Those focusing on controlling population growth have often advocated for programs that are coercive and violate women's rights and are ineffective at reducing population growth. A statement by the Committee on Women, Population, and the Environment claims that

> Environmental degradation derives from complex, interrelated causes. Demographic variables can have an impact on the environment, but reducing population growth will not solve [environmental] problems. In many countries, population growth rates have declined yet environmental conditions continue to deteriorate. Moreover, blaming global environmental problems on population growth helps lay the groundwork for the re-emergence and intensification of top-down, demographically driven population policies and programs which are deeply disrespectful of women, particularly women of color and their children.[23]

The reason neo-Malthusians cause problems for women of color is that

> Because so many of their activities have been oriented toward population control, rather than women's reproductive health needs, they have too often involved sterilization abuse; denied women full information on contraceptive risks and side effects; neglected proper medical screening, follow-up care, and informed consent; and ignored the need for safe abortion and barrier and male methods of contraception. Population programs have frequently fostered a climate where coercion is permissible and racism acceptable.[24]

This view, echoed by Betsy Hartmann in her book *Reproductive Rights and Wrongs: The Global Politics of Population Control*, is becoming more widely accepted with time, and family planning and development programs are increasingly concerned with women's empowerment as a path to eliminating poverty and to lowering rates of population growth.

Thinkers such as Hartmann argue that it is far more important to improve quality of life for the poor than it is to coerce them to have fewer children. As long as they are very poor, it is often in their interest to have many children, and no amount of education about and access to birth control changes that. People in these societies rely on their children to take care of them when they are old, and they know that many of their children will die young. Further, in many agrarian societies, children are actually economic assets, contributing economically to the family at a young age. In such societies, it is often a wise choice to have many children. Only changing the conditions of their existence changes that equation.

Sustainability

If the life-supporting ecosystems of the planet are to survive for the future, then consumer society will have to dramatically curtail its use of resources—partly by shifting to high-quality, low-input durable goods and partly by seeking fulfillment through leisure, human relationships, and other nonmaterial avenues.[25]

Members of the Global Scenario Group (GSG) in their report "Branch Points: Global Scenarios and Human Choice," describe three general possibilities for human development.

One involves a development of the status quo, with markets being the major force driving social development. According to that scenario, "During the next century, population more than doubles and economic output increases by more than eleven-fold as developing regions gradually converge towards socio-economic patterns in the rich countries."[26] Because of the dramatic increase in economic activity, with no change in the type of development involved, this scenario results in extreme destruction of the environment—continued species loss, continued rise in toxic pollution, and accelerated destruction from global warming.

GSG also posits a "breakdown" scenario, in which the world's inequality increases and social and political unrest destabilize the world. This scenario leads to a political "fortress world" in which there is much famine and warfare.

Finally, the group poses the possibility of a "great transition" in which nongovernmental organizations and transnational institutions are able to force a change in values and policies. According to this scenario,

> equality and sustainability, rather than economic growth, come to define development. Material sufficiency becomes the preferred lifestyle, while ostentatious consumption is viewed as primitive and a sign of bad taste. . . . Under popular pressure organized locally, nationally, and globally, governments and corporations begin negotiations around a New Planetary Deal. Building on intentional reductions in material consumption in rich countries, agreements are reached on international mechanisms for the redistribution of wealth. . . . Integrated settlement patterns place home, work, shops, and leisure activity in closer proximity. Automobile dependence is reduced radically, and a sense of community and connectedness is reestablished.[27]

This plan involves major social reorganization and the development of some new technologies. It can only be realized with an increase in popular pressure to control corporations and governments.

Lifestyle changes

Environmentalists interested in a social justice perspective argue that the consumption patterns of people in wealthy countries are the most serious cause of environmental problems. But it is not simply a matter of the personal choices of the wealthy. Rather, it requires deep transformation of the social patterns of the wealthy and middle classes of the world.

There is a strand in the environmental movement that focuses on individual lifestyle choices as the answer to environmental problems. This view is most strongly expressed in the book *50 Simple Things You Can Do to Save the Earth*. The book claims in its introduction that "*50 Things* empowers you to get up and do something in your day-to-day life to help solve global environmental problems. And even the most 'intractable' environmental problems march toward a solution when everyday people get involved."[28] In some ways, that's true—when people advocate for change, many important things can happen. But what matters is the nature of people's actions and the changes for which they advocate.

The book includes suggestions for growing a lawn using less water and recycling aluminum cans, but it doesn't ask its readers to take collective action. This lifestyle approach to environmentalism is dominant in the popular consciousness. Lifestyle environmentalism can feel very good to the individual. And there are some important ways that individual lifestyle changes can sometimes add up to significant social change. An individual's choice to become a vegetarian, for example, might spur others to stop eating meat. If the practice spreads widely, it could end up having a dramatic impact on the amount of meat eaten. And, since a meat-based diet uses much more grain than a vegetarian one, the environmental impact of a widespread shift to a diet lower in meat could be considerable.[29]

The important thing to note here is that individual lifestyle changes are significant when they are taken up by larger numbers of people. It is important to distinguish things that make us feel good about ourselves from things that will change the destructive social patterns we want to change. Knowing the difference is often difficult, and much in our cultural system encourages us to think in individualistic and moralistic terms rather than in strategic and institutional ones.

In practical terms, it is often hard to tell whether or not an individual lifestyle change will have a broader impact. The key question is whether the lifestyle choice has a chance of being broadly embraced. An individual's choice to travel by bicycle will have limited impact on overall energy use if public transit remains abysmal and bike riders have to risk their lives to compete with cars for space on roads. Bike riding becomes significant when it is accompanied by a push for streets to be engineered to accommodate bikes. In communities all across the country, organizations of bike riders have done this, often beginning with mass riding events that disrupt automobile traffic.

Lifestyle changes can be valuable, but they need to be understood in terms of deeper questions about the causes of a particular problem and the most effective means of solving that problem. The politics of fighting for urban growth barriers and public transportation is vastly different from the politics involved in choosing to drive less. And, many in the environmental justice movement have argued, it is much easier for the privileged to make lifestyle choices, such as buying a fuel-efficient car, than it is for the poor. A focus on developing systems of public transportation also builds a coalition between the poor and wealthier environmentalists, whereas a focus on individual choice often alienates low-income people.

Lobbying, lawsuits, direct action, and coalitions

In his 1995 book *Losing Ground*, Mark Dowie argues that "unlike the other new social movements of the 1960s and 1970s (women's, peace, civil rights, and gay liberation), which are essentially radical, the ecology movement was saddled from the start with conservative traditions formed by a bipartisan, mostly white, middle-class, male leadership. The culture they created has persisted until very recently and hampered the success of the movement."[30] Dowie claims that people in the movement used their privilege to advocate for reforms from the state. In the beginning, this was accomplished by lobbying and educating and without making too many waves. In the 1970s and '80s, this movement was often challenged by deep ecologists and environmental justice activists who took a more militant approach. They did not believe in the ability of the system to make significant changes, and they often used direct action tactics to stop the sorts of behavior they opposed.

The environmental movement has a long history of using militant tactics. In 1971, Greenpeace launched a flotilla of twelve small boats to draw attention to and disrupt US atomic tests in Amchitka, Alaska. For many years, deep ecologists engaged in property destruction to stop logging. The idea behind direct action is to go straight to the source of a problem and confront corporations and transnational institutions directly. In some ways, this strategy has developed as compensation. When you can't get a change by pressuring government, then you go around government and directly to the problem.

Environmental justice advocates have been critical of both the mainstream and deep ecology tendencies. They have argued that the liberals put too much faith in nonconfrontational action, and that the deep ecologists are naïve about the social forces they are confronting. When environmental concerns are pursued without attention to the social context in which they take place, environmentalists can alienate the people they need on their side to win.

A new wave of direct action developed in the fight against the Keystone XL pipeline. That movement has been very thoughtful about the race and class implications of its actions, and it has been very successful at building broad coalitions. The first phase of the pipeline was completed in 2010; its purpose was to move the incredibly dirty tar sands oil from Alberta, Canada, through the United States to market in the Gulf of Mexico. Burning those sources of oil would be devastating for the climate. And their extraction has been devastating to indigenous people in Alberta. The fight against the pipeline has brought together unlikely coalitions of ranchers in Nebraska, climate justice activists from the cities, as well as indigenous people from Canada and the United States.

The protests against the project are part of a broader transnational movement that Naomi Klein calls "Blockadia." Which she says "is not a specific location on a map but rather a roving transnational conflict zone that is cropping up with increasing frequency and intensity wherever extractive projects are attempting to dig and drill, whether for open-pit mines, or gas fracking, or tar sands pipelines . . . what unites Blockadia to is the fact the people at the forefront—packing local county meetings, marching in capital cities, being hauled off in police vans, even putting their bodies between earth movers and earth—do not look much like your typical activist, nor do the people in one Blockadia site resemble those in another. Rather, they each look like the places where they live."

One way that people in these movement have kept their coalitions together is by doing research on how few jobs the extractive projects create, and how many more jobs could be created by investing in more sustainable projects.

Coalition work is often very difficult and requires an incredible openness to hearing the other side and to allowing one's own most deeply felt beliefs to be challenged. It usually requires the development of deeper political analyses of the issues than those presented as common sense through the media.

Work time reduction is another powerful example of the potential of coalitions around environmental politics. In his book *Sharing the Work, Sparing the Planet*, Anders Hayden argues that one way to work toward a dramatic reduction of consumption levels in the countries of the North, without lowering living standards, would be to reduce the amount of time people work. His point is that as people work more hours, they tend to buy more things to satisfy their desires in quick and easy ways.

"Breaking out of the 'work and spend' cycle would create abundant time for a wide variety of self-directed activities."[31] It would also contribute to gender equity, as families would have less of a time crunch and be more able to divide household labor fairly. And it could help lead to lower rates of unemployment, as employers shift to hiring more workers to work for less time. Building a movement to reduce working hours without lowering wages would help develop a coalition between labor, environmentalists, and feminists.

These sorts of coalitions are never easy to build. But their potential is amazing. They have an especially strong impact on the development of popular consciousness and support for the movements. If people must choose between labor and the environment, some will go each way, but neither movement can become very strong. If they must choose between a labor and environmental coalition on the one side and business and a polluted environment on the other, environmental concerns are much more likely to win.

Conclusion

The environmental problems before us are immense. Solving them will require a deep transformation of the capitalist tendency to hold no one responsible for protecting the common good. Global survival will require the development of transnational mechanisms, such as the very successful Montreal protocol on ozone depletion, that force national governments to keep companies from producing chemicals that destroy the atmosphere. It will require the phasing out of fossil fuels as the primary energy source for industrial, home heating, and transportation applications. And it will require new ways of meeting the needs of the global population while addressing the economic aspirations of low-income people in the Global South.

Most people are concerned about the environment and want to see policies enacted that will protect it. Environmental issues might serve as an important unifying set of interests for people to work together for a better world for everyone. This will only happen if people are brought to understand the ways that their fates are tied together with the fates of those living in the Global South and the nonhuman parts of the biosphere.

People all around the world are fighting against trade deals that favor transnational corporations, against genetically modified organisms, and for sustainable and just economic policies. There is still time to make the transitions required for a sustainable planet, and more people are seeing with more clarity what is needed to get us on that path.

CHAPTER 8

Whose Side Is the Government On?

ON JUNE 6, 2013, THE *WASHINGTON POST* AND THE BRITISH NEWSPA-per the *Guardian* began to publish stories about an extensive spying program operated by the National Security Agency (NSA). Edward Snowden, an analyst working for a firm that contracted with the NSA had decided to act as a whistle-blower and share important details of this secret program with journalist Glenn Greenwald. It turns out that the NSA was keeping records of every phone call made by anyone in the country and was going further and looking into the content of phone calls all over the world.

In the wake of the 9/11 attacks, the United States was thrown into a state of panic, and the government was able to pass the Patriot Act that allowed for enhanced government surveillance. But the programs Snowden exposed go far beyond what the Patriot Act allowed.

Some US citizens feel that it is all right for the government to spy on them, because they believe that the government would only look at things it had a reason to look at, and since they are doing nothing wrong, there is no reason to worry about being watched.

Most of us who have been involved for a long time in social justice work see it differently. We are aware of the ways that the FBI spied on Martin Luther King Jr., among others, and used the information they gained to discredit him. In the 1980s I was involved with a peaceful antiwar organization that we later learned was infiltrated with FBI agents spying on our activities. Often agents in groups such as ours act to distort the work of those groups, sometimes acting as *agents provocateurs*, trying to move a group to engage in illegal activity.

Snowden was charged with breaking the Espionage Act, a law passed in 1917 to prevent opposition to military recruitment and operations during World War I. For those of us who oppose many of the wars the United States gets involved in, it is frightening to think how quickly speech that is protected by the First Amendment can be turned into criminal activity, and how few limits there are on our government's ability to spy on us.

The "war on terror" that has engulfed the world and led to major wars in Afghanistan, Iraq, Libya, and Syria has meant a dramatic rollback of civil liberties at home and a major escalation of aggressive behavior against other countries. Where once communism was the reason given for intervening in other countries, now antiterrorism is the framework used to rationalize long-term goals in places as far flung as the Philippines, occupied Palestine, and Colombia.

Critics of this militarism and repression wonder: Did President Obama continue to pursue George Bush's "war on terror" because it was somehow good for capitalism? Did he do it because he was politically indebted to the military-industrial complex? Or was it all about elections and his fear of looking weak?

In terms of foreign policy, the US government often looks like one unified force, with most mainstream politicians supporting illegal NSA spying operations; supporting the harsh treatment of whistle-blowers; allowing the illegal prison camp in Guantánamo, Cuba, to continue holding prisoners in violation of international law; supporting targeted killings of suspected terrorists; and supporting drone strikes wherever a terrorist threat can be claimed. Patriotism and the fear of terrorism are used to silence opposition, both in the government and in the population as a whole. And the political system seems fairly unified in supporting an aggressive foreign policy agenda.

Yet there are other times when the two parties in power fight with one another, and some forces in the government pursue progressive agendas. The US government acts to regulate some of the worst behavior of corporations, to build low-income housing and to tax the rich and use that money to support the poor. While President Obama pursued the war on terror aggressively, he also worked for some social programs that serve society as a whole.

Given these different roles, should social justice activists demand that we "smash the state," meaning get rid of existing governments entirely? Or should we demand that government develop a strong social safety net? When we want to protect the environment, should we insist that the government rein corporations in, or should we take direct action against polluters? Are schools in capitalist societies small enclaves of socialism, or are they instruments for producing workers for the capitalist class? Am I colluding with capitalism if I work for a government-run community mental health agency? Is it politically valuable to try to use government resources to help people? Should we support taxation when taxes go to pay for social goods, such as parks, medical access, and services for the poor? Or should we oppose taxes as giving more strength to the government?

Democracy

Most people in the United States, no matter what their political perspective, support democracy, and argue that the government should be democratic. While democracy is one of the most cherished values among social justice advocates, mainstream Americans, and right-wing Americans alike, exactly what it means is much more complex than it might appear at first.

Early European and European-American theorists of democracy took many of their ideas from the experiences of the colonists in the Americas. Large parts of the US Constitution were inspired by the Great Law of Peace, the constitution of the Iroquois.[1] Early European explorers of the Americas told Europeans amazing stories of large societies in which everyone needed to be consulted for decisions to be made. Thomas More's *Utopia*, one of the first European books to deal with democracy, was inspired by such travelers' tales.

While the concept of democracy that developed during the Enlightenment had deep roots in non-Western societies, the standard story tells us that democracy was invented by Europeans in Greece during the classical period around 500 BCE, and then rediscovered by Europeans during the Enlightenment.

Those supporting Western expansion will often talk about spreading Western values to the rest of the world. Because democracy arose in Europe in the period of the Enlightenment when capitalism was also on the rise, many Western thinkers associate the two.

In *Democracy and Capitalism*, Bowles and Gintis argue that capitalism is antithetical to democracy. Capitalism is based on the principle that people who own private property should have the ability to do what they want with their property. Many people think this right to private property is part of what democracy means. Yet for those who don't own property, it means that they must sell their labor in order to survive, giving up their rights to self-determination to the person who gets to decide how they will act for eight hours a day. Whole aspects of society that are crucial to people's survival are not in the domain of things that are expected to be democratic: they are expected to be the private decisions of the owners of capital.

Theorists of democracy have made a few distinctions that are helpful for understanding the concept of democracy. Democracy can be formal or substantive; it can be representative, direct or "monitory"; and the idea can be understood as applying only to politics, or it can be applied to economics and culture as well.

In the United States, we have a limited formal democracy rather than a substantive democracy. It is formal in the sense that there are clear rules for how people make decisions, and people are able to elect representatives to make and change those rules. To have a substantive democracy would mean putting ordinary people in a position to make decisions about the important things affecting their lives. Largely as a result of social movements, we have some level of substantive democracy in the United States. Laws apply to everyone, regardless of race and gender, to a greater extent than they did at the time of the country's founding.

Substantive democracy in the United States is very limited, however. There is nothing to guarantee that the people who are elected into positions of power will act in the interests of the majority. And people don't have as much impact on who gets elected as they could because of the money involved in campaigns, the way our two-party system functions, and the influence of commercial media on our political culture.

Social justice advocates usually favor direct over representative democracy. For people to really rule their lives, they need to be actively involved in making decisions about things that impact them. There are many challenges and tradeoffs between efficient use of people's time and levels of participation. Anarchists tend to favor higher levels of involvement, and socialists are often more concerned with the outcome of a decision-making process than about the process itself.

In his book *The Life and Death of Democracy*, Australian political Theorist John Keane argues that in the middle of the twentieth century a new form of democracy began to emerge that was based on the ways that social movements and transnational organizations hold systems of power accountable by monitoring and challenging them. He calls that new form "monitory democracy."

> The years since 1945 have seen the invention of about a hundred different types of power-monitoring devices that never before existed within the world of democracy. These watchdog and guide-dog and barking-dog inventions are changing both the political geography and the political dynamics of many democracies, which no longer bear much resemblance to textbook models of representative democracy, which supposed that citizens' needs are best championed through elected parliamentary representatives chosen by political parties. . . . Power-monitoring and power-controlling devices have begun to extend sideways and downwards through the whole political order. They penetrate the corridors of government and occupy the nooks and crannies of civil society, and in so doing they greatly complicate, and sometimes wrong-foot, the lives of politicians, parties, legislatures and governments. These extra-parliamentary power-monitoring institutions include—to mention at random just a few—public integrity commissions, judicial activism, local courts, workplace tribunals, consensus conferences, parliaments for minorities, public interest litigation, citizens' juries, citizens' assemblies, independent public inquiries, think-tanks, experts' reports, participatory budgeting, vigils, "blogging" and other novel forms of media scrutiny.[2]

Keane claims that the representative principle of "one person, one vote, one representative" is being supplemented by "one person, many interests, many voices, multiple votes, multiple representatives"[3]

If democracy is everyone's goal then we can understand different schools of political thought as favoring different aspects of democracy. Their view of the purpose of government, or what political scientists call "the state," are different, and their views of what governments relationship to democracy is also differ.

Conservatism

Generally conservatives want people to be individually responsible for their own well-being, and see democracy as being served by a government that does as little as possible to allow people the autonomy to rule themselves. They see a social safety net as making people weak and dependent. They generally advocate for small government, yet most mainstream conservatives support high levels of government spending for the military and for surveillance. They support strong government in terms of national security because they believe that individuals and their private property must be protected for individuals to have liberty and freedom.

Conservative US libertarians argue that, without a state, people will be free to do whatever they want. They believe that people who own private property should be allowed to do what they want with it. They see taxes as the state stealing people's private property. They are believers in extreme versions of the philosophies of Adam Smith and John Locke. For them the most democratic society is the one where individuals have as much liberty as possible, and they believe that this is consistent with capitalism. Libertarians and mainstream conservatives are often on opposite sides of arguments about government surveillance.

In extreme versions of libertarianism, such as the philosophy of Ayn Rand, the argument isn't even that this is best for everyone, but rather that it is best for the best people. Rand argued for a social Darwinist view that the best thing for humanity is for the "best" to be given what they want and the rest to fend for themselves. Randian libertarians often do not favor democracy. Rather they favor a society developed for the strong.

Anarchism

Anarchists sometimes call themselves libertarian socialists and use the word "libertarian" to mean someone who believes in personal liberty. They are sometimes confused with right-wing libertarians because of some superficial similarities in their positions. Both believe in the importance of people being "free" and both see government as limiting individual freedom. The important difference is that anarchists don't believe in the sanctity of private property. They focus on freedom as freedom from domination, rather than freedom as freedom from interference. For them, if you smash the state but allow capitalism to remain, you are in essence saying that the rich should be able to do what they want with society's resources. Because this leaves people who don't own capital unable to determine the conditions of their existence, there is no personal freedom, and it isn't an anarchist society.

Anarchists also point out that the libertarian ideal of capitalism without a nation-state wouldn't really work, since capitalism requires the state to protect private property and engage in repression. The state is a gatekeeper institution that enforces an unjust social order. Without the state, they argue, other forms of injustice would be relatively easy to abolish. Thus, for anarchists, getting rid of the state is an important step in getting rid of capitalism.

Organizations such as Food Not Bombs, a transnational network of over four hundred independent groups, have used this approach to the state in their work challenging poverty. Rather than demanding that the government offer more food services for the poor, Food Not Bombs makes food in someone's kitchen and goes out and gives the food to people who need it. They do this without permits or officially recognized kitchens. In doing this, they are promoting the development of a society based on what the nineteenth-century Russian anarchist Peter Kropotkin called *mutual aid*—or people helping one another freely out of their natural sense of interconnectedness.[4]

According to anarchist organizations such as Food Not Bombs, people should work to solve social problems communally rather than asking the state to solve them. On another level, by naming themselves Food Not Bombs, they are pointing out the injustice of spending billions on the military in a country where millions of people routinely go hungry. Members hope that, through this form of political struggle, they can both live a good communal life in the here and now and help to undermine the legitimacy of the state.

Anarchists usually advocate strong forms of participatory democracy as a way of developing communal bonds, and for fostering people's ability to jointly work out solutions to social problems. They usually see representative democracy as empty and formal, and they argue that governments exist to reinforce unequal and undemocratic power relations.

One of the main criticisms that anarchists have of the state is that they see it as the base from which large-scale violence is perpetrated and justified. As the nation-state has risen as a social form over the past few centuries, governments have been the source of tremendous amounts of violence. Much of the violence perpetrated by states has been done to protect private property, as in the case of the early days of police forces in the United States.

Internationally, much state violence been motivated by the desire to create wealth through colonialism and slavery. State violence has been a core aspect of states since the beginning of the development of nation-states. And even as the world is moving past colonialism and its successor neocolonialism, state-sponsored violence in the form of runaway militarism is becoming embedded in the ways many states function.

Colonialism and neocolonialism

In the 1870s King Leopold of Belgium wanted to join in on the scramble for Africa. He wanted the wealth and prestige that a colony would bring. Unfortunately for him, the major European powers had a hold on much of the continent, and the people of Belgium weren't especially interested in colonization.

Leopold ended up developing an intricate scheme that used the famous explorer, Henry Morton Stanley, and a fake benevolent organization, the International African Association, to realize his dreams. In his book *King Leopold's Ghost*, Adam Hochschild tells an amazing story of one man's personal ambition and ruthlessness, and along the way he ends up telling us quite a bit about how colonialism worked, how the people of Europe went along with it, and how movements to end oppression can succeed. Hochschild writes that Leopold had learned from his many attempts to buy a colony that none was for sale; he would have to conquer a part of Africa held by Africans and create his own colony. Doing this openly, however, was certain to upset both the Belgian people and the major powers of Europe. If he was to seize anything in Africa, he could do so only if he convinced everyone that his interest was purely altruistic. In this aim, thanks to the International African Association, he succeeded brilliantly. Viscount de Lesseps, for one, declared Leopold's plans "the greatest humanitarian work of this time."[5]

Under cover of the benevolent organization, Leopold sent Stanley to the Congo basin to secure trading partnerships with many of the Congolese people. He did this by negotiating treaties that the Congolese believed were agreements to friendly cooperation, but which Leopold and his operatives knew to be agreements to turn Congolese land over to Leopold's trading company. These treaties worked to keep other European powers out of the Congo.

As for actually taking the land from the Congolese, the only thing that could accomplish that goal was brute force. Leopold set up a major military operation that forced the people of the Congo, one tribe at a time, to work for Leopold's company as slave laborers on rubber plantations.

> If a village refused to submit to the rubber regime, state or company troops or their allies sometimes shot everyone in sight, so that nearby villages would get the message. But on such occasions some European officers were mistrustful. For each cartridge issued to their soldiers they demanded proof that the bullet had been used to kill someone, not "wasted" in hunting or, worse yet, saved for possible use in a mutiny. The standard proof was the right hand from a corpse.[6]

Tswambe, a Congolese, describes an especially hated official of Leopold's company:

> All the blacks saw this man as the Devil of the Equator. . . . From all the bodies killed in the field, you had to cut off the hands. He wanted to see the number of hands cut off by each soldier, who had to bring him the baskets. . . . A village which refused to provide rubber would be completely swept clean. As a young man I saw [Fiévez's] soldier Molili, then guarding the village of Boyeka, take a big net, put ten arrested natives in it, attach big stones to the net, and make it tumble into the river. . . . Soldiers made young men kill or rape their own mothers and sisters.[7]

These brutal practices went on for many years, as Leopold was able to convince people in Belgium and the rest of Europe that he was helping develop the Congo through free trade and humanitarian missionizing. In part, he was able to do this because the people of Europe were inclined to believe in the mission of uplift. They believed this much as people in the modern industrialized nations continue to believe that "development" is taking place in the Third World at the present moment. Few ask for evidence, and the idea that the Western powers have something positive to offer to the "backward" people of the world is taken as a given.

Leopold also succeeded for as long as he did by controlling the information that came out of the Congo. His empire started to unravel when he lost that control. In the 1890s, E.D. Morel, a shipping company clerk, noticed that rather than the expected goods for development—fabric, tools, health and educational equipment—the ships going to the Congo were laden with chains, guns, bullets, and other military gear. Morel hooked up with several other people who had suspected that Leopold's operation was not humanitarian, and together they began what Hochschild calls the first human rights campaign in the Western world. After many years, they succeeded in exposing the company and having Leopold's empire brought down.

The result was that Leopold's personal empire Congo Free State was taken over by the government of Belgium and turned into the Belgian Congo, which, while stopping some of the most brutal practices of Leopold's regime, continued its basic practices of colonial exploitation.

In 1961, Patrice Lumumba came to world prominence as a leader of the movement that freed the Congolese from Belgian colonial rule. As the Belgians left, the Democratic Republic of the Congo was thrown into turmoil, and Lumumba reached out to the socialist world for help. That put him onto a collision course with US policy, and the CIA worked with Congolese forces to overthrow and assassinate Lumumba.

The coup that preceded the assassination brought US ally Mobutu Sese Seko to power. Mobutu ruled as a brutal and corrupt dictator until 1997. In those four decades, he became enormously wealthy, while the people in this resource-rich country remained in desperate poverty. The United States maintained its support for Mobutu throughout his years in power. The instability that followed left the country in a state of civil war. More than five million people died as a result of that war, mostly dying of diseases such as malaria and diarrhea from unclean water. Now the Democratic Republic of the Congo is rich in natural resources particularly in cobalt, copper, and diamonds, and it is the site of intense struggles over who will control access to and get wealthy off of those resources.

The Democratic Republic of the Congo has fallen victim to the "resource curse" many observers have noted, where countries with very valuable resources end up with high levels of corruption, and therefore governments with low levels of accountability. Often the finding of a valuable resource in a country is correlated with a steep decline in living standards for most people.

The current "backwardness" of this resource-rich country is intimately related to the politics of colonialism and neocolonialism. In a general sense, colonialism means the domination by one people over another. Sometimes colonizers leave a people's culture intact and merely control their political and economic systems. In other cases, the colonizers attempt to incorporate the conquered people into their way of life. Sometimes the conquered are integrated as subordinated peoples and sometimes they are mostly killed.

Colonialism has existed in a variety of forms for thousands of years. The Aztecs of Mexico colonized many other indigenous groups and extracted wealth from them. In the twelfth century, people from Mongolia conquered much of Asia and subordinated the local people to their direct political control.

The colonial relations most important for understanding the modern world have their roots in the projects that began with Europe's colonization of the Americas and the enslavement of the people of Africa in the sixteenth century. That wave of colonization provided the foundations for capitalist domination over earlier economic and social systems and greatly expanded the world system that we are living under today. By the middle of the nineteenth century, European powers had colonized almost all of the Americas and Africa, and had colonial relations with much of Asia.

The primary motivation for colonization is profit. If one country controls some foreign territory, it can administer it for purely economic interests. It can extract wealth and control the labor conditions in brutal ways not possible in the home territory. It can gain access to resources not available in the home territory, and it can keep others from having access to those resources.[8]

In some cases, colonization for profit was carried out by companies chartered by governments they were involved with, as in the case of the British East India Company. At other times, such as the Spanish conquest of the Americas, the government itself profited directly from the enterprise. In the case of the Belgian venture in the Congo, colonization was carried out at the behest of one person, King Leopold, who profited personally from the colony, at considerable expense to the Belgian government.[9]

One of the most powerful writers on colonialism was Aimé Césaire, born in Martinique in 1913. He was a poet, politician, playwright, and essayist. He was one of the first authors from a colonized country to write in ways that valued African traditions. This work sparked the arts movement called Negritude. Césaire was also deeply involved in movements to end French colonialism.

In his book *Discourse on Colonialism*, first published in 1950, Césaire discusses the purpose of colonialism, beginning with a definition of what it is not:

> Neither evangelization, nor a philanthropic enterprise, nor a de-
> sire to push back the frontiers of ignorance, disease, and tyranny,
> nor a project undertaken for the greater glory of God, nor an at-
> tempt to extend the rule of law. To admit once and for all, without
> flinching at the consequences, that the decisive actors here are
> the adventurer and the pirate, the wholesale grocer and the ship
> owner, the gold digger and the merchant, appetite and force, and
> behind them the baleful projected shadow of a form of civilization
> which, at a certain point in its history finds itself obligated, for
> internal reasons, to extend to a world scale the competition of its
> antagonistic economies.[10]

Césaire points out that for as long as there has been colonialism there have
been attempts to justify it in humanitarian terms. But, fundamentally, colonialism involves one group taking the resources of another by force. The
colonial powers have been motivated by the search for wealth. They use
military, political, and economic means to get it.

"Imperialism" is the word used in the Marxist tradition to describe the
ways that countries expand their domination from the national to the world
scale. While "colonialism" is the word people tend to use when describing
economic domination, they often use the word "imperialism" when wanting to emphasize the use of military power to conquer a national territory.
The word came into common usage to describe the British empire which
had a worldwide reach that included direct rule, military control, and economic domination in territories as far-flung as Australia, India, southern
Africa, Palestine, Jamaica, Canada, and Hong Kong. The saying "the sun
never sets on the British empire" only stopped making sense in the postwar
period when the economic and military power of the United States began to eclipse the trading habits of the increasingly politically independent
Commonwealth states.

Many colonies, such as the United States and Australia, were settler
colonies. This means that the local people were to a large extent murdered to
make way for a new country populated by immigrants from the home country and their descendants. Those places have largely become well-integrated
parts of the wealthy Global North. The other dominant pattern was for
European powers to import slaves, and a relatively small number of people
from the home country.

As a result of the anticolonial struggles of millions of people, beginning with the liberation of Haiti in 1804, most colonial regimes have been overthrown, with the exception of a few important cases such as Puerto Rico. Unfortunately, they were often replaced by neocolonial regimes. Most colonies were class divided, with some subset of the subordinated population helping the colonial power rule over the rest. This elite group, because its members were more educated in the ways of the colonizers and already occupied positions of privilege, often became the rulers in the new post-colonial society.

In many countries, this new ruling class ended up running society in much the same way as the old colonial powers. Because the colonial economy was built around providing goods and services to the colonizing country, cutting off that relationship would starve the newly independent nation of its primary source of capital. Unless it is able to radically transform the economy, the newly independent society has tended to do things the way they were done before. Though they are nominally independent politically, neocolonial countries remain economically dependent upon either their former colonizers or other foreign capitalists. Thus, even though they are not colonies, these neocolonial governments allow imperialism to continue.

The US government has worked alongside other Western powers to keep neocolonial regimes in power, to develop Western imperialist relations, and to keep those people who would run their countries in the interests of the poor out of power. The poor countries of the Global South continue to play a vital role in the world economic system, providing raw materials and labor at low costs.

This is changing significantly as some formerly colonized countries have begun to develop better systems of governance, and have begun to shift their economies to better serving their own populations. As the legacy of the Cold War fades, we are entering a period where it is increasingly difficult for the United States to keep dictators and neocolonialists in power.

The former colonial powers continue to exert their influence on postcolonial nations through rigged elections, invasions, and more subtle tactics such as manipulating trade union movements. The United States has played a major role in this process, even in countries where it did not have direct interests in the colony before independence.

US foreign policy and militarism

In 1986, Jeff Paterson graduated from high school in the small central California town of Hollister. Looking for adventure, a sense of meaning, and a way to make a living, Paterson signed up for the Marine Corps. After a while, his optimism about the military as an honorable establishment whose purpose was to defend democracy began to fade. Paterson began to see the racism of his fellow soldiers and the negative impacts the military had on the lives of the people living near US bases overseas, especially the women.

Then, in 1990, Paterson was called up to serve in the Persian Gulf in the war against Iraq. By then, Paterson had learned about US foreign policy in Central America and had grown more disillusioned. He knew enough about the US military to suspect that the purposes for fighting in the Persian Gulf were not to protect democracy, either in Kuwait or in the United States. Paterson refused to go.

Paterson was the first person in the US military to publicly oppose that war, and he started a newsletter called *The Anti-WARrior*. The military estimated that, all told, 3,500 members of the military refused to serve in the Persian Gulf. For his organizing work, Paterson was given a "less than honorable" discharge from the Marines. After that, Paterson dedicated much of his time to speaking out against US militarism and helping people to see the role the military plays in US imperialism.[11]

When World War II was over, General Eisenhower gave a speech in which he expressed concern about the development of a "military-industrial complex" that would come to rule the nation. "The conjunction of an immense military establishment and a huge arms industry is new in the American experience. The total influence—economic, political, and even spiritual—is felt in every city, every state, house, and every office in the federal government. . . . In the councils of government, we must guard against the acquisition of unwarranted influence, whether sought or unsought, buy the military-industrial complex."[12]

In the time since that speech, military spending has continued to be an enormous part of the US government spending, accounting for more than 30 percent of the total federal budget.[13] According to Ismael Hossein-Zadeh, in his *The Political Economy of U.S. Militarism*, in 2006, the United States had around six thousand domestic bases, one thousand overseas bases, 1.5 million military personnel, and "the official Pentagon budget for the 2005 fiscal year, which does not include the cost of war in Iraq and Afghanistan, stands at $419 billion."[14]

The United States accounts for 47 percent of global military spending. And much of the rest of the world buys its military hardware from us. There are eighty-five thousand companies in the United States that profit from military contracting. Hossein-Zadeh argues that ever since the end of World War II there has been a conjuncture of interests between the Pentagon, the civilian military agencies that shape foreign policy, militaristic think tanks, and these contractors. Together they have formed a vortex of influence that is always looking for conflicts to keep its profits and influence flowing.[15]

Many analysts have argued that the push toward war from this military-industrial complex, is an important factor in understanding how the United States deals with any particular foreign policy crisis. Another important motivator behind US militarism is the role that has emerged for the United States since World War II, as the dominant force for maintaining conditions conducive to capital accumulation around the globe. As governments arise that might threaten the ability of global corporations to extract wealth, the United States has usually been there to make sure that those governments were toppled. It has done this through support for dictatorial governments, such as the Somoza regime in Nicaragua and the Suharto regime in Indonesia, and it has done it through indirect means, such as supporting coups d'état in countries such as Iran, Chile, and Guatemala.

In 1951, the people of Guatemala elected Jacobo Árbenz as president. Árbenz was a moderate socialist who attempted to take unused land away from landowners. One of the largest of these landowners was the US-based company United Fruit. Árbenz's plan was to give the land to the poor to help fight poverty. United Fruit pressured the US government to do something. Soon the CIA was training disgruntled members of the Guatemalan military to overthrow the government.

In 1954, Árbenz was deposed according to plan. Since that time, Guatemala has been wracked by civil war, and the majority of its people live in crushing poverty. It has been ruled by a series of military dictatorships and civilian regimes subordinated to the military. And while many of the terrible things that have happened in that country since Árbenz's ouster are related to internal dynamics in Guatemala, the US government has consistently played a crucial and negative role.

This story has been repeated over and over in the second half of the twentieth century. The US government helped bring to power people who would later become its enemies, such as Manuel Noriega and Saddam Hussein. It trained the terrorist Osama bin Laden, helping him fight the Soviet Union in Afghanistan. Often a willingness to fight against perceived threats to global capital or regional stability is all that is required to qualify for US support. The US government is not concerned with the humanitarian credentials of its allies.

Increasingly, the US government has wanted to have as much freedom as possible to play its global role, without constraints from transnational bodies such as the United Nations (UN) or the World Court. Militarism has guaranteed US dominance in the world economy, and US leaders have worked hard to protect that position. While the United States occasionally works with transnational institutions, more often it fights to undermine international treaties and transnational bodies that might hold it accountable.

In the early 1980s, the US government was caught mining the harbors of Nicaragua as a part of the war it was waging through its surrogate force, the contras. The government of Nicaragua brought the United States before the World Court and won. The United States decided to ignore that ruling. In 1987, the UN passed an antiterrorism resolution that exempted national liberation struggles from the definition of "terrorist." The United States and Israel were the only two countries to oppose it, citing their opposition to the antiapartheid struggle in South Africa and the Palestinian movement in Israel's occupied territories. Yet in the 1990s, the United States supported the use of the International Criminal Tribunal for the former Yugoslavia to try Serbian leader Slobodan Milosevic.

The US government has, in general, chosen to act independently, building what coalitions it can to support its actions, but opposing international agreements that are widely supported by other nations around the world. This has led many people in the rest of the world to see the United States as the ultimate force responsible for maintaining oppressive rule in their countries, particularly in Middle East. They see the US government supporting oppressive governments in the region; imposing brutal sanctions on the people of Iran; starting wars in Afghanistan and Iraq; and supporting the state of Israel no matter what it does to the Palestinian people.

In most cases, those close to the foreign policy establishment are fully aware of what they are doing and of the negative human rights consequences of their policies. Their own justification is usually based on the belief that it is important for the United States to be in a position of political dominance in the world, in order to protect US interests. And they usually believe that what is in the interest of US-based corporations is in the interest of US citizens.

In the past, US citizens were mostly told that military intervention was necessary to fight communism. To get public support for these interventions more recently, the US government and mainstream media tell stories that usually involve protecting democracy, human rights, and freedom, and increasingly the war on terror.

Throughout the second half the twentieth century, most US intervention could be explained as attempts to keep neocolonial regimes in power, or to keep countries from moving into the Soviet orbit or to provide models of functioning noncapitalist economies. As the Cold War fades from memory and many of the corrupt governments that were held in place by either the United States or the Soviet Union have been transformed, new dynamics are developing.

The post 9/11 state of fear among the US population was packaged into the "war on terror" and became a vector for allowing the part of the US ruling class that was allied with the military-industrial complex to pursue adventures whose purpose was not especially clear.

After the World Trade Center was bombed on September 11, 2001, George Bush invaded Afghanistan saying that it was to pursue Osama bin Laden, the mastermind behind the attack. He quickly used the rhetoric of the war on terror to argue for an invasion of Iraq, a country with a dictator in charge, who had nothing to do with the 9/11 attacks, but who was troubling to US policy-makers. For the next ten years the United States was actively involved in wars in Afghanistan and Iraq, leading to a deep breakdown of both of those countries.

The legacy of those years has been a national security state, with unprecedented levels of spying against US citizens; a prison in Guantánamo Bay, Cuba, where a few hundred people have been kept for over a decade, many without ever being charged; and license to kill people using drone strikes with almost no limit in many countries in Middle East.

In 2010 Mohamed Bouzazi, a fruit vendor in Tunisia, had his scales confiscated by the government in an act of petty harassment. Asking for them back, and getting no response and out of frustration at the corruption of the government of Tunisia, he called out, "How do you expect me to make a living?" doused himself with gasoline and set himself on fire. This sparked a protest movement in Tunisia that led to the overthrow of the corrupt US allied government there.

That set off a series of people's movements in many neighboring countries, dubbed the Arab Spring. Many of those countries have deeply corrupt neocolonial regimes, kept in power as part of the Cold War. Many of those governments stayed in place by offering relatively easy access to education, but very few job opportunities. Having many well-educated young people with no sense of an economic future for themselves was part of the recipe for the revolts. When the WikiLeaks files showed just how corrupt and controlled by the United States those government were, it didn't take much for the old political systems to become unstable. Using old-fashioned forms of organizing, supplemented by some increased ability to network using social media, powerful revolts broke out all across the region.

Those movements were very inspiring to people all around the world, and for a while it looked as though amazing change would happen very quickly. After about a year the joy faded as it became clear that in countries such as Egypt there was a "deep state" that remained stable as the people at the top changed.

As some of those countries ended up in civil war, radical Islamist groups have become larger forces. According to Hossein-Zadeh, while many in the Muslim world have been, and continue to be, receptive to Western approaches to politics and economics, "after a century and a half of imperialist pursuits and a series of humiliating policies in the region . . . the popular masses of the Muslim world turned to religion and the conservative religious leaders as sources of defiance, mobilization, self-respect."[16] The roots of the reactionary, and deeply violent, radical Islamist movement that is wreaking havoc in much of Middle East can be seen in the call, supported in no small part by the CIA, to fight the Soviets in Afghanistan in the 1990s. According to David Cook in his book *Understanding Jihad*, "The campaign was the first time in centuries that people from all over the Muslim world had gathered together—irrespective of their ethnic differences—to fight exclusively *for the sake of Islam*. Thus, the battlefield of Afghanistan was the religious and social incubator for global radical Islam in that it established contacts among a wide variety of radicals from Muslim anti-governmental and resistance movements and fused them together."[17]

According to Peter Mandaville in his *Global Political Islam*, the first generation of members of Al Qaida were veterans of that fight. The second generation "tended to have strong connections to the West. Many were recruited in Europe (and to some extent North America) or were citizens of Muslim countries who had spent some time living, studying, or training in the West as expatriates."[18] He argues that most young Muslims with connections to the West grow into a cosmopolitan identity. For others, however, they can come to see themselves as part of a global Muslim community that is under assault.[19]

Not only are many young people attracted to the millenarian vision of radical Islamist groups, but those groups are very well funded by wealthy individuals who support their causes. The groups are well armed through those funding mechanisms and by capturing arms from the wide variety of wars raging in the region. Many are led by military commanders who were trained in toppled regimes, such as that of Iraq.

Functionalist Marxist theories of the state

In *State and Revolution*, written in 1917, Lenin argues that the state is the repressive arm of the owning class.[20] The state serves the ruling class by building roads, regulating trade, producing trained workers through schools, and by repressing the working class through police and military action. Lenin argues that revolutionaries must completely destroy the state. For him, parliamentary democracy was nothing but a sham—it existed to give the illusion of democracy to a fundamentally undemocratic institution.[21] He hoped that his Bolshevik party, in overthrowing the Russian government, acting as a vanguard of the people, would lead the workers to communism. Communism was the ultimate goal of human society; with true communism there would be a commonality of interests between all members of society and a state would no longer be necessary. Of course it didn't turn out what way, and the Soviet Union that was the result of the Russian Revolution ended up having a very powerful and repressive state.

French Marxist Louis Althusser had a view of the state similar to Lenin's. Writing in the 1970s, he took this basic Marxist-Leninist view and developed it in more detail. Althusser argues that society is made up of three sets of institutions that are intricately combined to form the structure of society—the economic, the political, and the ideological.[22] While each has some independence from the other, they all work together to support the dominant economic system. The state, according to this view, exists to support the interests of the ruling economic class. It does this through two types of mechanisms: repressive state apparatuses and ideological state apparatuses.[23]

By repressive state apparatuses Althusser means the military and police forces and the legal system. These state-run institutions are prepared to use violence and other forms of force whenever necessary and exist to make sure that dominant interests are served. In the United States, the police began unashamedly as a repressive force acting to protect capitalist interests. The United States began to have organized professional police forces in the mid-nineteenth century. From the beginning, controlling labor unrest was a significant task of the police. They were used as strikebreakers and for riot control. Similarly, a significant role of the FBI is to engage in spying on political dissidents.

Althusser defines ideological state apparatuses as the religious system, the educational system, ideological aspects of the political and legal systems, trade unions, the press, and culture.[24] For Althusser, these systems are extensions of the capitalist state. In some ways, Althusser's theory of ideological state apparatuses is similar to Gramsci's theory of hegemony. Like Gramsci, Althusser sees different social forces as contending for control over ideological institutions.

> The class (or class alliance) in power cannot lay down the law in the [ideological state apparatuses] as easily as it can in the (repressive) State apparatus, not only because the former ruling classes are able to retain strong positions there for a long time, but also because the resistance of the exploited classes is able to find means and occasions to express itself there.[25]

Unlike Gramsci, however, Althusser argues that the ruling class will always get its way in these struggles as long as capitalism exists. Thus, where Gramsci might see public schools as a place where hegemonic and counter-hegemonic forces fight for control, Althusser sees them as a site of ideological formation working in the interest of the ruling class.

Althusser's theory of how people experience the world is also much more one-sided than Gramsci's. For Althusser, subjectivity—people's sense of self, their desires and beliefs—is created through ideological state apparatuses. Althusser's theory has been widely criticized as overly functionalist. He sees everything that the state does as an expression of the needs of the capitalist class. And in his theory, the capitalist class always wins.

Liberal pluralist theories of the state

Political liberals tend to see the state as a positive force whose purpose is to serve social needs. Liberals tend to see the state according to the theories put forward by pluralists. Pluralism is the main theory of the state taught in political science classes in the United States. For pluralists, government in a nominally democratic society is seen to represent the interests and desires of voters. For them formal representative democracy leads to substantively democratic results over time.

In his early work, liberal theorist Robert Dahl argued that the form of state found in advanced capitalist countries is basically democratic. He concedes that the political process is very complex and most voters are not interested in most of the decisions that the government makes. But, he argues, elections are

> crucial processes for insuring that political leaders will be some-
> what responsive to the preferences of some ordinary citizens. But
> neither elections nor interelection activity provide much insur-
> ance that decisions will accord with the preferences of a majority
> of adults or voters. Hence we cannot correctly describe the actual
> operations of democratic societies in terms of contrasts between
> majorities and minorities. We can only distinguish groups of vari-
> ous types and sizes, all seeking various ways to advance their goals,
> usually at the expense, at least in part, of others.[26]

According to Dahl's view, different social forces put forward their preferences and the government acts by mediating between these different interest groups. Pluralists tend to be optimistic about the state serving the interests of people in society. They often work with an implicit view that, with time, states become more democratic and efficient in meeting the needs of all members of society.

Institutionalist theory of the state

The optimism of liberalism is challenged by institutionalists. For them, the state is an arena where different social interests come into conflict and competition with one another. As in Omi and Winant's theory of racial formation, these thinkers see the structures of the state as being determined by the history of real struggles. They look at the way power relations play themselves out, as well the ways that social structures are formed in these historical processes. The main difference between institutionalists and pluralists is that institutionalists are interested in how power relations impact the ways that social forces interact and lead to particular outcomes. For them, it is when monitory forces push formal democratic systems for more accountability that they become substantively democratic.

Theda Skocpol, director of the Center for American Political Studies at Harvard University, writes,

> Pluralists fail to offer (or seek) well-developed explanations of how economic and political institutions variously influence group formation and intergroup conflicts. Nor do they feel the need to go beyond vague evolutionist schemes that posit institutional change in politics as an inevitable progression of ever-increasing democracy, governmental effectiveness, and the specialization of smooth, adaptive responses to the "modernization" of the economy and society.[27]

Institutionalists such as Skocpol focus on the ways that power differences impact the ways states function and argue that power inequalities become entrenched in state institutions. While the state is a site where different classes vie for influence, those with more power have more influence over the state, unless this power is checked by popular mobilization.

In their very influential 1982 article "The Crisis of Liberal Democracy in Capitalism," economists Sam Bowles and Herbert Gintis argue the modern state—both in the United States and in other industrialized societies—is not just a tool of the capitalist class, as functionalist Marxist theories had assumed, but rather something more complex.

> Following World War I . . . and in some capitalist countries even earlier, the long-standing struggle of workers for political

representation came to fruition. The classical liberal state, which vested the right of participation in the owners of *property*, gave way to the liberal democratic state, which vests these rights in *persons* by virtue of citizenship.[28]

Thus, the theory of the state needs to deal with a more complex situation in which the working class and subordinated people in general, have some power and influence over governmental action. The question then is to understand how that influence works and how it is limited. Bowles and Gintis argue that the relationship between the state as a mechanism for guaranteeing capitalist accumulation and the state as a democratic institution needs to be understood historically.[29]

The contemporary US state

Bowles and Gintis see the post–World War II era as characterized by "an accord between capital and labor." In this period, the capitalist class and the working class found a way to reach an accommodation in which the interests of each were served to some extent by avoiding conflict and through a particular set of compromises. This accord granted workers the possibility of real distributional gains, while at the same time ensuring the continued dominance of capital within the site of capitalist production.[30]

Thus, the owners of the means of production were allowed to control the labor process in exchange for workers making relatively high wages. The accord is characterized by labor laws that permitted unionization but restricted its scope. During this period, working-class wages rose significantly, but the political power of the working class was severely limited as radicals were purged from trade unions. "The evolution of a conservative, hierarchical, and economistic trade-union movement was important in this process, but it was more an effect than a cause."[31]

As part of the accord, capital also supported a stronger role for the state in mediating the economy and the lives of workers and the poor. The "welfare state" that developed during these years was not named after the specific policies we now know as welfare but around the concept of state investment in the overall welfare of its citizens. Higher taxes resulted in a social safety net to protect the unemployed, a GI bill to open access to higher education, rural electrification, Medicaid to insure the health and well-being of the old, and other significant social improvements.

Bowles and Gintis argue that the idea of a liberal democratic state and the rising standard of living supported by the accord helped nurture the rise in demands by the poor in the 1950s and 1960s, especially people of color, for better living conditions. "Access to a decent standard of living and to adequate housing and medical care was promoted as a natural right."[32] This push for a higher standard of living through state action became the fight for a *social wage*.

In western Europe, with its stronger trade union movement and weaker tradition of individualism, social democratic governments went much further than the United States in offering a social wage. There governments provide health care, old-age pensions, support for public transportation, some support for childcare, and unemployment protections.

Living in a society with a high social wage can take a huge amount of pressure off of everyday life. It is hard for most people in the United States to imagine a life in which all of these things are considered basic rights for everyone. It means that people don't need to worry about their own survival in the same desperate ways they do in the United States. They live in a society where levels of crime and general misery are considerably less, since they aren't surrounded by people unable to have their basic needs satisfied.

The end of the accord

Until 1973, US workers saw a steady rise in both their wages and their standard of living. This domestic shift in resources coincided with a global rise in competition that left US-based capitalists feeling threatened. By the late 1970s, the US right had built an impressive coalition to challenge the notion that the state was primarily responsible for maintaining the social wage. The 1980 election of Ronald Reagan and George H.W. Bush signaled the strategic unity of capital with the religious, antistate right, the collapse of the accord between capital and labor, and decades of relentless assaults on the social wage, and on the role of the state as helping get a fair deal for working people from business owners.

The Reagan-Bush coalition was able to build popular support for its attacks on the social wage in part by playing on divisions among the population, especially racist ones, and on social anxieties, especially regarding gender and sexuality. This can be seen in the shifts in the rhetoric surrounding taxes. Before this "Reagan revolution," it was generally believed that people paid their taxes so that the government would provide for social goods. It was assumed that public schools, parks, roads, and libraries were things that everyone wanted and that, if people paid their taxes, these and other services could be provided for everyone. With the development of the Reagan revolution, taxes came to be seen as a way that the government was taking hard-earned money from working people and giving it to people who did not deserve it.

Thus, much political rhetoric focused on the services that were provided to the poor, and the poor were represented as people of color, especially as African Americans and as women. Suddenly, it became commonplace to believe that government programs were wasteful. Trying to improve a public school by increasing its funding was called "throwing money at a problem," even though studies showed that there is a strong correlation between funding levels and quality of education.

In his book *Lockdown America: Police and Prisons in the Age of Crisis*, Christian Parenti argues that the crisis in corporate profits due to increasing international competition set the stage for Ronald Reagan's assault on social spending: "In 1982 alone Reagan cut the real value of welfare by 24 percent, slashed the budget for child nutrition by 34 percent, reduced funding for school milk programs by 78 percent, urban development action grants by 35 percent, and educational block grants by 38 percent."[33]

Parenti argues that this approach to economic policy led to a major shift from the ideal of a welfare state that is supposed to manage the fates of the poor, to a state more reliant on prisons. "In fact, Reagan created whole new classes of poor and desperate people. It was in response to this social crisis, created by the elite response to the profit crisis that a new wave of criminal justice crackdown began."[34]

This challenging of the accord eventually led to President Bill Clinton's destruction of the system of welfare support for single women with children in 1996.

Elections

If the pluralists were right, you would expect the action of the government in the United States to reflect the opinions of the majority of the people. We know this isn't true, as strong majorities support increasing the federal minimum wage, and strong action on climate change, yet the majority of national politicians do not see those actions as necessary. The gap between what people want and how politicians vote is very high, and one reason for that is the impact that money has on our electoral system. That problem was made larger by the 2010 Supreme Court decision in the *Citizens United* case, which took away Congress's ability to limit campaign spending, claiming that political spending is a form of free speech, and since corporations are legally people, the government cannot limit their spending.

Many other countries have strong limits on the amount of money that can be spent on elections, and the public airwaves are used to allow a variety of political parties to express their views. And in most other countries of the world, parliamentary systems allow small parties to contest elections and grow as they move from small victories to larger ones. Governments are formed by coalitions of parties with similar views, so that people with views that are less popular can have those views be part of the conversation. In the United States, because we have a winner-take-all system it is much more difficult for smaller parties to grow.

Our two major political parties are deeply indebted to large donors to win elections, yet they must also appeal to people who have interests different from those large donors for votes. Politicians from both parties are in institutional positions where they must mediate between the influences of those paying for their elections and the people who vote for them. Some politicians in both parties are largely motivated by those corporate interests and are very cynical in the way they package their views to get votes. Others, in both parties, are genuinely motivated by the concerns they campaign on, and find it painful the ways they end up needing to compromise their beliefs to achieve what is possible in terms of passing legislation.

In recent years Republicans have tended to rely strongly on the "Southern strategy" of appealing to the resentments of white people who blame their problems on the rise of people of color. They have also appealed to people's view of government as an oppressive force and have won votes by saying they are in favor of less government.

In both of Obama's presidential elections, Democrats were able to represent themselves as being a more welcoming party, and a necessary alternative to the Republicans. When Obama was elected in 2008 there was a powerful excitement among people from the overlapping demographic groups that have tended to vote in lower numbers because they do not see the political system as representing their interests: people of color, poor people, and young people. Obama ran on a campaign of hope for change. By the time of his second election, there was more cynicism as many saw him pursuing pro-corporate and pro–Wall Street policies not very different from what would be expected from Republicans. Yet many people vote for Democratic candidates as the lesser of two evils and as people who will often support policies such as a strong social safety net, some regulation of corporations, and some protection for the environment.

There are other political parties that run candidates in the United States, such as the Green Party on the left and the Libertarian Party on the right. Both of those parties have been frozen out of national debates, and it is hard for them to gain support when votes for their candidates often lead to fewer votes for a Democrat or a Republican. Voting for a "third party" in close elections can end up splitting the support and lead to the election of a candidate a third-party voter may like even less than the competing mainstream alternative.

In presidential elections it is very difficult for any candidate not supported by huge amounts of money to get any traction. At other levels, elections are forums where social justice advocates do sometimes win, and those wins can be meaningful for social change. Bill de Blasio's victory as mayor of New York City meant a sea change there in how issues of poverty are dealt with there. One of the first things he did once elected was to set up a universal program for after-school care for children in the city's schools.

In the state of New York there is a system of fusion voting, where third parties can get on a ballot and either run their own candidate, or ask their supporters to vote for another candidate. New York's Working Families Party has been able to get concessions from Democratic Party candidates to get them to support more progressive policies, and they were an important force in de Blasio's election.

Similarly, in several major cities in the United States there is a system of instant-runoff voting (IRV), whereby people can vote for the candidate they prefer as their first choice and give a second preference to their second choice, etc. This allows people to vote for the candidate they prefer, without being afraid that their vote will split support for candidates who are likely to win, and lead to the election of someone whom they really don't like.

Government policies can be impacted by electing people who represent particular interest, and they can be impacted by influencing those elected with pressure. When the economic crisis of 2008 hit, many observers compared President Obama's actions to those of President Roosevelt during the Great Depression of the 1930s. Both were moderately liberal presidents with strong connections to dominant economic interests. Both had some level of compassion for people hurt by the crisis they were dealing with. And both were beholden to large donors. Roosevelt pushed for and enacted many amazing pieces of legislation that founded most of the social safety net we still rely on. Obama, on the other hand, acted mostly in ways that were beneficial for the very elites who had caused the crisis. The difference was not in the individual personalities, or the political forces that had elected each of these two presidents. What Roosevelt faced that Obama did not was a powerful and mobilized set of social movements protesting vigorously for change.

Intuitionalists encourage us to look to the networks of power operating at any time and that structure the possibilities of any given political moment. When social movements are strong politicians need to respond to them. When people who believe in social justice are in positions of power they can use those positions to enact progressive policies, but only if they have support from below.

The state in utopian society

The disasters of so-called state socialism—in the form of the Soviet Union and its satellites—forced many social justice advocates to wonder about the role of the state in an ideal society. Where Marx and Engels, as well as Lenin, had argued that as class antagonisms disappeared, the state would no longer be necessary, the actual experience of those societies was just the opposite: over time, these states became more powerful and more repressive. Free speech was severely limited, along with other political rights; industries were developed in ways that were devastating to the environment; government elites continued to enjoy class privileges; and educational systems and other cultural institutions were highly propagandistic.

Marx focused on capitalist exploitation as the core of social oppression. Implicit in his philosophy is the idea that, as class antagonisms disappear, people will find ways to live well together. For this reason, Marx never wrote much about what his ideal society would look like, and he never analyzed the kinds of problems that would develop in a society that wasn't class divided.

Many Marxists have argued that Marx's philosophy is inherently democratic. This can be seen most strongly in *The Economic and Philosophic Manuscripts of 1844*, in which Marx argues that a truly fulfilled human life is one in which people's work and their relations with one another are not alienated. That is, they see themselves as expressive beings, and work is something like unfettered artistic production in that it has inherent meaning.

According to this vision, social relationships are also part of an expressive whole, such that people work for society because they care about the well-being of their fellow people. In this view, the ideal society is one in which all people participate in forming the policies that impact their lives. Yet Marx never explains what kinds of mechanisms might foster that sense of empowerment and cooperation.

Marxists have done a great job explaining the ways that class divisions get in the way of this communist ideal. Feminists, antiracists, and gay liberationists have challenged Marxism's narrow emphasis on class-based oppression and have argued that, in the move toward a liberated society, other dynamics of oppression must also be challenged. Each of these liberation movements looks at one of the mechanisms through which power becomes embedded in social relations.

Anarchists argue that there is something inherently oppressive about government, separate from the problem of class division. Others, such as German sociologist Max Weber, argue that bureaucracy contains, within itself, forms of domination.

Bureaucracy

In her book *The Feminist Case Against Bureaucracy*, Kathy Ferguson argues that while bureaucracies have a long history, dating back a few thousand years in China, bureaucracy is increasingly one of the more insidious forms of power operating in modern society. Bureaucracies have a tendency to be self-perpetuating, to set up systems of rules that protect their power even when there is no one in particular who supports them. This bureaucratic power works through impersonal structures that turn people into passive participants in society. This passivity, in turn, helps promote the power of the bureaucracy.

Ferguson uses this analysis to argue for the abolition of bureaucratic structures. This raises some hard questions for those interested in the question of whether or not a society without oppression is possible and what goals social justice advocates should be trying to move society toward.

A large-scale society needs complex mechanisms for building infrastructure, such as sewage and water systems; coordinating transportation systems; and coordinating health care. It isn't clear how these things can be done without some level of bureaucracy—or rule-governed systems of administration. And bureaucracy often works to keep systems accountable. They can protect people against the arbitrary actions of those with power.

Many Marxists argue that there is nothing inherently wrong with a bureaucratically organized society, as long as there are some mechanisms for democratic input. Bureaucracies can be excellent for getting things done. What they don't do well is set goals; they tend to simply replicate things as they are and to perpetuate themselves. As long as there are democratic mechanisms for setting the goals of bureaucracies, a society can be both bureaucratically organized and nonoppressive.

An anarchist can be against the state entirely yet still argue for the need for democratic mechanisms and ways to prevent the accumulation of power by members of society. Where they disagree with Marxists most fundamentally is in the level of participation that social institutions require. Many Marxists are content with a situation in which state institutions administer social needs, as long as they are administered fairly and in the interest of society. Anarchists oppose the creation of an "administered society" and argue for active participation in the creation and re-creation of social forms. For them, democracy is one of the most important values.

Making demands on the state

During the years following the Great Depression, when the accord between capital and labor was in place, the working class had much more success demanding a higher social wage from the state than it did from confronting capital. Thus, in this period, social justice advocates became accustomed to making demands for a better life from the state, and they did less to directly challenge capital's "right" to run society.

The welfare rights movement can be seen in this context. Throughout the 1960s and 1970s, poor people, especially women who were recipients of a social wage from the state, struggled with the state over demands for better support and better conditions. Feminists have argued that, as the patriarchal nuclear family declined in social importance, the state has increasingly come to take over many of its functions. Because women continue to be disproportionately responsible for raising children, they have needed more direct support from the state than have men.

For Bowles and Gintis, there is nothing wrong with social justice advocates demanding that the state give more to the working class. In fact, for them, one of the major ways to challenge capitalism is by forcing the state to work more in the interests of the working class and less in the interests of the ruling class. When the state is able to deliver something we want, we should take it, and when the state is working to protect the interests of the ruling class, we need to oppose it.

Some social justice advocates have argued against supporting the welfare state. For years, especially when the welfare state was strong, many argued that the systems of support for the poor were paternalistic, condemning people to a powerless and subordinate position. Instead of supporting welfare programs, they wanted a situation in which no one needed welfare. In the days when those programs were relatively strong, many focused on the ways that the state controls people through them.

According to the functionalist Marxist view, it is in the interest of the capitalist class that the state take care of the poor to some extent, in order to make sure that people are not pushed into open rebellion. Some functionalist Marxists argue that the social wage mutes the revolutionary potential of the working class and adds to the legitimacy of the state. Similarly, some anarchists think that asking the state for help leads to passivity and dependence on the state. Other anarchists, such as those associated with the magazine *Love and Rage*, have argued that, for tactical reasons, it is important to fight cutbacks that have negative impacts on people's lives.

It's easy to say that welfare is just a way to pacify the masses when welfare programs are strong. From the 1960s through the 1970s, when the welfare state was expanding, it seemed reasonable for social justice activists to argue that the state was primarily an institution of capitalist rule and that their most fundamental goal should be the elimination of capitalism and the procapitalist state along with it.

As the social wage came under concerted attack beginning in the 1980s, an increasing number of social justice advocates argued that even if protecting the welfare state was "reformist," the goal of improving people's living conditions could not wait for a revolution. The idea of overthrowing the capitalist system seemed impossible.

In trying to understand the relationship between reformist and revolutionary goals, Gramsci developed the concepts *war of position* and *war of maneuver*.[35] Overthrowing a capitalist state by outmaneuvering its armed forces in a military way is what Gramsci termed a war of maneuver. But Gramsci also urged revolutionaries to engage in a war of position in the short term, during nonrevolutionary times. The war of position means that radical forces are constantly trying to transform the state and the conditions of society into what they want. Struggles for the state to take care of people's basic needs, such as public housing, food stamps, and health care, should be seen as battles for a good life that must be fought for all the time.

This war of position focuses simultaneously on ways to transform the institutions of power and get benefits out of them. The ultimate goal of poor people and their allies is a society in which no one will need welfare. But until that time, state support for the poor is required. It is often tricky to frame short-term demands in ways that foster a continuous effort toward a more deeply transformed society.

If we use Bowles and Gintis's terms for understanding the state, we can see that there are two main sets of functions of the state in the contemporary United States. It is both a mechanism for guaranteeing capitalist accumulation and, to the extent that popular movements have made it so, a mechanism for democracy.

The state works as a mechanism for guaranteeing capitalist accumulation by providing stable conditions for capitalist investment. It does this through the legal system, which enforces contracts and passes laws that make business possible. The state also builds and maintains systems of transportation. The police and military play important roles by maintaining the social conditions for appropriation, both domestically and in other countries. The state is also an important direct investor in businesses such as the arms trade. Yet the state in contemporary "democratic" capitalist countries is also more than this. As Bowles and Gintis argue, as a result of popular movements, the contemporary state in the United States does much that is in the interests of groups besides the capitalist class.

Public schools are an interesting example of this contradictory nature of the capitalist state. On the one hand, the state does an enormous amount of work for the capitalist class by developing an educated and prepared labor force in the public school systems. On the other hand, much of the impetus for public schools has come from working-class people demanding access to a free educational system whose goal has also been to provide access to the knowledge and skills needed to be full members of a democratic society.[36]

Right now we are seeing a major struggle over the purpose of education. On one side are those who want to justify educational spending on the grounds that it is good for the economy—that is, that we need good schools because we need a trained workforce. On the other side are the humanists who see education as good for human development and want to see money spent on education so that people will have better lives. This humanistic rhetoric is fading into the background, and many students in college at the present moment have no idea that the educational system ever had any purpose other than job training.

How schools actually function is influenced by a wide variety of social factors, such as the struggles of parents, teachers, students, taxpayers, and grassroots organizations, as well as the demands of business and government officials. It isn't inevitable that capitalist interests will always win out.

Shifting targets, shifting alliances

As the political landscape changes in the struggles between capital and labor, and between antioppression advocates and their opponents, the targets that social justice advocates choose to focus on change as well. There have been many times when the state has seemed like a poor target for social change. Sometimes, the most sensible thing to do has been to challenge companies directly. This was true for the early days of the labor movement in most industrialized countries. In those struggles, workers were able to challenge their companies for better working conditions. Only when it was clear that striking workers had companies on the run did the government step in to try to set up conditions for "labor peace." It worked to stabilize economic relations by instituting legal changes that would give each side something and make the process of strikes less volatile.

In the 1970s, on the other hand, US environmentalists were amazingly successful at demanding changes directly from the government. Interestingly, the movement was very strong during the Nixon administration. Even though Nixon was unsympathetic to environmental interests, the size and popularity of the movement forced powerful governmental regulations, such as the Clean Air Act and the Endangered Species Act.

After the rise of neoconservatism, the US government seemed immune to this sort of pressure for reform. This was in part because the movement changed in the intervening period and began to play a more insider game of lobbying and lawsuits and partially because the government became less responsive to pressure from environmentalists. Neoconservatives denigrated environmentalists as one more "special interest group," just like the people of color, feminists, labor organizers, antimilitarists, and gay men and lesbians it was strategizing against.

Radical elements of many movements then shifted to strategies of more direct pressure on corporations. If governments wouldn't regulate corporations, then radicals would go after them one at a time, often choosing the worst offender in a given industry to make an example of. Boycotting companies became an effective tactic. When enough people hear about the damaging practices of a company, the company's image can be severely tarnished, sometimes irretrievably destroyed.

Church and labor groups pressured corporations into adopting "corporate codes of conduct" that companies would agree to in order to avoid bad publicity or shareholder actions by groups that had bought their way to a place at the table.

The rising power of multinational corporations and transnational organizations raises new possibilities for action. On the negative side, they have made reforms gained from pressure on governments less meaningful, as transnational bodies undermine national environmental and labor legislation and as multinational corporations move production to evade laws they find inconvenient. Yet people are still able to fight through their national government against pro-corporate trade policies and for policies that are good for people.

We may be entering a period where the possibilities to make a difference through elections, are increased. In several European countries and many in Latin America, there have been surprise victories by parties, some of them very new parties, that have been able to connect with people's frustration at the polices of austerity and neoliberalism. In the United States there are many positive changes being made in cities that have elected progressive mayors, and there may eventually come a time when candidates for higher levels will be ones who represent people's interests. Until that time it will remain important to keep the pressure up through grassroots organizing.

CHAPTER 9

What Do We Want and Why Do We Want It?
Media and Democratic Culture

WITH THE DEVELOPMENT OF THE INTERNET WE ALL HAVE ACCESS TO practically all of the knowledge developed over all of human history at almost any time and any place. We can quickly search and find answers to a huge number of questions instantaneously. That does not mean, however, that we have a well-informed society or a culture that serves us well.

Like most people of my age group, I think is important for people to be knowledgeable about what is happening in the world. People in my generation tend to believe that crucial to being a responsible member of our local, national, and global communities is to keep current about what is happening in terms of politics and economics, science, and general social trends. Recently I asked my students how they kept up on the affairs of the world. Most said that they think it is a good idea to be informed, and many said that they do keep informed through their use of the internet. Some use aggregating sites to bring them information about the issues they care about. Others read the headline news that goes along with some of the sites they regularly visit. Virtually none read a newspaper, and one of my students said that one day while reading the school newspaper, she reflected that she felt like an old lady doing so.

We are all embedded in cultural processes that help determine what we know, what we think is important, how we interact with each other, and how we interact with the social and political structures we are embedded in. Before the age of mass culture, people developed a sense of meaning, purpose, and identity through direct face-to-face interactions. Music was something many people made and they shared and enjoyed it without anyone needing to profit from it.

In the course of the twentieth century, culture came to be deeply commodified. A few giant corporations controlled almost all movie production and distribution; most television production and distribution; most radio stations, and most newspapers. Those corporations tended to favor content that was devoid of engagement with deep and serous questions, it tended to focus on celebrity, fun, and cynicism when it got close to political, economic, or environmental issues.

While it is still true that those forms are largely controlled by those same few dominant corporations, new and more unruly forms are emerging, where corporate control is weaker, and where people are finding their own voices in interesting and surprising ways. We're entering an age when many people interact with media that allows for a "do it yourself" culture, where people make and distribute their own videos, and shows become popular just on the basis of friends sharing with friends; where thousands of people blog about issues of concern to them; and where information about issues can spread across the internet like wildfire.

Are we entering a period of extremely democratic cultural production? Or are we in a period better characterized by the fact that fewer and fewer people are reading and producing serious investigative news; where a few corporate behemoths control the infrastructure of communication which is also thoroughly watched by the National Security Agency; and where those corporate behemoths are constantly figuring out newer and better ways to make money off of our aimless wanderings?

The fights in 2015 over net neutrality were an important battle in the struggle over the future of the internet as a democratic space. Millions of people weighed in and said very clearly and forcefully that they wanted the internet to be a place of free speech, not a place where the interests of profit could determine who had access to what information.

Media have important political implications. Our senses of what's interesting, beautiful, exciting, and just are all mediated by the images and ideas we take in when we watch TV, go to the movies, watch YouTube, surf the net, view Instagram, listen to the radio, and see billboards. We are influenced by the real role models we find in our lives, but all of us are also influenced by the lives we see in the media. To some degree, the range of what we think is possible is defined by our popular culture.

One of the attitudes toward life that's most popular on television as I'm writing this is cynicism. Connecting with real people involves emotional vulnerability, and knowing about the world takes work. To protect oneself from either of those challenges, it's attractive to adopt a worldview that says all human connections are corrupt and that the outside world isn't worth knowing about; that the world is corrupt and unchangeable, so informing oneself about it won't do any good; that anyone who cares about anything is a sucker; and that people involved in social movements are a bunch of hypocrites and won't accomplish anything anyway. Therefore, the best strategy is to be aloof, to make fun of people who try to take the world and their existence in it seriously, and to find pleasure and humor in distancing oneself from everything. While in many ways this cynicism appears to be a safe strategy, it rarely compensates for the loss of personal integrity and the social isolation that come with it.

Cynical programming does succeed in generating income for television producers, however. Television needs to remain uncontroversial in order to keep its sponsors, its prime reason for existence. Cynical programming hooks viewers who identify with the meaninglessness and despair they see portrayed. How have we ended up with media that are so cynical and a population that is so addicted to that cynicism? How is it that dominant social groups have been able to gain such high levels of complacency and consent within a system of domination? How have modern states been able to maintain systems of domination with relatively little direct force? As we shall see in this chapter, there are many ways that people are convinced that they want what dominant systems need them to want. This work of creating consent is done by governments, by elite groups consciously acting to promote their own interests, and, in complex and subtle ways, through culture.

One of the most powerful mechanisms for creating consent is the mass media. From the time we are small children we hear messages that tell us that capitalism is fine, that white ways and heterosexual ways are normal, that elderly people and the disabled should not be seen, and that men are important social actors, while women are decorative parts of the scenery. We receive these messages through television, radio, books, newspapers, plays, and music. We reproduce these ideas in our families and social lives, our artistic productions, and by responding positively to the media and its corporate sponsors.

This chapter looks at three different approaches social justice theorists have taken to understanding media and culture: the propaganda model, the US cultural studies model, and a Marxist cultural studies approach.

The propaganda model has been dominant in the US left. You can see aspects of it in the work of Noam Chomsky and Ben Bagdikian, and a wide variety of leftist thinkers. Cultural studies, as developed in the United States in the 1980s, is heavily influenced by the French postmodernists, especially Foucault, and based largely in academia. It tends to focus on the complex workings of culture and desire, and on the ways that power influences everyday experience. Finally, there is a powerful school of cultural analysis that is based in the work of Stuart Hall, who draws much of his analysis from the work of the Italian Marxist Antonio Gramsci, while incorporating elements of the propaganda model and US cultural studies.

Propaganda

According to the propaganda model, what mainstream media and popular culture portray as common sense and objective reality are in fact only sensible and unbiased according to the definitions of dominant groups. The power of the press belongs to those who own one, so to speak. Media bosses hire sports reporters who won't raise racial issues, such as graduation rates for college athletes, and news reporters who won't question why drone strikes would be purported to solve a complex social problem. From Disney to the *Daily Planet*, media consumers are trained to take for granted conceptual frameworks that favor elites.

One of the more blatant tools dominant interests use is public relations. In the book *Toxic Sludge Is Good for You*, John Stauber and Sheldon Rampton write about the ways that individual corporations will hire public relations firms to convince the public that the things they are doing are good and, often, to strategize ways to undermine oppositional organizations. Public relations firms flood the media with press releases that make it easy to write stories that favor their clients. They set up fake grassroots organizations (derogatorily called "astro-turf") that create the appearance of public support for corporate interests. And they work to discredit organizations and individuals who speak out against them. In some cases, corporations engage in this propaganda individually, but Stauber and Rampton also describe instances in which corporations in the same industry will band together to form groups that develop campaigns to support common interests.[1]

Advertising works in a similar way. Companies spend billions to ensure that people associate their products with deep human needs. Any message, repeated enough times, will have a deep effect on people's thoughts and behavior. Dreams of new cars and beautiful lovers and great friends and pristine scenery all go together in our minds, despite the way the car culture has facilitated the dissolution of the multigenerational family structure, resulted in the paving of massive acres of natural environment, and increased isolation as the majority of commuters spend more time in their cars than they do with their children, let alone their lovers and friends.

One of the most influential books that develops the propaganda model is *Manufacturing Consent* by Edward Herman and Noam Chomsky. In it, they explore the ways that the media presents elite interests in order to make them commonly accepted as the interests of all.

In describing what they mean by propaganda, Herman and Chomsky write,

> the U.S. media do not function in the manner of the propaganda system of a totalitarian state. Rather, they permit—indeed, encourage—spirited debate, criticism, and dissent, as long as these remain faithfully within the system of presuppositions and principles that constitute an elite consensus, a system so powerful as to be internalized largely without awareness.[2]

They argue that money and power "are able to filter out the news fit to print, marginalize dissent, and allow the government and dominant private interests to get their messages across to the public."[3] Whereas many governments have tried to control the media directly, US elites have learned that there are much more effective ways to establish control. And the great virtue of these indirect forms of control is that they can exist in the context of a theoretically "free press" that helps to legitimate the political system.

Herman and Chomsky argue that there are five major filtering systems for the media in the United States: (1) the size, concentrated ownership, ownership wealth, and profit orientation of the dominant mass-media firms; (2) advertising as the primary income source of the mass media; (3) the reliance of the media on information provided by government, business, and "experts" funded and approved by these primary sources and agents of power; (4) "Flak," or strong disagreement put out by elites to a view which opposes them, as a means of disciplining the media; and (5) "anticommunism," or a belief in the benevolence of a free-market economy, as a national religion and control mechanism.[4]

They argue that these five mechanisms work together to yield powerful results. Atrocities for which the United States is responsible, such as human rights abuses in Guatemala in the 1980s, will be described as unfortunate events with no understandable cause. Human rights abuses perpetrated by enemies of the United States will be explained as the result of the actions of oppressive governments. Those who are killed by opponents of the United States will be seen as "worthy victims" who merit attention, whereas those killed by pro-US forces are presented as unworthy of concern and compassion.

> Thus, for example, the torture of political prisoners and the attack on trade unions in Turkey will be presented in the media only by human-rights activists and groups that have little political leverage. The US government supported the Turkish martial-law government from its inception in 1980, and the US business community has been warm toward regimes that profess fervent anti-communism, encourage foreign investment, repress unions, and loyally support US foreign policy (a set of virtues that are frequently closely linked). Media that chose to feature Turkish violence against their own citizenry would have had to go to extra expense to find and check out information sources; they would elicit flak from the government, business, and organized right-wing flak machines, and they might be looked upon with disfavor by the corporate community (including advertisers) for indulging in such a quixotic interest and crusade. They would tend to stand alone in focusing on victims that, from the standpoint of dominant American interests, are *unworthy*.[5]

Herman and Chomsky's work has been very influential, and their model is consistent with the most popular forms of media analysis on the left. Ben Bagdikian and Norman Solomon have used similar approaches to analyze the mass media, and Michael Parenti uses similar analytical tools to investigate the ways that corporate interests come to dominate the political system. These thinkers have been very effective in exposing the internal workings of elite-dominated systems.

While the propaganda model has many virtues and explains quite a bit about how the media work, it also oversimplifies the picture in some troubling ways. Theories that focus on elite power have a hard time explaining where resistance comes from and often give the impression that elites are all-powerful. This model has been criticized by many as overly functionalist, in that the needs of the dominant system are identified and the rest of social reality is analyzed in terms of how it fulfills these needs.

These theories tend to leave the reader justifiably outraged about the evils of dominant systems, but without much indication of how the systems might be fought. Left unanswered are many important questions: Are there conflicts between members of the elite groups? Are class elites and gender elites and racial elites all always on the same side? Are consumers of media always duped by it? If not, what allows some people to see through the lies and others not to? And why do so many people, radicals included, love to consume commercial media?

Cultural studies in the United States

Focusing less on news media and more on popular entertainment than the propaganda model does, cultural studies tries to answer some of these questions. By looking at the ways that audiences construct their own counterhegemonic meanings of popular culture, cultural studies theorists argue that media consumers influence media producers and, to some degree, reshape the public meaning of the producer's message.

Thinkers in this school often focus on the contradictory nature of mass media products such as television shows, and argue that part of their appeal lies in their openness to interpretation. Thus, Horace Newcomb and Paul Hirsch argue that television

> presents a multiplicity of meanings rather than a monolithic point of view. It often focuses on our most prevalent concerns, our deepest dilemmas. Our most traditional views, those that are the most repressive and reactionary, as well as those that are subversive and emancipatory, are upheld, examined, maintained, and transformed. The emphasis is on process rather than product, on discussion rather than indoctrination, on contradiction and confusion rather than coherence.[6]

Consumers of media often resist dominant interpretations and construct the meaning of media products in their own ways. In their study of a situation comedy about a wealthy black family, *The Cosby Show*, popular in the 1990s, Sut Jholly and Justin Lewis examine how audiences interpreted the show. They found that

> different viewers responded to *The Cosby Show* in divergent ways. For many black viewers, its positive portrayal of a successful black family was a feature of its appeal since it contrasted with the often-negative ways in which African Americans were portrayed on television. However many white viewers found in the series a reassuring confirmation that racism had become a thing of the past, making it possible for anyone to prosper and succeed in American society.[7]

In the influential article "Is the Gaze Male?" E. Ann Kaplan argues that mainstream movies are generally shot from the point of view of a male viewer. This work led to a whole school of media analysis that concentrated on ways that women are constructed in media as a male projection and how women are rarely shown as active subjects with complex thoughts and feelings of their own.[8]

In addition to thinkers such as Kaplan, who focus on the ways that the media excludes women, other feminists began to focus on the ways that mass media are attractive to women. These thinkers showed the ways that female consumers of media find characters to identify with and resist dominant systems of meaning in the things they view. This school of interpretation has also been influential among theorists of color and queer theorists. These writers have shown the complex ways that people in these nondominant groups find pleasure in interpreting popular media in nonconventional ways, demonstrating the openness of systems of meaning.

These approaches to media have been important for developing theories that explain the media's appeal. They show ways that media respond to audiences rather than just constructing them.

This complex interplay is necessary if we are to understand advertising. Ads do not simply say "buy this car" over and over again. Rather, they attempt to tap into audiences' systems of desire. They offer the viewer satisfaction of some sort. Usually, ads work by appealing to some sort of desire and making the claim, usually false, that buying the product will satisfy that desire.

" Cognitive Disodence"

They also work by creating new forms of desire, which they *can* satisfy. If I want to feel like the type of person in the ad, I can buy the outfit and adopt the identity, which has a particular sort of feel to it that I find appealing. And I can successfully *be* that type of person.

Some famous Nike ads of the mid-1990s were artistically produced and showed women athletes working hard, older people engaged in sports, and people of color depicted in ways that were often culturally sensitive. In these ads, people from these nondominant groups were shown in positive but realistic lights. They always looked cool and powerful, and they were shown to be rebels, working hard for what they thought was right. Many of the ads appealed to a rebellious consciousness on the part of the audience.

On the one hand, there is something positive about seeing rebellious images on television, and the extent to which this shows the power of sub-cultures to influence mainstream meanings shouldn't be underestimated. While Nike was appropriating popular culture for exploitative reasons, the style of the ads was a testament to the power of that rebellious spirit in the culture at large. This demonstrates that dominant forces do not completely construct social reality. Rather, in important ways, they are also constantly responding to our initiatives.

These ads also made Nike vulnerable, as young people of color began to call Nike to task for ripping off their cultures in order to sell them over-priced shoes, and by exploiting the people of color around the world who make the shoes. The same rebellious spirit that Nike was trying to cash in on eventually turned on the company.

Cultural studies approaches to media analysis tend to focus on complexity and political ambivalence. This can be helpful for generating analyses that explain the appeal of mass media and allow us to see our own ability to resist and take initiative. In stressing these ambivalences, however, cultural studies theorists often lose their political clarity. Suddenly, resistance is everywhere and the mass media come to look like places where people's democratic interests are served. The propaganda approach is often more satisfying in the ways it describes corporate control.

Marxist Cultural Studies

The work of Stuart Hall, which was influenced by influenced by Italian Marxist Antonio Gramsci, has some of the best features of both the propaganda model and US cultural studies. Its approach is complex yet still has political clarity.

In the work he wrote while imprisoned by fascists in Italy in the 1930s, Gramsci explored the ways that culture works as an important part of political struggle. Gramsci argued that systems of domination require a certain amount of consent from the governed to survive. They manage to accomplish this through dominating the society's systems of meaning, building what he called hegemony—the way that idea systems come to legitimize, or support, the interests of ruling groups in society. Much of the work of a cultural critic, according to Gramsci, is to analyze the ways that dominant groups construct hegemonies and the ways that subordinated groups create counterhegemonies.

Marx and Engels argued that the ruling ideas in any society are the ideas of the ruling class. Gramsci's work attempts to explain how this happens and where resistances to it come from. By breaking the problem down and not seeing it so globally, Gramsci opens the way for a less functionalist form of explanation, which is much more helpful for seeing possibilities of resistance.

In his essay "The Study of Philosophy," Gramsci argues that all people are philosophers. What he means by this is that we all create meaning and have ways of making sense of the world. The meaning systems that we create grow out of the systems we are born into. Thus, while culture is constantly changing, it is also something that carries with it strong influences from the past. As Gramsci writes, "The starting-point of critical elaboration is the consciousness of what one really is, and is 'knowing thyself' as a product of the historical process to date which has deposited in you an infinity of traces, without leaving an inventory."[9]

Gramsci argues that most people's thought processes are reliant on what comes to be seen as "common sense." He writes,

> common sense is not something rigid and immobile, but is continually transforming itself, enriching itself with scientific ideas and with philosophical opinions which have entered ordinary life. "Common sense" is the folklore of philosophy, and is always halfway between folklore properly speaking and the philosophy, science, and economics of the specialists.[10]

Gramsci argues that dominant groups in society try to make the world make sense from their perspective; that is, they try to gain hegemony. But they are always working within a field of ideas not of their own making. They are working with the raw materials of a culture's common sense, and everyone in a society is a part of the creation of these idea systems. This means that what happens and which ideas become dominant is always subject to political struggle.

Gramsci called ideas that support the ruling elites *hegemonic* and ideas that challenge them *counterhegemonic*. He saw developing forms of counterhegemony as an important part of the working-class movement. This means that he saw cultural development as an important part of politics. Members of the working class must be engaged in processes whereby they re-create systems of meaning so that the common sense of their culture develops into a "good sense," whereby they can see clearly the social relations around them and decide for themselves where they want society to go.

Jamaican-born cultural theorist Stuart Hall drew heavily on Gramsci. Hall found Gramsci's theories of hegemony and counterhegemony very fruitful for engaging in intersectional analysis. He was interested in analyzing how race, class, and gender dynamics are reproduced in culture. While Gramsci himself only analyzed class domination, his analytical tools were flexible enough to be very useful to those wanting to analyze race and gender politics as well.

For Hall, hegemony, or the dominant ideology, is not one thing that exists simply as an outgrowth of the needs of the ruling class. Instead, following Gramsci, Hall sees hegemony as a task that ruling groups are always trying to accomplish, in different ways, and that different ruling groups will have elements of their interests represented at different times. While they are vying for domination among themselves, they are also always being challenged from below by various subordinate groups. Which ideas are hegemonic is an open question that is constantly being struggled over.

But for Hall, these struggles over hegemony are always related to political and economic reality—they do not take place just in the world of ideas. In Hall's view, culture and systems of meaning are related to but not determined by economic reality.

In the more simplistic Marxist tradition, often called orthodox Marxism or Marxist materialism, economic reality is seen as determining the nature of social reality. While it is indisputable that Marx himself argued that previous philosophers had overstressed the extent to which ideas themselves determine social reality, just how far Marx meant to go with his calls for attention to material reality is hotly disputed among Marxists.

In its crudest form, Marxist materialism claims that economic reality determines social reality. In terms of politics, this often means that people's consciousness is taken to be determined by their class position. People from the working class see the world in terms of their interests, and people in the ruling class see it in terms of theirs. These Marxists have then had to deal with the fact that most working-class people do not see the world in the revolutionary anticapitalist terms that Marxists hope for. The solution to this dilemma is the notion of false consciousness. According to this theory, workers' consciousness is clouded by the confusions of bourgeois ideology. Once they were exposed to the "truth" of a Marxist analysis, these clouds would disappear and they would be able to achieve unity between their perception of the world and how the world really is: they would have class consciousness as members of the working class.

In trying to understand how this process of confusion of class interests works, Althusser developed the ideas of *interpolation* and *ideological state apparatuses*. According to Hall, Althusser "put on the agenda the whole neglected issue of how ideology becomes internalized, how we come to speak 'spontaneously' within the limits of the categories of thought which exist outside us and which can more accurately be said to think us."[11] Hall claims that one of Althusser's most important contributions to social justice theory was his attention to the discourses—or systems of meaning—that structure consciousness and create human beings with a sense of self that works for the capitalist system.

Hall rejects much of Althusser's thinking as too functionalist, but takes from him this idea that systems of meaning construct our sense of self in deep ways, and that social justice must work from within these systems of meaning. Culture is not something simple that people can be shown the way out of. There is no concise set of ideas that people can be taught that will make them understand the oppressive nature of reality. Hall argues that

> events, relations, structures do have conditions of existence and
> real effects, outside the sphere of the discursive; but only within
> the discursive, and subject to its specific conditions, limits and
> modalities, do they have or can they be constructed within mean-
> ing. Thus, while not wanting to expand the territorial claims of
> the discursive infinitely, how things are represented and the "ma-
> chineries" and regimes of representation in a culture do play a

constitutive, and not merely a reflexive, after-the-event, role. This
gives questions of culture and ideology, and the scenarios of representation—subjectivity, identity, politics—a formative, not merely
an expressive, place in the constitution of social and political life.[12]

According to this theory, culture is not merely a reflection of material reality. Rather, society is structured through multiple systems, and cultural
reality is one of those systems. Ideas do not only reflect and organize reality;
they are a part of actively creating it. Michel Foucault developed the idea of
discourse to refer to a sort of system of power that is constructed through a
combination of cultural and material practices.

Thinkers using these concepts are often referred to as postmodernists. A
modernist is someone whose thinking is influenced by the ideas coming out
of the Enlightenment, when there was a faith that we could get to truth and
freedom by using reason. Postmodernists claim that the world is more complex than that, and that reason is always wrapped up in discourses of power.

One important implication of this approach is that it acknowledges that
social justice advocates themselves are constructed by complex networks
of power. This helps to explain the ways that the left in the United States
is often dominated by white cultural ways. White social justice advocates
often have a tough time understanding the ways that they reproduce power
relations in their political practice. Assuming that having a radical analysis
makes them able to see the lies of the dominant system, they can miss the
ways they themselves act out dominant positions of power. So, for example,
anarchists sometimes don't see the ways they carry the dominant view of
individualism, radical feminists can miss the ways they accept dominant
ideas about gender, and Marxists can misperceive the ways their analysis
assumes a modernist notion of progress.

Hall writes about this multiple nature of power in the following terms:

> More and more of our everyday lives are caught up in these forms
> of power, and their lines of intersection. Far from there being no
> resistance to the system, there has been a proliferation of new
> points of antagonism, new social movements of resistance orga-
> nized around them—and consequently, a generalization of "poli-
> tics" to spheres which hitherto the Left assumed to be apoliti-
> cal: a politics of the family, of health, of food, of sexuality, of the

body. What we lack is any overall map of how these power relations connect and of their resistances. Perhaps there isn't, in that sense, one "power game" at all, more of a network of strategies and powers and their articulations—and thus a politics that is always positional.[13]

If we take Hall's view seriously, then we are left with a view of the world that cannot be divided easily into political structures and cultural systems that support them or help tear them down. Instead, material and cultural practices are all part of the complex networks of social reality that shape our experiences and political potentials.

Cultural politics

Sometimes when social justice activists think about doing political work, they don't think about culture. Yet how people experience their world—what they desire, their sources of information, their sense of what they like and don't like, who they believe and don't believe, and what makes them happy—are all crucial parts of the political world.

In analyzing culture, Marxists tend to focus on the ways that capitalism turns everything into a commodity to be bought and sold and encourages us to desire increasing numbers of commodities. We often think of the desire for high levels of consumption as a part of human nature, but according to the economist Juliet Schor, "In the nineteenth- and early twentieth-century United States, there is also considerable evidence that many working people exhibited a restricted appetite for material goods. Numerous examples of societies where consumption is relatively unimportant can be found in the anthropological and historical literature. Consumerism is not an ahistorical trait of human nature, but a specific product of capitalism."[14] Since the early days of capitalism, this tendency has increased, with ever more of our culture being taken over by desires of consumption.

Capitalism creates this unquenchable desire for more in a few different ways. One way is that people are so busy working that they are unable to engage in other social forms of bringing pleasure to their lives.

Another way is advertising. The ruling class in a capitalist society has an interest in making people feel that buying products will satisfy their desires. Thus, Marx writes that in a capitalist society, every person speculates on creating a *new* need in another, and so as to drive him to a fresh sacrifice, to place him in a new dependence and to seduce him into a new mode of *gratification* and therefore economic ruin. Each tries to establish over the other an *alien* power, so as thereby to find satisfaction of his own selfish need. The increase in the quantity of objects is accompanied by an extension of the realm of alien powers to which man is subjected, and every new product represents a new *potency* of mutual swindling and mutual plundering.[15]

Advertising makes us feel insecure and convinces us that the empty feeling we have inside will be satisfied if only we buy something. Many people feel their anxiety is calmed when they shop. We are also sold forms of identity through shopping. Certain lifestyles and attitudes toward life (even antimaterial ones such as the hippie subculture) are associated with certain products, and we can tap into a certain cultural feel through our purchases. Yet all three of the frameworks above—overwork, advertising, and identity formation—tell us something about the kinds of political work that would be helpful.

Those following an orthodox Marxist path and those following the propaganda model have often engaged in cultural practices that are about enlightenment. The idea is that people need to be told what is wrong with society. The hope is that, when they are told the problem, they will see the truth and join the opposition. In terms of culture, the hope is that they will find ways of expressing their authentic class perspective through popular culture.

In the traditional Marxist approach to culture, mass or capitalist culture is often opposed to popular culture, which is the authentic voice of the working class. If we think that people's desires are something simple that are connected to their interests, then we could believe that when people understand their true interests, when they are not confused by false consciousness, they will create cultural artifacts and systems of meaning that express the truth of who they are. Their culture will be authentic. The political practices that follow from this sort of analysis are usually focused on the development of popular culture and the dissemination of information to help people see through the lies of the dominant media and information systems.

Artists and media activists working out of the propaganda model tend to create their own counterpropaganda. Forms of art such as socialist realism present the truths hidden by the dominant discourse, tell the stories of people's struggles for liberation, and show ways of living that run counter to the dominant discourse. Working to counter the hegemony of mainstream media, the organization Fairness and Accuracy in Reporting (FAIR) keeps track of who owns which media outlets and the ways ownership influences reporting. The anti-WTO protests in Seattle in 1999 brought attention to another media activist movement: the Independent Media Centers. These centers for alternative journalism have sprung up all around the world, using the internet and digital video to provide sources of information that are more accurate and closer to the protest movements than the mainstream.

These forms of art and media have been crucial for keeping people on the left informed about the realities they are fighting for, and many people have been moved to action by their messages.

Counterpropaganda can sometimes be overly didactic or teacherly. It tends to preach to its audiences rather than trying to appeal to them. Those working out of the propaganda model are often influenced by a certain Enlightenment point of view that sees people as primarily rational. They attempt to present the truth in a convincing way and to appeal to people's rational selves for belief in the truth.

Followers of Gramsci and of postmodernism would argue that there is no such thing as authentic culture. Cultural practices are always caught up in a complex of systems of meaning, and discourses of power are always present in everything we do.

In *Consumers and Citizens*, Néstor García Canclini, who teaches urban studies in Mexico, argues that who we come to be as people is increasingly defined by our status as consumers. And, he argues, culture is increasingly produced for a global market. This, he claims, is leading to a radical shift in people's sense of identity: "Ever less shaped by local and national loyalties and more and more by participation in transnational or deterritorialized communities of consumers (youth in relation to rock; TV viewers of CNN, MTV, and other satellite-beamed programs)."[16] And, according to Canclini, along with this has come a shift

> from the citizen as a representative of public opinion to the consumer interested in enjoying a particular quality of life. One indication of this change is that argumentative and critical forms of participation cede their place to the pleasure taken in electronic media spectacles where narration or the simple accumulation of

anecdote prevails over reasoned solutions to problems. Another indication is the ephemeral exhibition of events instead of a sustained and structural treatment.[17]

Canclini is critical of those who would say that consumer culture is not culture and try to find "real" culture in nostalgic forms of folk production. He claims that our culture is increasingly a consumer culture, and much of our active engagement in life is as consumers. From his perspective, there is no authentic Mexican culture that exists outside of this complex reality. Even "folk culture" has become commodified through the trade in art for tourists. Whether we like it or not, this is the reality of our culture. It is the core of how we relate to the material objects around us and how we relate to one another.

Most of us exist in cultural contexts that are mediated by commercial practices. If we want to understand our culture, we need to understand the ways that dominant discourses of power, especially commodification, impact cultural processes. People influenced by cultural studies argue that people's desires and their sense of what is true, or even what is rational, grow out of complex power-laden systems of meaning. As a result, we cannot know in any clear way what the correct and true path toward liberation is. And there is no way to get outside of systems of power to analyze them objectively. People who are influenced by this approach tend to value desire as a mark of what people want and will often value forms of commercial culture by seeing resistance and subversion everywhere. This is sometimes taken to the extreme that watching television and shopping are seen as subversive practices when they satisfy people's desires.

An approach consistent with Hall's and Gramsci's theories would focus on ways to create new forms of meaning that allow people to experience the world in new ways, helping them to transform the oppressive aspects of society, while not giving up on what is desirable or fun. Counterhegemonies need to be developed, and new senses of aesthetics and meaning need to be woven out of what exists and formed into something new.

People rarely switch political perspectives simply because someone has convinced them of the truth of some proposition. Rather, as Gramsci says, our beliefs are wrapped up in networks of meaning and forms of life. Switching political perspectives involves a radical shift in one's values, cultural orientations, and worldviews. Getting people to make these shifts involves appealing to people's senses of desire. The alternative worldview must be appealing to the passions as well as to the mind.

New social media

With the rise of new social media, the ways that those systems of desire circulate is being deeply disrupted. Where for most of the past fifty years, corporations had ever-increasing control over the mass media, now, fewer people are watching network television, and more are watching videos created by other people for the pure fun of it. Messages that are counter to dominant norms are now able to circulate if people find them attractive and interesting. This presents huge opportunities for social justice activists working in the realm of culture. Now, if a message is interesting and attractive, it can find a huge audience without having to go through the filters that the older forms of media imposed.

One example is Annie Leonard's video *The Story of Stuff.* Leonard and her collaborators figured out a way to package a deeply anticonsumerist message in a very short video that was funny and visually appealing. It has been viewed by millions of people and has an important influence on our culture. The Color of Change is a web-based organization that challenges media misrepresentations of people of color. It has been very impactful in a few campaigns, and was a major player in the fight over internet neutrality.

There is a lot of potential for counterhegemonic culture to be spread via the internet. Yet most of what circulates on the internet is pornography, cute videos of cats, and celebrity gossip.

We have within our reach the ability to communicate across vast distances, and to build sense of meaning and purpose uncontrolled by corporate gatekeepers. The extent to which we are able to use that for building a better world remains unclear, and as struggles such as the one over net neutrality show, much of that struggle has to be over who controls the physical infrastructure for and rules governing all of that disembodied free-floating content. But much of it also needs to involve the creation of ways of experiencing and understanding the world that help us to transform it for the better.

CHAPTER 10
Organizing to Make a Difference

WHEN I FIRST GOT INVOLVED IN SOCIAL JUSTICE POLITICS IN THE 1980s, I didn't have to work hard to figure out what to do or how to get involved. I was becoming concerned about the state of the world in general when I read an article in the local entertainment weekly about what was going on in El Salvador. The article talked about the brutal situation for the people there and US support for the military. The article mentioned an organization trying to stop US aid to El Salvador and gave its contact information.

That week, I called the Committee in Solidarity with the People of El Salvador (CISPES) and asked if I could volunteer. At that time, I assumed that a person like me would be expected to come to an office and prepare materials and things like that. As it turned out, they wanted me to help some other people who had called them to start a chapter of the organization where we lived.

A Salvadoran exile came out to talk with the few of us who had volunteered. He impressed upon us how important our work would be and how much support we would get in figuring out how to do the work. Although I was frightened by the level of responsibility they wanted me to take on so quickly, I immediately liked the other people I was working with. The group turned out to be great for me. I learned organizing skills more quickly than I could have imagined. Being in the group began to transform the rest of my life, as I gained confidence and a sense of myself as an active participant in world affairs.

Much social justice work involves focusing on an issue where there is a serious social problem and challenging entrenched powers that are responsible for the problem. Sometimes social justice work involves finding new and better ways to live, or building positive economic structures, or community assets such as worker-owned co-ops, or community gardens. Social justice work also involves the development of ways of experiencing and understanding the world that sustain people and inspire them to engage with making a difference At different times these three core elements of social change—challenging the old, building the new, and developing cultures of resistance—are more predominant within a social movement, and some people are attracted to different ways of making the world a better place.

As the internet has made connecting with others around social change easier, there is a whole range of levels of involvement open to us: from "clicktivism" where a person shares information or opinions with friend on the internet, or signs a petition, all the way to becoming a professional organizer. Most of the work that most of us do is in between those extremes, with people going to protests, engaging as volunteers on particular campaigns, creating social spaces in which people can experience the world in more positive ways, producing oppositional culture, or starting a local organization to take up with work that is shared by people in other places, often supported by staff who provide resources.

Currently I am involved with the fossil fuel divestment movement, which began in 2010 when students at Swarthmore College began to pressure their board to sell off all stocks invested in fossil fuels. While the college has repeatedly rejected the students' request, their struggle sparked a movement that caught fire all around the country, at other colleges and in intuitions such as cities and pension funds. As I write this, the fossil fuel divestment movement is the fastest-growing divestment movement in history. Several organizations with paid staff are helping with the organizing. Those organizations are developing and sharing materials, and they have hired some paid organizers to help with local campaigns. The movement is spreading, as people in different institutions hear about the idea and decide to work on it themselves.

There is a similar dynamic happening around police violence. After a series of high-profile murders of black men by police, communities all around the country are taking up the work of transforming local police practices.

National attention to the issue opens up a space for organizations that have been struggling with this issue for years to have more traction and gain some victories.

For any particular issue, people can go for years without a lot of high-profile action, and without a sense that their work is moving forward very well. Then moments come where the issue gains traction more broadly and where dispersed communities begin to feel like they are part of a movement. That is when the work is usually the most exciting, and where large-scale transformations can take place, and sometimes quite quickly. It is often impossible to know when the slow work people do that seems to be going nowhere can turn into a movement where anything seems possible.

For a movement to grow, people's commitments to it have to grow. That usually happens when people form friendships with other activists, when they feel they are gaining a bigger picture of the way the world works, and when they have an expanded sense of themselves as important actors in the drama of social transformation. In times of rapid social change, those movements can pull people in and transform their life paths in profound ways. In slower times, it is quite hard for people to sustain their commitments to a better world, and they often feel isolated and out of step with the society around them. Larger transformations in people's consciousness and sense of commitment tend to grow when people are part of participatory organizations, where they get to help to define what the organization does and how it goes about doing its work.

Today's loose networks are in stark contrast to the main style of organizing popular in the early part of the twentieth century, when social change activists were interested in forming stable organizations with very clear goals. That fairly rigid model was strongly rejected by many activists in the 1960s, '70s, and '80s. Activists during those decades favored more informal organizational structures and thought they should be vehicles for the expression of the people involved.

Before looking in a deeper way at the current possibilities, it is helpful to look at those older ideas about organization.

The Old Left

People involved in the movements of the 1960s began to look back at the movements that predated them and defined themselves in contrast to what had been before. The term "New Left" came to be a description for much of what was going on at that time, and it was meant to stand in contrast with the "Old Left." When people talk about the Old Left, they are mostly referring to the Communist Party, which was a dominant force in social justice politics for much of the early part of the twentieth century.

The term "Old Left" is a bit misleading since there were many social justice organizations besides the Communist Party at that time. Anarchism was popular and very influential. Civil rights groups such as the NAACP were very active and radical at that point. There were many pacifist groups and organizations working to improve people's lives in specific ways, such as the co-op movement. The Socialist Party and many smaller Trotskyist parties were also quite active.

Still, the Communist Party was a clear symbol for 1960s activists to define themselves against, and there has been much historical discussion of the differences between these two periods and the types of organization that characterize them.

The Communist Party had a formal structure, and members were expected to follow party policy in very disciplined ways. The party started many organizations and took over many organizations that were working on a very broad range of issues. The party sometimes let people in those organizations know what it was doing and sometimes it did not.

Only party members were in on the analysis that was driving the direction of those organizations, and only people who seemed to really understand the political issues at stake were invited to join the party. The Communist Party was able to accomplish quite a bit in its efforts to make trade unions more radical and in many cases more multiracial, in its work on racial justice in the South, and in its involvement with many single-issue organizations trying to improve people's lives.

The Communist Party was a vanguardist party. Parties work by trying to build support for a specific set of principles and are organized through a membership committed to adherence to those principles. A vanguardist party is based on the idea that its principles should be used to lead the rest of society. In a vanguardist party, a small number of people are educated in the analysis of the organization. This select group then makes sure that the party's analysis influences the actions of a much broader part of the population by working within other organizations only loosely connected with the party.

Vanguardism

The word "vanguard" comes from the French word for the advanced guard of an army. A vanguard is the group of people who are out ahead of everyone else in terms of figuring out the nature of the problems and the best solutions to them.

"Leninism" is another word often used to describe vanguardist theories. That's because Vladimir Ilyich Lenin was the most important theorist of this approach. A leader of the Bolshevik Party that overthrew the Russian government in 1917, he was known as a brilliant political strategist as well as an important Marxist theorist of revolution and imperialism. His ideas have formed a core around which debates about radical social change centered for most of the twentieth century.

Reflecting on the practice that would eventually bring his Bolshevik Party to power in the Soviet Union, Lenin argued that a revolutionary party needs a highly trained core. This core would be made up of people who had studied the issues seriously and who had committed themselves to a certain amount of party discipline—they would work to come to agreement on their analysis and would abide by the analysis of the group. This analysis would then be used as the basis for the party's organizing. Some of the analysis would be shared with the base—or the more general members of the organization, and some of it would be used to inform the actions of the leaders, who would decide the best ways to explain what was going on to everyone else.

In the book *What Is to Be Done?*, Lenin compares making a revolution to building a house with bricks. He argues that the leadership should facilitate the work of the bricklayers by using

> a line to help them find the correct place for the bricklaying; to indicate to them the ultimate goal of the common work; to enable them to use, not only every brick, but even every piece of brick which, when cemented to the bricks laid before and after it, forms a finished, continuous line. . . . If we had a crew of experienced bricklayers, who had learned to work so well together that they could lay their bricks exactly as required without a guideline (which, speaking abstractly is by no means impossible), then perhaps we might take hold of some other link. But it is unfortunate

that as yet we have no experienced bricklayers trained for team-work, that bricks are often laid where they are not needed at all, that they are not laid according to the general line, but are so scat-tered that the enemy can shatter the structure as if it were made of sand and not of bricks.[1]

Leninism has been the dominant organizational philosophy among Marxist activists. This vanguardist approach assumes that there is some objective truth about how society should change and about the nature of the social problems being addressed. The goal of the leaders is to get everyone else on board to work toward that objectively knowable goal by following the party's "line."

In his book *Revolution in the Air*, Max Elbaum writes that one of the virtues of Leninism is that it pushes people in an organization to work to-gether in a disciplined way. Commenting on the successes of Leninist parties in the United States in the 1970s, Elbaum writes,

> Leninism's requirement that every member participate in advanc-ing an agreed upon program allowed groups to coordinate multi-sector, nationwide campaigns and fostered genuine camaraderie. The Leninist stricture that every revolutionary must be respon-sible to a party unit served as a positive corrective to the problems many had experienced in looser New Left groups, whose work was badly hurt by the unaccountable actions of media-created leaders or by the refusal of a numerical minority to abide by the will of the majority.[2]

This approach sees the question of what is in people's interest in very simple terms. It supposes that it is possible to analyze what would con-stitute liberation of the people and that a small group of people who had figured this out could lead the population to freedom. As we saw in Chapter 1, there are two major problems with this approach. One is that it is hard to see how to get people involved in a revolution if they don't really know what they are fighting for. The other is that it is easy for a small group to develop a partial understanding of the situation and focus on issues that reflect their own situated reality as opposed to the interests of everyone.

Rosa Luxemburg was one of the most eloquent critics of Leninism at the time when these debates were raging in the Marxist movement in Europe. She was a leading activist and intellectual of the German Social Democrats, the party that Marx had belonged to fifty years earlier. Born in Poland in 1871, she fled imprisonment and, after living for years in Switzerland, moved to Germany in 1898. She wrote several books and gave hundreds of speeches to party members. Both Jewish and a feminist, Luxemburg was part of a tendency that opposed the nationalism of the mainstream of the party. She struggled, unsuccessfully, to get the Social Democrats to oppose World War I. After the war, she was a leader of an uprising against the German government. In 1919, she was murdered by German troops.

Long before the Russian revolution turned into an authoritarian police state, Luxemburg criticized Leninist vanguardism. She was a believer in the idea that revolutions are highly unpredictable, that consciousness changes as movements develop, and that therefore leaders need to be very open to contingencies and changes in people's consciousness that occur as a movement develops. No one can know what issues are going to be of passionate concern to people involved in social change. Leaders who stick too closely to their analysis will miss the spontaneous force of a group of people in motion.

In her influential 1904 pamphlet *Leninism or Marxism*, Luxemburg writes, "Let us speak plainly, historically, the errors committed by a truly revolutionary movement are infinitely more fruitful than the infallibility of the cleverest Central Committee."[3] This is because, she argues, political consciousness grows organically through the process of political struggle. The objectives of struggle and the ways that it is analyzed must develop together.[4]

While the New Left defined itself in opposition to the vanguardism of the Communist Party, many vanguardist parties developed at that time, as members of the New Left became more and more impatient with the pace of social change in the United States. Some of the organizations that arose at that time are still around today. Part of their appeal is that they offer their members clear and unambiguous analyses.

Revolutionary parties have played important roles in movements throughout the world. They offer their members a strong sense of belonging in an often hostile world, they are usually committed to the political education of their members, and they help put the day-to-day work of organizing into a broader context.

In the contemporary United States, they have sometimes been able to sustain radical vision at times when other groups have focused so much on fighting for what is attainable that they have lost a larger sense of what they were fighting for. On the more negative side, they often position themselves as more radical than other groups and spend much of their time criticizing multi-issue and democratically organized groups for being wishy-washy. Those opposed to these Leninist forms usually refer to them as sectarian organizations, implying that they operate like sects or cults.

US vanguardist groups today usually define themselves as followers of Lenin, Mao, or Trotsky. In actual practice, the differences between the groups are not always directly connected to the theorist they take as their namesake. Maoist organizations, such as the Revolutionary Communist Party (RCP), tend to focus on Third World liberation struggles. Theoretically, they follow Mao in believing that a radical change in people's consciousness can lead to rapid radicalization of masses of people. Maoists believe that even though it seems like most people in the United States are quite conservative, in fact, if the movement does the right things, revolution could be made right now. This set of beliefs has led their opponents to characterize Maoist politics as "voluntarist," meaning that the success or failure of a movement is dependent upon the wills of organizers rather than being determined by external conditions.

Voluntarism can lead members of an organization to be overly concerned with having just the right analysis, which can lead to sectarianism, where people fight with those whose ideas are only slightly different from their own. According to Elbaum, who spent many years in organizations influenced by Maoism, "Mao's idealist slogan 'The correctness or incorrectness of the ideological and political line decides everything' was gospel for many United States Maoists, and it stacked the deck in favor of purism and ultraleftism."[5]

Organizations that call themselves Trotskyist are extremely diverse. Leon Trotsky was one of the leading intellectuals of the Russian revolution. After Lenin died, Trotsky was pushed aside by Stalin in a power struggle. Trotsky was critical of Stalin's authoritarianism and was assassinated while in exile in Mexico in 1940 by agents working for Stalin.

Some groups calling themselves Trotskyist, such as the International Socialist Organization are among the most sectarian of the vanguardist organizations. Others, such as Solidarity, are the most democratic and participatory. Both tendencies find their roots in the ideas and practice of Trotsky, who was interested in a democratic form of socialism but who also was fundamentally a Leninist.

One of the things that vanguardist groups have in common is that they tend to believe that they have an internal process for coming up with a correct analysis of the present political situation. And they are usually organized internally according to fairly strict hierarchical principles. Externally, they often try to recruit new members into their organization and to influence the rest of the movement by getting larger, more open groups to adopt their line. Often, they are not open about either of these goals, and they can play a destructive role in large coalitions by creating huge amounts of strife through struggles over the analysis a larger group should adopt. By seeing their own organizational development as more important than the goals of a particular coalition or organization they are involved with, they often act in ways that tear organizations apart.

Prefigurative politics

In her book *Community and Organization in the New Left, 1962–1968*, Wini Breines argues that, in the movements of the 1960s, there developed a whole new way of thinking of politics that was opposed to the vanguardism of the Communist Party, which she calls *prefigurative politics*.

> The term *prefigurative politics* is used to designate an essentially anti-organizational politics characteristic of the movement, as well as parts of new left leadership, and may be recognized in counter institutions, demonstrations and the attempt to embody personal and anti-hierarchical values in politics. Participatory democracy was central to prefigurative politics. "Anti-organizational" should not be construed as disorganized. Movements are organized in numerous obvious and often hidden ways. My use of the term anti-organizational should be understood to mean principally a wariness of hierarchy and centralized organization. The crux of prefigurative politics imposed substantial tasks, the central one being to create and sustain within the live practice of the movement, relationships and political forms that "prefigured" and embodied the desired society.[6]

In other words, we should act right now as if we were living in the better world we are fighting for. Prefigurative politics is based on the belief that we are creating the new world we are advocating as we go, and so we should try to build in the present the institutions and social patterns of the society we are working toward.

This is one of the reasons that movements growing out of the social justice movements of the latter part of the twentieth century were often very concerned with internal processes. As an intersectional approach has become the norm, it has become an increasingly important part of social justice politics to insist that people in organizations pay attention to race, class, and gender dynamics within the organization, and to work toward democracy in group processes.

Those operating out of a vanguardist framework are usually less concerned about how we live in the present. They often see these issues as an unnecessary luxury. What matters is the political action taken and the goals achieved. They use a structural analysis that looks at what needs to be changed and use any means necessary to achieve that change. If we can overthrow the state using undemocratic means, we can then build a democratic society afterward. For them, there is no necessary connection between how we act in the present and what we are trying to achieve.

Those who believe in prefigurative politics, on the other hand, believe that the means we use in the present are intimately connected with the world we are creating, and they see means as deeply connected with ends. It is crucial for people in a social justice movement to treat one another with respect and care. In prefigurative movements, we are reweaving the social fabric. We are creating an alternative social world, and the relations we create along the way lay the foundation for the relations we will have after we achieve our goals.

People who are interested in prefigurative politics often focus on the aspects of social justice work that have to do with building the new world, rather than on the parts related to challenging systems of domination. When you are building a community garden, or developing a worker-owned cooperative, it is important to live the values you are working toward. People engaged in working to oppose a free trade agreement, and similar work aimed at challenging systems of domination, do often pay attention to their internal dynamics, and try to build positive interactions and relations in their process, but the need for it is generally not as obvious.

The revolutionary subject

The civil rights movement began in the 1940s and influenced a whole string of movements that flourished over the next forty years. Each of these social justice movements focused on different problems, and each had its own culture and ways of organizing. They are often grouped together and referred to as the social justice movements of the 1960s, even though some, such as the civil rights movement, began in the 1940s, and others, such as the women's and gay and lesbian liberation movements, didn't really develop until after 1970.[7]

Each of these movements focused on making changes for a particular group of people. For the Communist, Trotskyist, and Socialist parties, and the anarchists of the period before the social justice movements of the 1960s, it was assumed that the most important group for making major social transformation was the working class. People from all of these different approaches made analyses of the world that argued that capitalism was the main problem facing society and that the group most negatively impacted by capitalism was the working class. In Marxist terms, the working class was the revolutionary subject, or the active force that would make change happen.

Activists in the social justice movements of the 1960s tended to write off the working class as hopelessly attached to the high wages that many sectors of the work force received in post–World War II United States. They were interested in forms of social change that related to the quality of people's lives. The issue wasn't the wages earned in capitalist production, but the form of life people were experiencing in a more general sense. The student movement focused on free speech on campuses, an education relevant to people's experiences, and an end to the universities acting as a training ground for business. The civil rights movement challenged the systems of racial apartheid that existed at the time. As the Black Power movement, the Chicano Moratorium, and other people of color liberation movements developed, they focused on issues of respect and cultural representation, as well as access to good jobs.

The women's movement of that period focused on a whole range of issues, some having to do with equality in personal relationships, some having to do with media representations and legal limitations such as divorce law, child support, and the right to abortion. Issues surrounding equal pay for equal work, which was a more traditional trade union issue and was related to women as a part of the working class, were only part of what people were mobilizing around.

People in all of these movements struggled with the ideas of the Old Left. Many of those involved advocated for party organizations to challenge the status quo, and many tried to fit new issues into the old frameworks of liberation. But this was also an incredible time for the development of new ideas. People in these movements developed new ways of understanding how social change happens and which people were most relevant to making it happen.

Identity politics

Many people involved in the social justice movements of the 1960s were deeply critical of the oppressive dynamics within movements for social change. Young people in the civil rights movement created the Student Nonviolent Coordinating Committee (SNCC), in part to avoid domination by their elders. Women formed NOW after experiencing sexism in the civil rights, antiwar, and student movements. Women of color challenged the racism of the women's movement and sexism in the Black Power organizations. Movements based on sexuality and physical and mental ability asserted that those issues, too, should be addressed.

The period roughly from 1975 through 2000 is often characterized as dominated by "identity politics." What people mean by this expression is a politics based on the interests of groups of people who share something important in terms of their sense of self. People critical of this political form rejected it by arguing that it was about superficial issues of personality rather than about serious issues such as economics and social structures. They saw it as more focused on psychology than structural transformation.

Those using the term "identity politics" in a negative way are usually operating out of a model of politics that is founded on the idea of a split between society's "base" and its "superstructure." The base is the economic foundation of society, and the superstructure refers to the ideas and cultures of society. This model grew out of a crude form of Marxism, sometimes referred to as vulgar or orthodox Marxism. Many operating out of this framework think that the problems of the white male working class best represent the problems that need to be solved in society's base. They see attention to concerns outside the economic interests of the working class as distractions from "real politics."

In contrast to these economistic Marxists, Gramscian Marxists, such as Stuart Hall, have argued that it is positive for movements to work in the interests of specific groups and to look in detail at how social power operates in constructing and restricting people based on these types of group memberships. Feminist multi-issue groups, such as the Women's Pentagon Action in the early '80s, provide women with an opportunity to fight militarism, environmental destruction, patriarchy, and heterosexism, without having to struggle with sexist men in their organization. Even single-issue groups rarely stay single-issue. Fighting antigay discrimination, for example, involves challenging discrimination in the workplace and in military recruiting, as well as legal claims for health insurance coverage, freedom from violence, and gender and sexual liberation for all people.

Civil rights and disability

Movements that are based on the common identity and experience of a particular group often draw their inspiration from other movements. The example of the civil rights movement helped people with disabilities see themselves as members of an oppressed community whose rights were not being respected.

Before the advent of the civil rights movement, there were two general tendencies among the disabled and their advocates. The most common one, even today, is based on the idea that the disabled are persons in need of care and support, and that society should be generous enough to care for them.

While much good work has been done under this idea, many disabled people see it as paternalistic. It requires people with disabilities to assume the role of victims of their fate, dependent upon others for help. Often, along with this caregiving approach goes an attitude that people with disabilities should be passively grateful for any help they receive. People with disabilities are often appreciated and seen as heroes when they make few demands on their caregivers or on society.

A more radical tradition argues that the problems encountered by the disabled are intimately connected with other social problems and should be looked at through political lenses. The most famous advocate of this approach was Helen Keller. Born in 1880 in Alabama, she had an illness as a baby that left her blind and deaf. The story of how Ann Sullivan worked with Keller to teach her to read and write, and thus to be able to communicate with other people, is a famous one. Less well known is that Keller was a committed socialist.

Keller saw that many disabilities were caused by unsafe conditions in the workplace and lack of health care for the poor. Keller was acutely aware of the narrow set of views acceptable for people with disabilities.

> So long as I confine my activities to social service and the blind, the [newspapers] compliment me extravagantly, calling me "archpriest of the sightless," "wonder woman" and "a modern miracle." But when it comes to a discussion of poverty, and I maintain that it is a result of wrong economics—that the industrial system under which we live is at the root of much deafness and blindness in the world—that is a different matter. It is laudable to give aid to the handicapped. Superficial charities make smooth the way of the prosperous; but to advocate that all human beings should have leisure and comfort, the decencies and refinements of life, is an Utopian dream, and one who seriously contemplates its realization must indeed be deaf, dumb, and blind.[8]

Keller focused on the social causes of disabilities, and she argued for people with disabilities to be able to be more than passive victims. While she was a strong advocate for women's rights, Keller herself didn't think of disability issues in terms of rights.

It wasn't until after the civil rights movement that people began to understand disability issues in terms of civil rights. Inspired by the ideas of the civil rights movement, which argued that systems of oppression could be challenged by demanding equal rights, people with disabilities began to understand many of the problems they experienced in terms of discrimination and oppression. Attention shifted away from a focus on the physical or mental disability and onto the way society treated the person with disabilities.

One of the originators of the disability rights movement was Ed Roberts. In his book *No Pity: People with Disabilities Forging a New Civil Rights Movement*, Joseph Shapiro writes about Roberts's involvement in the origins of the civil rights approach to disability organizing.

In the fall of 1962, James Meredith, escorted to class by US mar-
shals, integrated the University of Mississippi. That same school
season, a postpolio quadriplegic named Ed Roberts entered the
University of California at Berkeley. Just as surely as Meredith ushered in an era of access to higher education for blacks and a new
chapter in the civil rights movement, Roberts was more quietly
opening a civil rights movement that would remake the world for
disabled people. The disability rights movement was born the day
Roberts arrived on the Berkeley campus.[9]

Roberts and his mother had to fight for him to be able to graduate
from high school. His principal insisted that he needed to complete driver's
education and physical education to graduate. When he tried to go to the
University of California at Berkeley, the Department of Rehabilitation at first
refused to pay for his education, arguing that since he would never be able to
work, his education would be wasted. UC Berkeley also required students to
live on campus, but did not have any dorm rooms that could accommodate
his eight-hundred-pound iron lung.

In each of these cases, what was blocking Roberts's progress was less
his physical limitations and more the refusal of others to allow for them.
Eventually, Roberts was joined at Berkeley by other disabled students, and
they began to work together.

By 1967 there were twelve severely disabled students living in
Cowell [Hospital, which eventually became their dorm]. They
called themselves the "Rolling Quads." In late-night bull sessions
on the hospital floor, Roberts and his friends, in their wheelchairs
and iron lungs, would strategize constantly about breaking down
the common barriers they faced—from classrooms they could not
get into to their lack of transportation around town—and dissect
the protests for self-determination of minority students.[10]

This group eventually went on to found the Center for Independent Living
in Berkeley. The center was based on the principles of self-determination
and independence. By framing the issue as one of civil rights rather than
requests for more services, this group began a revolution in how people with
disabilities and their allies think about these issues.

In recent years, this movement has focused increasingly on issues surrounding mental disabilities. One group that has done much work on this is the National Alliance for the Mentally Ill. Mental disability is more strongly stigmatized than physical disability. People with mental problems are often thought to be responsible for their illnesses, and they are often seen as dangerous. Even though people with mental disabilities are no more prone to violence than the population as a whole, the stigma of violence is often used as a justification for taking away their rights.[11]

The Support Coalition International is fighting against forced institutionalization and forced use of psychiatric medication and for choice in medical care. They want people with mental illness to be able to control their care to the fullest extent possible.

People working for the rights of the mentally and physically disabled eventually won passage of the Americans with Disabilities Act in 1990. One of the revolutionary things about the ADA was that it was a civil rights bill. The ADA outlawed discrimination based on ability and required that "reasonable accommodations" be made in employment and government. It focused on the ways that discrimination marginalizes people with disabilities. Business fought the ADA bitterly. Many people with disabilities and their allies protested and lobbied hard for its passage. Since it has been in effect, many of the barriers that limit the lives of people with disabilities have been torn down. Yet many remain, chief among them the attitude that people with disabilities should not be accepted as full members of society.

Empowerment

The power of people acting for justice on their own behalf was made very clear through the tumultuous years of the civil rights movement. In place of the Old Left's tendency toward vanguardism, *empowerment* became a central organizing premise throughout the social justice movements of the 1960s. According to this idea, as oppressed people begin to take themselves and their own needs more seriously, they develop the resources needed to fight for social change.

In *Women and the Politics of Empowerment*, published in 1988, Ann Bookman and Sandra Morgan explain that the term "empowerment" has come to have a less political meaning than it once did. "Empowerment is currently a fashionable term, particularly as it refers to individual self-assertion, upward mobility, or the psychological experience of 'feeling powerful.'" Bookman and Morgan argue that, in its political context, empowerment may involve these things. But for women in the feminist movement of the 1970s, "empowerment begins when they change their ideas about the causes of their powerlessness, when they recognize the systemic forces that oppress them, and when they act to change the conditions of their lives."[12]

In the women's movement, this idea was associated with consciousness-raising groups. In these leaderless groups, women got together and talked about the issues that concerned them. Through these discussions, the participants began to see patterns in their experiences and to develop theories of the sources of their problems in larger social structures. Feminists developed a politics based on the idea that people should be given a chance to speak about their own reality and to develop analyses based on that experience. In contrast to vanguardism, empowerment theorists argued that political programs should grow organically out of the wishes and desires of those affected.

The Brazilian educator Paulo Freire developed a similar perspective based on his work in education. Freire was a professor of the philosophy of education in Recife, Brazil. He was jailed, briefly, by Brazil's military government in 1964 and spent many years in exile. Eventually, Freire became one of the leading theorists of political education, and his book *Pedagogy of the Oppressed*, became essential reading for social justice advocates throughout the decolonizing world.

Freire rejected what he called a "banking theory of education," whereby a teacher deposits information into the brain of the student. Instead, he saw education as dialogical, or based on dialogue. The goal of education is to develop people's consciousness of themselves as knowledge producers. His method involved posing problems to his students about their own lives.

> Problem-posing education, as a humanist and liberating praxis, posits as fundamental that men subjected to domination must fight for their emancipation. To that end, it enables teachers and students to become Subjects of the educational process by overcoming authoritarianism and alienating intellectualism; it also enables men to overcome their false perception of reality.[13]

In his work with the rural poor, Freire would ask people what their concerns were and then ask a series of questions that would engage them in an investigation of the roots of those concerns. Through this process, students developed their own analyses of the sources of their poverty and a program for doing something about it. They experienced a deep transformation of their view of themselves and their place in the world, coming to see themselves as intelligent and resourceful rather than as passive victims of inevitable misfortune or insurmountable oppression.

Freirean teachers guide the direction of their students' analyses by the sorts of questions they ask. The important difference between Freire's approach and the Leninist model of political education is that Freireans work in dialogue with those affected, and the analysis that develops has much stronger ties to the lived experience of those people.

In contrast to the rigid leadership of the Leninist model, and also to Freire's teacher-student model, empowerment in US radical politics is sometimes taken to mean that the people affected by a system of oppression are the only ones who know that system and that whatever they have to say about it must be right. This idea can lead to an unfortunate anti-intellectualism, where no analysis needs to be developed because the oppressed know from their experience what is wrong and what strategies will improve their lives. Of course, oppressed people often understand their own situations better than those who don't have that experience. However, people can be confused about their own situations.

Freire and other theorists of empowerment believe that experience is an important starting point for the building of analysis, but that knowledge does not grow directly out of experience. Experience needs to be reflected on and analyzed. In describing the relationship between teacher and student, Freire focuses on the need for the teacher to be open, but he is also very clear about the important role played by critical intellectuals in the process of developing leadership.

While the leaders may have

> a level of revolutionary knowledge different from the level of empirical knowledge held by the people, they cannot impose themselves and their knowledge on the people. They cannot sloganize the people, but must enter into dialogue with them, so that the people's empirical knowledge of reality, nourished by the leaders'

critical knowledge, gradually becomes transformed into knowledge of the *causes* of reality.[14]

Thus, the Freirean perspective argues for leadership that is very open to changing its goals, strategies, and tactics as a result of dialogue, and that is more likely to lead by facilitating clarification of the issues than by formulating them at the outset.

The nuances of Freirean leadership remain ambiguous. When Freirean organizers come into a community in an attempt to build a movement, they cannot set aside their own analysis of what would be best for the community. Yet some of Freire's followers believe that analysis developed through Freirean practice grows completely from the students themselves. They don't see the ways that their own power operates to affect the situation. And those who use Freirean techniques and really avoid injecting their own analysis can end up with work that leads nowhere. Students will not necessarily develop a point of view that a social justice advocate would be happy with.

Radical Christians in Latin America used Freire's methods in groups called *comunidades de base*, or "Christian base communities." These Bible study groups incubated radical consciousness and helped ignite revolutionary movements in Central and South America. And while those movements had strong Leninist elements in them, they also contained Freirean, anti-Leninist elements. Freire's work was also influential in the United States, especially in the women's movement and among social justice educators, where it worked as an antidote to the authoritarian tendencies that predominated in the Old Left.

Violence

Members of the Communist Party, and members of most vanguardist parties, have argued for the necessity of a violent revolution. For members of the Old Left, there wasn't a problem with the morality of violence, since the most important moral imperative was to overthrow the oppressive system. In this case, the ends justified the means. Those involved in the social justice movements of the 1960s were more hesitant about the use of violence. For anyone interested in the idea of prefigurative politics, ends are intricately entwined with means. Freire, while concerned about the connections between ends and means, did not rule out violence. Here, Freire is more in line with traditional Marxists who argue that, because the ruling groups will defend their power until forced to give it up, violence is sometimes necessary to make radical changes.

In his book *The Wretched of the Earth*, the anticolonial thinker and activist Frantz Fanon takes this idea one step further. Published in 1961, the book had a dramatic impact on the anticolonial movements of the 1960s and '70s, particularly in Africa. Fanon was from the Caribbean island of Martinique and went to Algeria to work as a psychiatrist. There he became involved in the movement for independence from France.

Fanon argues that the colonial situation is a brutally violent one, in which colonized people are devastated by the violence of the colonizers. Only by turning taking their lives into their own hands and decolonizing their consciousness and seeing themselves as subjects will the colonized purge the violence and degradation from their systems and become ready for liberation. This process sometimes involves violence.

In a famous speech, the great abolitionist leader Frederick Douglass expresses his view of the necessity of agitation and the importance of a willingness to engage in violence:

> Those who profess to favor freedom and yet depreciate agitation are men who want crops without plowing up the ground, they want rain without thunder and lightning. They want the ocean without the awful roar of its many waters. . . . This struggle may be a moral one, or it may be a physical one, and it may be both moral and physical, but it must be a struggle. Power concedes nothing without a demand. It never did and it never will. Find out just what any people will quietly submit to and you have found out the exact measure of injustice and wrong that will be imposed on them, and these will continue until they are resisted with either words or blows, or with both. The limits of tyrants are prescribed by the endurance of those whom they oppress. In light of these ideas, Negroes will be hunted at the North, and held and flogged at the South so long as they submit to those devilish outrages, and make no resistance, either moral or physical. Men may not get all they pay for in this world; but they must certainly pay for all they get. If we ever get free from the oppressions and wrongs

heaped upon us, we must pay for their removal. We must do this by labor, by suffering, by sacrifice, and if needs be, by our lives and the lives others.[15]

Malcolm X, who was himself not involved in any revolutionary violence, made the famous statement that blacks should use "any means necessary" to achieve liberation. His point was that the racist situation in the United States was completely illegitimate. There was no moral compact between blacks and whites. You don't owe ethical obligations to people who are oppressing you.

In his writings about nonviolence as a tactic, Martin Luther King Jr. was very aware of the criticism that nonviolence looks like a weak approach to social change. King argued that nonviolence did not mean weakness. Rather, a tactic of nonviolent civil disobedience would be the most powerful means for transforming US society.

In *Where Do We Go from Here: Chaos or Community?*, published shortly before his death in 1968, King writes that nonviolent civil disobedience would create a deeply transformative ethical position that would have its own sort of power.

> One of the greatest problems of history is that the concepts of love and power are usually contrasted as polar opposites. Love is identified with a resignation of power and power with a denial of love. . . . What is needed is a realization that power without love is reckless and abusive and that love without power is sentimental and anemic. Power at its best is love implementing the demands of justice. Justice at its best is love correcting everything that stands against love.[16]

King argues that "power and morality must go together, implementing, fulfilling and ennobling each other."[17] For King, it was crucial for those in the civil rights movement to maintain the moral high ground. This moral position would forge an ethical unity in the movement that would operate as the core of its transformative power. It is not that King believed that the ethical beliefs themselves would make change. Rather, he felt that the movement's deep ethical foundation would motivate its participants and undermine the ability of oppressors to retain support within the passive majority of society.

This breaking of the legitimacy of the hegemonic worldview would open up the space for the demands of the movement to be met.

King addresses those involved in the civil rights movement who were influenced by Fanon's argument about violence. King's response is that violent overthrow is only possible when the majority of the population no longer accept the legitimacy of the government.

> Few if any violent revolutions have been successful unless the violent minority had the sympathy of the nonresisting majority. Castro may have had only a few Cubans actually fighting with him, but he would never have overthrown the Batista regime unless he had had the sympathy of the vast majority of the Cuban people. It is perfectly clear that a violent revolution on the part of American blacks would find no sympathy and support from the white population and very little from the majority of the Negroes themselves.[18]

Most people on the left agree with King that a successful armed struggle against the US state is not a possibility in the near future, but debates continue about the role of US-based activists in supporting armed groups in other countries. The movements to stop US intervention in Central America in the 1980s, and those working in solidarity with the Zapatistas in Mexico, have faced the question of the moral and practical validity of violence.

The Central America movement had two different tendencies within it: those who were against US intervention in the affairs of another country and those who actively supported the revolutionary movements there. For some, the choice of which position to take was purely a practical question of which would get the most support among the larger population. Anti-intervention was a much less controversial position.

But for many people, there was also a deeper question about revolutionary movements. Pacifists argued that violence was never justified. They did not support the revolutionary movements in El Salvador, Nicaragua, and Guatemala. Instead, they simply opposed the violent imperialism of the United States.

Others, however, were passionate supporters of the armed struggle. They saw the success of those revolutions as key steps in a worldwide process of decolonization and anticapitalism. This view was often based on evidence that armed struggle worked in anticolonial movements. While supporters of Gandhi argued that nonviolence is a better path for decolonization, many Indian radicals have pointed out the crucial role played by armed resistance in India.

Sometimes support for the revolutions of others can have a romanticized quality. Most of us working for social justice in the United States are operating in a context in which the only changes we can make are small and achieved through slow and painful work. The idea that we could stop talking to people who believe differently from ourselves and simply come out of the jungle with guns can have a real appeal. There is something exhilarating about watching movements in which people, using any means necessary, are making real changes in their societies. This perspective can make us lose sight of how much slow painful work takes place in situations in which people are also taking up arms.

On January 1, 1994, the Zapatistas surprised the world by launching an armed struggle against the Mexican government. Timed to coincide with the implementation of the North American Free Trade Agreement (NAFTA), under which Mexico was forced to abandon communal land holding, the Zapatistas demanded regional autonomy, democracy for all of Mexico, and the rights to farm communally.

With the charismatic and articulate Subcomandante Marcos as their spokesperson, the Zapatistas captured the imagination of social justice advocates all around the world. Their movement stood for a new approach to social transformation. Using traditional techniques of armed struggle, they were not attempting to take over a state, rather they were asking for autonomy from the state for indigenous people.

The image of the Zapatista militants, with ski masks covering their faces and guns over their shoulders, came to symbolize the movement. This image dominates people's sense of who the Zapatistas are and how they operate. Missing from the image of the armed militant is the reality that most of the work of the Zapatistas involved the slow process of consciousness-raising and community organizing.

The Zapatistas have worked for years building weaving cooperatives and other systems of mutual support to improve lives in the present and to develop lives that are autonomous from the Mexican government and capitalist agriculture. Often, what gets ignored by those who romanticize armed struggle is the political work done by women.

Disruption and protest

Those advocating for the use of violence often rely on ideas like those expressed by Frederick Douglass. They argue that violence is necessary because people with power will not give it up voluntarily. But there are other ways of challenging those with power besides violence.

Douglass was advocating agitation and pressure, even when it provokes opposition. The idea that one will keep on pushing, even when the other side becomes angry and begins to lash out, is one that often distinguishes radical advocates for social change from liberal ones.

Radicals believe that social injustices involve unequal power relationships and that those with power will protect their power. Liberals, on the other hand, often believe that if those wanting change speak up and let the rest of society know about the problems they are experiencing, change will happen. These different views of power lead to very different approaches to making change happen.

Liberals often favor education as the crucial aspect of social change, and radicals focus more on agitation. Agitation takes many forms. Violence is the most extreme. Short of violence, there are many ways that those advocating for social justice can put pressure on those with power.

Martin Luther King Jr. had a well-developed theory of how agitation works, and he was interested in analyzing how to maximize the resources of the oppressed and minimize those of the powerful. The basic idea behind King's nonviolent civil disobedience was that you should simultaneously push for what you believe is right and expose the tactics used by the other side in responding to you. Doing this, King was always interested in the message being sent out to the population as a whole. King was very adept at using the mass media. Keeping the moral high ground was one of his most important tools.

He believed that it was critical for activists in a civil disobedience action to act in ways that were morally consistent. For example, activists could decide that a particular law was immoral and that they would break that law and bear the consequences of breaking it. Because they were interested in affirming the humanity of all people, they would not antagonize the police. Rather, they would manifest their humanity throughout an action.

Through this sort of disciplined behavior, civil disobedience activists were able to build support for the movement, even while many people were denouncing it for causing chaos and violence. King always maintained that the police themselves were choosing to engage in violence and that his people had nothing to do with violence. Many other activists using civil disobedience have used this approach. Much of its effectiveness comes from its combination of moral appeal and pressure.

There are other ways of applying pressure to a political system that are not violent. In the 1970s, Saul Alinsky developed a theory of community organizing based on the idea of provoking one's opponents to actions that would discredit them in the eyes of the public. Alinsky was interested in pressuring opponents by focusing on individual people in a corporation or government and infuriating and frustrating them. In his book *Rules for Radicals*, Alinsky outlines some of the "rules" that organizers should follow:

> Always remember the first rule of power tactics, *Power is not only what you have, but what the enemy thinks you have.* The second rule is: *Never go outside the experience of your people.* When an action or tactic is outside the experience of the people, the result is confusion, fear, and retreat. It also means collapse of communication. . . . The third rule is: *Whenever possible go outside of the experience of the enemy.* Here you want to cause confusion, fear, and retreat. . . . The fourth rule is: *Make the enemy live up to their own rules.* You can kill them with this, for they can no more obey their own rules than the Christian church can live up to Christianity. The fourth rule carries within it the fifth: *Ridicule is man's most potent weapon.* The sixth rule is: *A good tactic is one that your people enjoy.*[19]

Demonstrations operate on a similar principle. Shortly before a set of major demonstrations at the Democratic and Republican national conventions in 2000, Michael Albert wrote a widely circulated article titled "Why Protest the Conventions," arguing that the main goal of a protest is to "raise the social costs" of a policy.

> It isn't that our demonstrations educate policy-makers so they then willingly change their choices. It isn't that our demonstrations awaken a moral sensibility in policy-makers so they then willingly change their choices. Policy-makers could be educated

or enlightened sufficiently to truly change priorities, conceivably, but the most likely outcome for a policy-maker whose comprehension or values changes so dramatically would be dismissal, not increased influence.

So how do demonstrations affect policies if not by enlightening or morally uplifting policy-makers to have different attitudes? Demonstrations coerce elites. At a given moment, elite policy-makers have a whole array of priorities. Change in policy occurs when policy-makers decide that not changing is not in their interest. Change occurs, that is, when movements raise the social costs that policy-makers are no longer willing to endure and which they can only escape by relenting to movement demands.

Tactical calculation about movement tactics runs like this: If receiving lots of critical letters and email messages doesn't bother elites, and if this doesn't lead to other actions that will bother elites, then writing letters is not useful. If, on the other hand, lots of mail does bother elites by making them nervous about their base of support, or for other reasons, or if it leads to other actions with these effects, then letter writing is a good choice for dissent. And the same holds for holding a rally, a march, a sit-in, a riot, or whatever else. If these choices, either in themselves or by what they promise in the future, raise lasting and escalating social costs for elites who are in a position to impact policy, or if they organize and empower constituencies to do additional things that in turn will raise lasting and escalating social costs for these elites, then they are good tactics for dissidents to choose.

Reciprocally, regardless of how militant or insightful or morally warranted, if a protest or rally or whatever else would diminish social costs over time, say by reducing the number of dissidents or by causing dissidents to fracture and in-fight, it is not a good tactical choice.[20]

In the book *Poor People's Movements: Why They Succeed and How They Fail*, Frances Fox Piven and David Cloward studied the impacts of poor people's movements throughout the history of the United States. They argued that while many negative things happen as a result of riots, they have been one of the most effective means for people to achieve social change.[21]

In line with Albert's view, they argue that those with power generally only give up that power when it is uncomfortable for them to maintain the status quo. Disturbances such as riots do that much more powerfully than well organized and disciplined marches.

The protests in Ferguson, Missouri, after Michael Brown was killed seem to bear this out. While many people were concerned that the property destruction that protesters engaged in would lose them support, the whole country watched and had a sense that something needed, finally, to change. The attention from that, negative as much of it was, kept attention on the issue and in this case, helped it gather momentum.

Those advocating that movements should sometime involve property destruction often use the phrase "diversity of tactics" to make the claim that it is all right for some people to engage in property destruction while others hold rallies that are less confrontational. In the United States and in many other countries, those advocating for the political efficacy of property destruction often call themselves the "black bloc," because generally they wear black clothing and black masks. Many black bloc activists show up to protests initiated by others and engage in property destruction, often against the express agreement of the action's organizers. Protest movements will often begin by getting a set of agreements for participants about what kinds of tactics are acceptable, and if they agree that property destruction is not an acceptable tactic, they will try to stop others from engaging in tactics that are outside of that scope.

In many of the Occupy encampments there were bitter struggles over this. Many participants wanted to maintain the occupations as places here people with children, or undocumented people would be safe, and where public support could be gained by acting respectfully. Others felt that engaging in property destruction was morally right, and that it would make movement more effective. The Oakland Occupy encampment was torn apart by these conversations, as many people engaged in property destruction, and those who disagreed with that tactic had few means to stop them.

The idea behind protest politics is that pressure must be applied to the social structure, and it must be applied in ways that maintain support for those making change happen. That is a tricky balance, and movements are well served by leaders and participants being very thoughtful about how to maintain that balance.

Education in movements for social change

While social justice advocates don't tend focus on education as something that can make social change happen all by itself, for many, education is a critical aspect of social transformation. People need to understand the situation that they are challenging. People in the rest of society need to be informed about the goals of the movement, and they need to be offered ways of understanding the kinds of transformations being advocated in ways that will make them as sympathetic as possible.

Hopefully as a movement develops, people who observe its activities become sympathetic to its message and withdraw their support for elite policies. This can happen through mainstream media attention or through the movement's own media. As the mainstream media become more homogeneous and entertainment-oriented, it is increasingly difficult for protesters to get favorable coverage.

How alternative political perspectives are disseminated to people not already involved is an increasingly difficult question. Some organizations, such as Greenpeace, specialize in mediagenic actions—ones that are so visually interesting and that tell such compelling stories that even the entertainment-oriented media will be tempted to cover them.

In addition to the problem of how to educate those outside the movement, educating those within it is also important. One approach to education of those within a movement is to form study groups and consciousness-raising groups. These are small groups, usually of people who know each other through an organization or as friends, who get together and read about or just discuss the ideas behind the issues they are involved in. A study group focuses more on reading, and consciousness-raising groups focus more on personal experience. To educate people outside their membership, many groups sponsor lectures and other regular educational events. There is also a growing alternative media network of radio stations, video distributors, and internet resources that brings radical information to people who otherwise get most of their news from the corporate media.

More serious education of movement activists has happened in what sociologist Aldon Morris has called "movement halfway houses." By that term he means stable institutions that provide organizer training and other sorts of development for activists. One of the most famous of these at the time of the civil rights movement was the Highlander Folk School, co-founded and led by Myles Horton in Tennessee in 1932.

Horton grew up in rural Tennessee. His parents were educators in a period when so few people had a formal education that the only requirement for teachers was having more education than the people they were teaching. As the standards began to rise, his parents lost their jobs and did odd jobs while Horton was growing up. Horton went on to get a graduate degree in education and decided that his goal in life was to form a school where people could be educated in things relevant to their lives.[22]

Like Freire, Horton believed that oppressed people have deep knowledge of their social situations based on their life experiences, knowledge made much more effective when it is sharpened and made more coherent through a group process.

> They've got much of the knowledge as a group. Not as individuals, but the group as a whole has much of the knowledge that they need to know and solve their problems. If they only knew how to analyze what their experiences were, what they know, and generalize them . . . they would begin to draw on their own resources.[23]

The Highlander Folk School used this philosophy to educate generations of movement activists. The Highlander School's most important contributions were the development of citizenship schools that were an early part of the civil rights movement and, later, leadership development for activists.

A key leader in the citizenship schools was Septima Clark. Clark had been a schoolteacher but was fired because of her involvement in the NAACP. She then joined the staff at Highlander. She initiated a program to teach literacy to African American adults. At that time, there were literacy requirements to vote in the South. People needed to answer complex questions about the United States and their state constitutions. There were official programs to teach people literacy, but most treated adult learners as if they were children.

The Highlander approach was to begin by engaging people in discussions of issues they were interested in, and then teach them to read about those complex issues. Respect was one of the keys to the program. Highlander's citizenship schools were incredibly successful, and their model was adopted all over the South.

Myles Horton was interested in having the Highlander Folk School be an incubator for programs such as the citizenship schools but not in being an administrator, so the schools became independent, with Highlander providing training for the teachers. Later, the school was one of the places where movement activists and leaders would go to learn organizing skills and meet to strategize. Rosa Parks spent a few weeks at the Folk School before her famous decision not to give up her seat to a white rider on a Montgomery, Alabama, bus in 1955.[24]

One newer movement halfway house is the Center for Third World Organizing (CTWO) in Oakland. CTWO describes itself as a "gateway to the movement—a central hub that links activists of color with organizing skills, political education, and visions of a just society."[24] CTWO has a program called "Movement Activist Apprenticeship Program" (MAAP), which was founded in 1985 and provides intensive internships for young activists of color.

Anarchists have developed a tradition of movement education through centers called Long Hauls, which work as social spaces where activists can learn about what is going on in a particular area, find literature, meet other anarchists, and have music shows and other events. These cultural spaces provide a place for people to learn about the anarchist movement and to live in a prefigurative way according to its values.

Micropolitics

People involved in social justice work in the present are working in the shadow of the social justice movements of the 1960s. In those days, there was a sense in the air that the complete transformation of society was just around the corner, and that everyone was talking about how to make society better. The culture of social movements and the ideas people have about how social change happens and how people should be organized remain very much influenced by that period.

The idea of a movement is something that looms large in the imagination of people doing social justice work. Many people have grown up with pictures of civil rights marches and the demonstrations against the Vietnam War. The image of thousands of people in the streets confronting the powers that be is an inspiration to many. Anyone who's been to a large demonstration has probably experienced the powerful feeling of being part of a group of people who share a set of ideas being together in a public place. It gives the sense of a new world being formed.

But if we hold up that sort of experience as *the* experience of a social change movement, then we miss the value of what most of us are doing most of the time. Social justice work is often more dominated by a micropolitics of subtle transformation than it is by a macropolitics of large-scale confrontation.

Part of the analysis growing out of the social justice movements of the 1960s was that the personal is political, that the texture of our everyday lives matters. That led to a large part of the movement being interested in challenging the oppressive dynamics in interpersonal relationships and in the structures we inhabit every day.

While the social justice movements of the 1960s lay the groundwork for thinking in terms of micropolitical relationships, when people look back at that time, they often focus on the large-scale confrontational politics that took place. It has taken many years for micropolitics to begin to be conceptualized as an important part of social justice work.

According to a micropolitical perspective, we are doing important social justice work when we stop someone at a party from telling a racist joke, when we build ways for people to express themselves in classrooms, when we find ways to get institutions to serve the interests of members of groups that have been excluded. These sorts of actions can change social institutions when many people are doing them at the same time. They operate as a subtle and persistent internal pressure.

In some ways, this action is the slow digesting into the social systems of the critiques raised by the social justice movements of the 1960s. The fact that many people engage in them grows out of the education that many people continue to do—in schools and through books, alternative media, and occasionally the corporate media—about how society should be and how people should act.

By working to transform the structures of the institutions we are a part of, we make those institutions serve the needs of everyone, and we stop oppressive dynamics from being reproduced by institutionalized racism, classism, and sexism. If we look around us, we can see enormous changes that have taken place in many institutions. Many churches have female and gay ministers and welcome gay and lesbian families into their communities. Many colleges and universities have transformed some of their curriculum to make it relevant to students' lives and to respect the knowledge that students bring to the classroom. Women are increasingly able to compete on an equal footing with men in the workplace, and family medical leave allows fathers to take time off to be with their children.

On a wider cultural level, racism is widely assumed to be wrong, even if it is practiced on a daily basis and structured deeply into the fabric of society. Many people also consider sexism to be wrong, and a charge that some behavior is sexist carries some weight in some circumstances.

The kinds of changes that grow out of micropolitical transformation are easy to underestimate. In his book *Doing Democracy: The MAP Model for Organizing Social Movements*, Bill Moyer argues that social movements generally go through a series of stages, from a small group of people attempting to bring an issue to public attention, through several stages in which protest is used to force the larger society to deal with the issue, to the point at which society has recognized the problem and it begins the slow process of transformation.[25]

Moyer claims that many social justice advocates see themselves as having failed when large-scale protest doesn't lead to immediate social transformation. He argues that the kinds of activities and organizations that are required to really transform society are not those of street protest. Instead, after the protests have done their job, there is a long period of slow transformation that happens through much smaller and less dramatic forms of action.

We don't have much of a language for that sort of micropolitical transformation, and because it lacks drama and a sense of being part of a movement, it is very hard to sustain. If we want to sustain work in this area, we need to get better at noticing and acknowledging the value of these types of changes. When we are able to celebrate our successes, we inspire ourselves and others to continue the work we are doing. When we look at these sorts of changes, we can see that for all of the good things that have happened, there is an incredible amount more to be done.

The work that has been done in the past thirty years to accomplish institutional transformation has been subtle and persistent. It has taken place through the filing of lawsuits by individuals and organizations. It has happened because individuals challenge institutions in their everyday practice. And it is accomplished when people discuss the issues with each other and change how they act toward the people they deal with personally.

There are many people who believe that simply being nice to people in their everyday lives changes society for the better. Sometimes New Age thinkers elevate this view to a sort of political program. A micropolitical analysis says that social change requires more than that. A kindness that stays within the boundaries of the social structures that continually reproduce themselves doesn't make much of a difference except to the people it touches. But when our small-scale challenges interrupt the reproduction of a system of oppression, then something more is happening.

If people in a workplace get the sense that they can't discriminate in hiring, then that workplace will change. And if that ethos spreads and is reinforced by lawsuits that punish employers who discriminate, then the change is reinforced on a larger scale. Institutions can be radically transformed by an accumulation of these sorts of pressures.

But that only works if there is a larger context in which these individual actions take place. Part of the danger of this approach to political change is that people can run out of steam challenging institutions, since they can feel isolated and get a sense that their small actions don't add up to much. There needs to be something larger going on that people can feel they are a part of. This work would probably be strengthened if we were to have more of a sense of its importance and if those interested in making change happen spent more time talking about how to do it.

Structure in organizations

Most political groups doing social justice work struggle between three positions of debate on organizational structure. Some advocate for freedom from structure, others are committed to very democratic processes, still others want clear forms of hierarchy and organization. Each of these positions has something to recommend it and some weaknesses, and most groups have members who at any given time wish the group were more toward one of these positions than the others.

The argument against structure comes from those wishing a group could function like a network of friends. In such an organization people do what they want, no one tells anyone else what to do, and if a job becomes unpleasant, it doesn't get done. Groups that work like this are often fun to be in and people feel like they are able to express themselves. The group becomes a refuge from a world of rules and obligations.

The downside, of course, is that sometimes little gets done. And even more seriously, oppressive patterns of interpersonal interaction can play themselves out. In a group in which people speak whenever they want, whites and males are likely to dominate. Charismatic personalities can hold sway, and cliques can easily develop. These groups often form patterns of behavior described by Jo Freeman in her influential article as "The Tyranny of Structurelessness."[26]

To avoid these problems, many organizations become deeply involved in discussing democracy and the mechanisms for promoting democratic practice. These groups tend to favor consensus process. They have rules for how the group is supposed to function and will often institute rules such as no one speaks twice before everyone has spoken once. Consensus differs from unanimity in certain ways, but in essence it empowers everyone with the ability to "block" the group from moving forward.

This can be a valuable approach for groups engaged in civil disobedience, a tactic that succeeds only when participants are highly committed, both to the action and to their fellow activists. Many civil disobedience actions are organized around a network of affinity groups: small groups of people who work intensely together to forge common agreements, and these affinity groups are often organized in networks of councils, which also operate on the basis of consensus. Sometimes, with this sort of organizing, decisions made by the councils must go back to the original affinity groups and everyone must agree for the decision to be valid.

This form is often effective for civil disobedience actions because it tends to foster the development of trust. If you are going into a dangerous situation, it is nice to know that all of your concerns have been heard and that you are going into a situation that you have completely agreed to. A lack of efficiency is the main downside of consensus. These groups tend to attract people willing to commit large amounts of time to the process.

Those interested in efficiency, for whom getting things done is the top priority, have often advocated for more traditional forms of organization. They believe in electing officers and making them accountable, in having a set process that is followed for making decisions, and in having clear guidelines for how people are to act. Many nonprofit organizations, which are an increasingly large part of social justice work, are organized this way, though many are relatively structureless, relying on the personal power of those who start them.

The downside to formal structure is that groups organized in this way can overlook the spontaneous creativity and enthusiasm of their members. Additionally, the process often isn't self-reflective enough to foster a culture of watching out for oppressive interactions around race and gender. Many social justice advocates oppose this form of organization because they see it as replicating the bureaucratic forms of the dominant society.

Coalition politics

One of the premises of this book has been that there are a variety of social problems that can all be challenged separately but that interact with one another in complex ways. This analysis fits with a politics based on forming single-issue groups that interact with one another in coalition.

The idea behind coalitions is that different organizations, each focused on a particular issue and rooted in a particular community, could come together for specific actions or campaigns. What is often exciting about coalition politics is that these specialized groups can focus on long-term work on the issues that they are the most passionate and knowledgeable about. They can increase their impact by coming together.

An early and influential article on coalition politics was written by Bernice Johnson Reagon, who had been deeply involved in the civil rights movement and was a founding member of the social justice singing group Sweet Honey in the Rock.

In "Coalition Politics: Turning the Century," first given as a speech in 1981, Reagon assesses the strengths and weaknesses of social justice politics based on creating spaces for people who completely share a worldview and identity, politics based on women separating themselves, or people of a given race or ethnicity separating themselves. She argues that these types of spaces can be very nurturing. She calls them the politics of home.

But, even a home like a women's-only space might not be so comfortable for women of color, because the sisterhood that is supposed to unify women is always influenced by the racism that divides women from each other. Thus, even a safe home is rarely that. And a politics of home can cut you off from transforming the whole society. Reagon argues for the need to develop political practices that take us beyond the places where we feel comfortable and into work with people who are different from ourselves. This is the basis of her critique of nationalism, which she sees as too focused on staying in a place where people are supposed to feel the same as everyone they work with. "At a certain stage nationalism is crucial to a people if you are going to ever impact as a group in your own interests. Nationalism at another point becomes reactionary because it is totally inadequate for surviving in the world with many peoples."[27] Reagon argues that the politics of home must be supplemented by a politics of coalition.

> Coalition work is not work done in your home. Coalition work has to be done in the streets. And it is some of the most dangerous work you can do. And you shouldn't look for comfort. Some people will come to a coalition and they rate the success of the coalition on whether or not they feel good when they get there. They're not looking for a coalition; they're looking for a home! They're looking for a bottle with some milk in it and a nipple, which does not happen in a coalition. You don't get a lot of food in a coalition. You don't get fed a lot in a coalition. In a coalition you have to give, and it is different from your home. You can't stay there all the time. You go to the coalition for a few hours and then you go back and take your bottle wherever it is, and then you go back and coalesce some more.[28]

For Reagon, then, coalition politics is necessarily uncomfortable, it challenges us to broaden our perspectives and to work with people with whom we don't completely agree on every issue, or who don't share our cultural ways or personal lifestyles.

Coalition politics has remained a key strategy for forging temporary and shifting alliances that allow us to respond to changing circumstances. Some theorists have argued for more stable organizational forms and broad-based movements to challenge the problems we confront. It may be that as oppositional politics pick up steam, such long-term and overarching organizations will emerge. But it is equally likely that we are entering a time when it will be important to get better at being able to shift alliances and build and rebuild coalitions.

Conclusion

One of the hardest choices for a person who sees that there is much in the world that needs changing is the choice not to do some things. It's impossible to change everything at once, and the choice to be involved with one thing implies the choice not to do many other things that you know are important.

When faced with the enormity of the social problems in the world, it is easy to become overwhelmed. The left has a long history of attracting people who dedicate their lives so passionately to social change that they exhaust themselves, becoming resentful and even reactionary. Some people find it hard to balance their political commitments with their personal needs for friendship, relationships, and taking care of practical things, such as getting a job that is sustaining, emotionally and financially.

Some movements foster a culture of martyrdom, in which anything that isn't part of making social change is considered trivial or selfish. Yet movements that sustain themselves over time find ways of being fun, of taking care of their members, and of encouraging people to do what they need to in order to be able to make a lifelong commitment to social change. Political activism can only be satisfying over the long term if we are able to integrate it into our lives.

Social change work can be one of the most personally rewarding parts of a person's life. It puts us in contact with amazingly inspiring people and gives us a sense of being a part of large historical processes that are powerful and transformative. Life becomes deeply meaningful, and our place in the scheme of things becomes more clear and satisfying.

One of the most memorable ideas that has been attributed to Gramsci is that we should have pessimism of the intellect and optimism of the will. By that, he meant that we should try to be clear in seeing the depth of the social problems around us. We should not let ourselves be fooled by dominant perspectives, which often tell us things are fine when they're not. But this negative intellectual perspective needs to be linked with a spirit that is always looking for the possibilities to make things better.

This optimism of the will is what keeps people working for social justice when the odds seem stacked against them. And it is only when people do this work of social transformation that social problems are solved. With hope for a better world and commitment to doing the necessary work, amazing things have happened. Dictators have been overthrown, segregation has been defeated in the United States, and apartheid has been abolished in South Africa. In the twentieth century, labor unions won the right to an eight-hour workday, women achieved increasing access to quality jobs, marriage equality is a reality for millions of gay men and lesbians, and discrimination against people with disabilities is illegal. The air we breathe and the water we drink have become healthier in many places, and maybe we will act in time to keep the climate to a livable temperature.

It is important not to lose sight of the fact that many of the things that make life good were gained by the hard work and dedication of the generations before us who committed their lives to social justice. We can be a part of that legacy and offer the same kind of gifts to those who come after us.

Notes

Chapter 1

1. Adam Smith, *Selections from the Wealth of Nations*, ed. George Stigler (Arlington Heights, IL: Harlan Davidson, 1957), 11.
2. Smith himself acknowledged the need for the government to work actively to help those the market does not serve—that is, those who do not have enough to exchange for what they need—but his ideas have been used by most modern economists and by many policymakers in the United States to undermine anticapitalist or liberal demands.
3. Robert C. Tucker, ed. *The Marx-Engels Reader* (New York: W.W. Norton, 1978), 160.
4. Howard Zinn, *Emma: A Play in Two Acts about Emma Goldman, American Anarchist* (Boston: South End Press, 2002), ix–xiii.
5. Emma Goldman, *Anarchism and Other Essays* (New York: Dover, 1969), 52.
6. Alix Kates Shulman, "Dances with Feminists," *Women's Review of Books* 9, no. 3 (1991). This article offers an interesting history of how the quote got turned into a shorter one for a T-shirt, even though Goldman herself never said it.
7. Goldman, *Anarchism*, 52.
8. Murray Bookchin, *Social Anarchism or Lifestyle Anarchism: An Unbridgeable Chasm* (San Francisco: AK Press, 1995).
9. The term "Western" refers to European societies and societies influenced by European ways. As more and more of the world falls under the influence of European ways, and as those societies, such as the United States, which have traditionally seen themselves as Western begin to focus more on their non-European roots, the term "Western"

begins to lose its meaning. For now, it is convenient shorthand for European influence.

10. Segun Gbadegesin, "Yoruba Philosophy: Individuality, Community, and the Moral Order," in *African Philosophy: An Anthology*, ed. Emmanuel Chulwudi Eze (Malden, MA: Blackwell, 1998), 133.

11. Ibid., 139.

12. Marx in Tucker, *Marx-Engels Reader*, 86. In much of the Western tradition, discussions of human nature focus on what distinguishes humans from animals, which has led to an overstatement of the difference. For a discussion of the similarities between people and animals, see Lesley J. Rogers, "They Are *Only* Animals," in *Reinventing Biology: Respect for Life and the Creation of Knowledge*, ed. Lynda Birke and Ruth Hubbard (Bloomington: Indiana University Press, 1995), 149–72.

13. Marx in Tucker, *Marx-Engels Reader*, 74.

14. Marvin Harris, *Our Kind* (New York: Harper, 1989), 383.

15. James Joll, *Antonio Gramsci* (New York: Penguin, 1978), 27–30.

16. Antonio Gramsci, *Selections from the Prison Notebooks*, trans. Quintin Hoare and Geoffrey Nowell-Smith (New York: International Publishers, 1971), 323.

17. Michel Foucault, *Power/Knowledge: Selected Interviews and Other Writings, 1972–1977* (New York: Pantheon, 1980), 58.

18. Theodor W. Adorno, *Negative Dialectics*, trans. E.B. Ashton (New York: Continuum, 1983).

19. Deborah K. King, "Multiple Jeopardy, Multiple Consciousness: The Context of a Black Feminist Ideology," *Signs* 14, no. 1 (Autumn 1988): 48–49.

20. Kimberlé Crenshaw, "Demarginalizing the Intersection of Race and Sex: A Black Feminist Critique of Antidiscrimination Doctrine, Feminist Theory and Antiracist Politics," *University of Chicago Legal Forum* (1989): 139–67.

21. Michael Omi and Howard Winant, *Racial Formation in the United States from the 1960s to the 1990s*, 2nd ed. (New York: Routledge, 1994), 55.

22. Carl N. Degler, *Neither Black nor White: Slavery and Race Relations in Brazil and the United States* (New York: MacMillan, 1971).

23. It is tempting but not quite accurate to say that sexism influenced racism. The problem is that this implies that the form of oppression

works like an independent social force, as if it were a thing with a life of its own. Of course sexism does not have a life apart from the historically specific ways it has come to be. Rather, powerful relations regarding gender become woven into the social fabric, along with power relations relating to race.

24. Helen Zia, *Asian American Dreams: The Emergence of an American People* (New York: Farrar, Straus and Giroux, 2000), 59.

Chapter 2

1. David Mulder, *The Alchemy of Revolution: Gerrard Winstanley's Occultism and Seventeenth Century English Communism* (New York: Peter Lang, 1990), 293.
2. Andrew Bradstock, *Faith in the Revolution: The Political Theologies of Müntzer and Winstanley* (London: Society for Promoting Christian Knowledge, 1990), 96.
3. Ibid., 106.
4. Christopher Hill, *The World Turned Upside Down: Radical Ideas during the English Revolution* (New York: Penguin Books, 1972), 132.
5. Ibid., 69.
6. Charles Mills, *The Racial Contract* (Ithaca, NY: Cornell University Press, 1997), 68.
7. John Locke, *Two Treatises on Government* (London: Everyman's Library, 1990), 119.
8. Ellen Meiksins Wood, *The Origin of Capitalism* (London: Verso, 2002), 106.
9. Locke, *Two Treatises*, 125.
10. Hill, *World Turned*, 15.
11. Janet L. Abu-Lughod, *Before European Hegemony: The World System A.D. 1250–1350* (London: Oxford University Press, 1989), 3–38.
12. Janet L. Abu-Lughod, "On the Remaking of History: How to Reinvent the Past," in *Remaking History*, ed. Barbara Kruger and Phil Mariani (Seattle: Bay Press, 1989), 114.
13. Abu-Lughod, *Before European Hegemony*, 361.
14. Marx in Tucker, *Marx-Engels Reader*, 435–36.
15. Robert Brenner, "The Origins of Capitalist Development: A Critique of Neo-Smithian Marxism," *New Left Review* 114 (1977): 78.

16. Robin Blackburn, *The Making of New World Slavery: From the Baroque to the Modern 1492–1800* (New York: Verso, 1997), 518.

17. One of the problems with the transition of Russia from state socialism to capitalism is that many people believed the capitalist ideology that says an economy works best when simply left alone. In this case, the legal system and infrastructure were not set up for a market economy and what resulted was an economic and political disaster.

18. Ngugi Wa Thiong'o, *Devil on the Cross* (Portsmouth, NH: Heinemann, 1980), 79.

19. Quoted in Howard Zinn, *A People's History of the United States* (New York: Harper Collins, 2003), 132.

20. David Harvey, *A Brief History of Neoliberalism* (Oxford: Oxford University Press, 2007), 156.

21. Ken Saro-Wiwa, *Genocide in Nigeria: The Ogoni Tragedy* (London: Saros International Publishers, 1992).

22. William I. Robinson, *Promoting Polyarchy: Globalization, US Intervention, and Hegemony* (Cambridge: Cambridge University Press, 1996).

23. Karl Polanyi, *The Great Transformation: The Political and Economic Origins of Our Time* (Boston: Beacon Press, 1944).

24. Zinn, *People's History*, 19–20.

25. Marx in Tucker, *Marx-Engels Reader*, 302–19.

26. Ibid., 210.

27. Marilyn Waring, *If Women Counted* (New York: Harper Collins, 1990). See also Margunn Bjørnholt and Ailsa McKay, eds., *Counting on Marilyn Waring: New Advances in Feminist Economics* (Ontario: Demeter Press, 2014).

28. Amartya Kumar Sen, *Choice, Welfare and Measurement* (Oxford: Blackwell, 1982).

29. Jonathan Teller-Elsberg, James Heintz, and Nancy Folbre, *Field Guide to the U.S. Economy: A Compact and Irreverent Guide to Economic Life in America* (New York: New Press, 2006), 166.

30. Ibid.

Chapter 3

1. Pooja Bhatia, "The Long Term Impact of Student-Loan Debt, *USA Today*, March 3, 2014, http://www.usatoday.com/story/money/personalfinance/2014/03/03/ozy-student-debt/5976111/.
2. National Coalition for the Homeless, *Factsheet on Employment and Homelessness*, 2009, http://nationalhomeless.org/references/publications/.
3. Stephen A. Resnick and Richard D. Wolff, *Knowledge and Class: A Marxian Critique of Political Economy* (Chicago: University of Chicago Press, 1987).
4. Harry Braverman, *Labor and Monopoly Capital* (New York: Monthly Review Press, 1974), 54.
5. Richard Edwards, Michael Reich, and Thomas E. Weisskopf, *The Capitalist System: A Radical Analysis of American Society* (Englewood Cliffs, NJ: Prentice Hall, 1986), 168.
6. William Robinson, *A Theory of Global Capitalism: Production, Class, and State in a Transnational World* (Baltimore: Johns Hopkins University Press, 2004), 119–20.
7. Andrew Prokop, "40 Charts That Explain Money in Politics," July 30, 2014, http://www.vox.com/2014/7/30/5949581/money-in-politics-charts-explain.
8. Jonathan Teller-Elsberg, James Heintz, and Nancy Folbre, *Field Guide to the U.S. Economy: A Compact and Irreverent Guide to Economic Life in America* (New York: The New Press, 2006), 11.
9. Zinn, *People's History*, 99.
10. Jan R. Carew, *Fulcrums of Change* (Trenton, NJ: Africa World Press, 1988), 23.
11. James W. Loewen, *Lies My Teacher Told Me: Everything Your American History Textbook Got Wrong* (New York: Simon and Schuster, 1996), 76.
12. Ibid.
13. Rosalinda Méndez González, "Distinctions in Western Women's Experience: Ethnicity, Class and Social Change," in *Feminist Frontiers* IV, ed. Laurel Richardson, Verta A. Taylor, and Nancy Whittier (New York: McGraw-Hill, 1997), 13.
14. Winona LaDuke, *All Our Relations: Native Struggles for Land and Life* (Cambridge, MA: South End Press, 1999).

15. Tomás Almaguer, *Racial Fault Lines: The Historical Origins of White Supremacy in California* (Berkeley: University of California Press, 1971), 33.

16. Ibid., 14.

17. Zinn, *People's History*, 403.

18. Scott Molloy, "Debs, Eugene V.," in *Encyclopedia of the American Left*, ed. Paul Buhle, Mari Jo Buhle, and Dan Georgakas (Chicago: University of Illinois Press, 1992), 186.

19. Cornel West, "Marxist Theory and the Specificity of Afro-American Oppression," in *Marxism and the Interpretation of Culture*, ed. Cary Nelson and Lawrence Grossberg (Urbana: University of Illinois Press, 1988), 19.

20. David R. Roediger, *The Wages of Whiteness: Race and the Making of the American Working Class* (London: Verso, 1991), 127–28.

21. Jeanne Boydston, "To Earn Her Daily Bread: Housework and Antebellum Working Class Subsistence," in *Unequal Sisters*, ed. Vicki L. Ruiz and Ellen Carol DuBois (New York: Routledge, 1994), 46.

22. Ibid., 54.

23. Ira Katznelson, *When Affirmative Action Was White: An Untold History of Racial Inequality in Twentieth-Century America* (New York: W.W. Norton, 2006).

24. Barbara Ehrenreich and Arlie Russell Hochschild, *Global Woman: Nannies, Maids, and Sex Workers in the New Economy* (New York: Owl Press, 2004). "Global North" and "Global South" refer to what in the past were more commonly called the First World and the Third World. Those terms are losing favor, especially among social justice activists in the Global South. Global North refers to the countries of the world where there are generally high levels of wealth, most of which are in the Northern Hemisphere.

25. Zinn, *People's History*, 328.

26. Ibid.

27. Ibid., 329.

28. Ibid..

29. Ibid., 329–30.

30. Ibid., 327.

31. Ibid., 339.

32. Ibid., 365.

33. James R. Green and Eric Foner, *The World of the Worker: Labor in Twentieth-Century America* (New York: Hill and Wang, 1980), 92.

34. Zinn, *People's History*, 399.

35. Green, *World of the Worker*, 150.

36. Zinn, *People's History*, 404.

37. Green, *World of the Worker*, 198.

38. Ai-jen Poo, *The Age of Dignity: Preparing for the Elder Boom in a Changing America* (New York: New Press, 2015), 114.

Chapter 4

1. Stephanie Guilloud, ed., *Voices from the WTO: An Anthology of Writings from the People Who Shut Down the World Trade Organization* (Olympia, WA: Evergreen State College, 2000), 6.

2. William Greider, "Sovereign Corporations," *The Nation*, April 30, 2001, 5.

3. David Bacon, *Illegal People: How Globalization Created Migration and Criminalizes Immigrants* (Boston: Beacon Press, 2008).

4. Jeremy Brecher and Tim Costello, *Global Village or Global Pillage: Economic Reconstruction from the Bottom Up* (Cambridge, MA: South End Press, 1998), 46.

5. Alejandro Portes, "Neoliberalism and Sociology of Development: Emerging Trends and Unanticipated Facts," in *From Modernization to Globalization*, ed. Timmons Roberts and Amy Hite (Malden, MA: Blackwell, 2000), 356.

6. Brecher and Costello, *Global Village*, 51.

7. Manual Castells, *The Rise of the Network Society* (Malden, MA: Blackwell, 2000), 137.

8. Ibid.

9. David Harvey, *The Condition of Postmodernity: An Enquiry into the Origins of Cultural Change* (Malden, MA: Blackwell, 1990).

10. Naomi Klein, "Reclaiming the Commons," *New Left Review* 9 (May–June 2001): 203–4.

11. James Mittelman, *Out from Underdevelopment: Prospects for the Third World* (New York: St. Martin's Press, 1988), 59.

12. Saskia Sassen, *The Global City: New York, London, Tokyo* (Princeton: Princeton University Press, 2001).

13. Elisabeth Cline, *Overdressed: The Shockingly High Price of Cheap Fashion* (New York: Penguin, 2013), 5.

14. Ibid.

15. For a look at the causes of life span increases in the twentieth century overall, see Jim Oeppen and James W. Vaupel, "Broken Limits to Life Expectancy," *Science* 296, no 5570 (May 2002): 1029–31.

16. Helena Norberg-Hodge, *Ancient Futures: Learning from Ladakh* (San Francisco: Sierra Club Books, 1991), 143–44.

17. Richard Layard, *Happiness: Lessons from a New Science* (New York: Penguin, 2005).

18. Norberg-Hodge, *Ancient Futures*, 149.

19. Wolfgang Sachs, *The Development Dictionary: A Guide to Knowledge as Power* (London: Zed Books, 1992), 3–4.

20. Naomi Klein, *This Changes Everything: Capitalism vs. the Climate* (New York: Simon and Schuster, 2015).

21. Walden Bello, Shea Cunningham, and Bill Rau, *Dark Victory: The United States and Global Poverty* (Oakland, CA: Pluto Press, 1999), 68.

22. Raymond W. Baker, *Capitalism's Achilles Heel: Dirty Money and How to Renew the Free-Market System* (New York: Wiley, 2005), 352.

23. The words "socialism" and "communism" are used in almost opposite ways in different contexts. For Marx, communism meant an ideal society with no government. Socialism included some authoritarian elements. For complex historical reasons, this is completely out of sync with the words people now use to identify their own political views. Communists tend to be those more inclined to accept some level of authoritarianism from the state and socialists tend to be more interested in democracy and personal liberties.

24. Paulo Freire, *Pedagogy of the Oppressed*, trans. Myra Bergman Ramos (New York: Continuum, 1982), 78.

25. Jon Lee Anderson, *Che Guevara: A Revolutionary Life* (New York: Grove Press, 1997).

26. Walden Bello and Stephanie Rosenfeld, *Dragons in Distress: Asia's Miracle Economies in Crisis* (San Francisco: Food First, 1990).

27. Robert Pollin, *Contours of Descent: U.S. Economic Fractures and the Landscape of Global Austerity* (New York: Verso, 2003), 128.

28. David Harvey, *A Brief History of Neoliberalism* (Oxford: Oxford University Press, 2007), 2.

29. Philip McMichael, "Globalization: Myths and Realities," in *From Modernization to Globalization*, ed. Timmons Roberts and Amy Hite (Malden, MA: Blackwell, 2000), 283.

30. Loïc Wacquant, *Punishing the Poor: The Neoliberal Government of Social Insecurity* (Durham: Duke University Press, 2009), 7.

31. Bello, Cunningham, and Rau, *Dark Victory*, 33–34.

32. Ibid., 52.

33. McMichael, "Globalization," 284.

34. Naomi Klein, *The Shock Doctrine: The Rise of Disaster Capitalism* (New York: Metropolitan Books, 2007), 195–216.

35. J.K. Gibson-Graham, *The End of Capitalism (as We Knew It): A Feminist Critique of Political Economy* (Malden, MA: Blackwell, 1996).

36. Grace Lee Boggs, *Living for a Change: An Autobiography* (Minneapolis: University of Minnesota Press, 1998), 180–81.

37. Ibid., 181–82.

38. The ILO Reader, "Social and Solidarity Economy: Our Common Road towards Decent Work."

39. Gar Alperovitz, *America Beyond Capitalism: Reclaiming Our Wealth, Our Liberty and Our Democracy* (Hoboken, NJ: Wiley, 2005), 88–89.

40. Juliet Schor, *The Overworked American: The Unexpected Decline of Leisure* (New York: Basic Books, 1993).

41. The most popular at this point seems to be the Genuine Progress Indicator. See also Quality of Life Indicator, Happy Planet Index, and Human Development Index. For an in-depth analysis of the strengths and weaknesses of these indexes and ideas for improvement, see Thomas M. Parris and Robert W. Kates, "Characterizing and Measuring Sustainable Development," *Annual Review of Environment and Resources* 28 (2003): 559–86.

42. Anders Hayden and John M. Shandra. "Hours of Work and the Ecological Footprint of Nations: An Exploratory Analysis," *Local Environment: The International Journal of Justice and Sustainability* 14, no. 6 (2009): 575–600.

43. Richards Layard. *Happiness: Lessons from a New Science* (New York: Penguin, 2005); Carol Graham, *Happiness Around the World: The*

Paradox of Happy Peasants and Miserable Millionaires (Oxford: Oxford University Press, 2009).

44. Gar Alperovitz. *What Then Must We Do? Straight Talk about the Next American Revolution* (White River Junction, VT: Chelsea Green), 146.

45. Adam Przeworski, *Capitalism and Social Democracy* (Cambridge: Cambridge University Press, 1993), 217. Productivity is defined as the measure how much value is created per hour of work.

Chapter 5

1. Michelle Alexander, *The New Jim Crow: Mass Incarceration in the Age of Colorblindness* (New York: The New Press, 2012).

2. Mab Segrest, *Memoir of a Race Traitor* (Boston: South End Press, 1994), 180.

3. Ibid., 4.

4. Michael Omi and Howard Winant, *Racial Formation in the United States from the 1960s to the 1990s*, 3rd ed. (New York: Routledge, 2015), 110.

5. Omi and Winant, *Racial Formation*, 2nd ed. (1994), 63–64.

6. Scott Malcomson, *One Drop of Blood: The American Misadventure of Race* (New York: Farrar, Straus and Giroux, 2000), 173.

7. Matthew Frye Jacobson, *Whiteness of a Different Color: European Immigrants and the Alchemy of Race* (Cambridge, MA: Harvard University Press, 1998), 46.

8. Omi and Winant, *Racial Formation* (2015), 141.

9. Omi and Winant, *Racial Formation* (1994), 89.

10. Jacobson, *Whiteness*, 75.

11. Ronald T. Takaki, *Strangers from a Different Shore: A History of Asian Americans* (New York: Penguin Books, 1989), 369–70.

12. Jacobson, *Whiteness*, 75.

13. Cynthia Kaufman, "A Users Guide to White Privilege," *Radical Philosophy Review* 4, no. 1–2 (2001).

14. Harvard Sitkoff, *A New Deal for Blacks: The Emergence of Civil Rights as a National Issue: The Depression Decade* (New York: Oxford University Press, 1978), 50.

15. Teller-Elsberg et al., *Field Guide to the U.S. Economy: A Compact and Irreverent Guide to Economic Life in America* (New York: The New Press, 2006), 6.

16. Debbie Gruenstein Bocian, Keith S. Ernst, and Wei Li, "Unfair Lending: The Effect of Race and Ethnicity on the Price of Subprime Mortgages," Center for Responsible Lending, 2006, http://www.responsiblelending.org/mortgage-lending/research-analysis/rr011-Unfair_Lending-0506.pdf.

17. James Loewen, *Lies My Teacher Told Me: Everything Your American History Textbook Got Wrong* (New York: Simon and Schuster, 1996).

18. Frantz Fanon, *Black Skin, White Masks* (New York: Grove Press, 1967), 129.

19. Joel Kovel, *White Racism: A Psychohistory* (New York: Columbia University Press, 1984), 18–19.

20. Roediger, *The Wages of Whiteness*, 321.

21. Gloria Yamato, "Something about the Subject Matter Makes It Hard to Name," in *Feminist Frontiers* IV, ed. Laurel Richardson, Verta A. Taylor, and Nancy Whittier (New York: McGraw-Hill, 1997), 28–29.

22. Ibid., 29.

23. Ibid.

24. Ibid., 30.

25. Omi and Winant, *Racial Formation* (2015), 196.

26. Ibid., 194

27. Alexander, *New Jim Crow*.

28. The Sentencing Project, Felony Disenfranchisement, 2015, http://www.sentencingproject.org/template/page.cfm?id=133.

29. This is a bit tricky, because antiracism is a contemporary concept. In prior periods, there were movements to abolish slavery, struggles of Native Americans to protect their land, and attempts by Chinese immigrants to repeal anti-Chinese legislation. At the time none of these were seen as antiracist.

30. Herbert Aptheker, *Nat Turner's Slave Rebellion* (New York: Humanities Press, 1966).

31. Zinn, *People's History*, 185.

32. W.E.B. Du Bois, *Black Reconstruction in America: An Essay toward History of the Part which Black Folk Played in the Attempt to Reconstruct Democracy in America 1860–1880* (Cleveland: World Pub. Co., 1964), 716.

33. Ibid.

34. Ibid., 82.

35.   Ibid., 83.

36.   Ronald T. Takaki, *A Different Mirror: A History of Multicultural America* (Boston: Little, Brown and Co., 1993), 48.

37.   Ibid., 414.

Chapter 6

1.   Neil Miller, *Out of the Past: Gay and Lesbian History from 1869 to the Present* (New York: Vintage Books, 1995), 336.

2.   What to call this movement or cluster of movements has been a very political question. It was called homophile, then gay, and then people began to feel that "gay" referred to men, and thus argued for a gay and lesbian movement. As bisexual and transgender people fought to be marked as distinct parts of the movement, one tradition began what would give an initial to each of the parts of the movement. Many people I know refer to this set of identities as LGBTQQIA: lesbian, gay, bisexual, transgender, queer or questioning, intersex, and asexual. In the 1980s, the word "queer" was taken as term to refer to anyone who doesn't fit into the dominant heteronormative framework. As I write this, these terms are very contested. I prefer the word "queer," as it highlights the radical political nature of the movement, for other ways of being, and it does not put people into specific boxes. It also calls out that this is a movement that is reclaiming and resisting stigmatization.

3.   Ibid., 369.

4.   Judith P. Butler, *Gender Trouble: Feminism and the Subversion of Identity* (New York: Routledge, 1990).

5.   Margaret Mead, "Sex and Temperament in Primitive Societies (1935)," in *Feminist Theory: A Reader*, ed. Wendy Kolmar and Frances Bartowski (Mountain View, CA: Mayfield, 2000), 130.

6.   Anne Fausto-Sterling, *Myths of Gender: Biological Theories about Women and Men* (New York: Basic Books, 1985), 37.

7.   Ibid., 8.

8.   Ibid., 130.

9.   Bruce Bagemihl, *Biological Exuberance: Animal Homosexuality and Natural Diversity* (New York: St. Martin's Press, 1999).

10.   Will Roscoe, *Changing Ones: Third and Fourth Genders in Native North America* (New York: St. Martin's Press, 2000), 4.

11. Sherry B. Ortner, *Making Gender: The Politics and Erotics of Culture* (Boston: Beacon Press, 1996), 149.

12. Michelle Zimbalist Rosaldo and Louise Lamphere, *Woman, Culture, and Society* (Stanford: Stanford University Press, 1974), 17–42.

13. Ortner, *Making Gender*, 176.

14. Barbara Smuts, "The Evolutionary Origins of Patriarchy," *Human Nature* 6, no. 1 (1995): 1–32.

15. Ortner, *Making Gender*, 177.

16. Stephanie Coontz, *The Way We Never Were: American Families and the Nostalgia Trap* (New York: Basic Books, 1992).

17. Zia, *Asian American Dreams*, 119.

18. Joan M. Jensen, "Native American Women and Agriculture: A Seneca Case Study," in *Unequal Sisters: A Multicultural Reader in U.S. Women's History*, ed. Vicki L. Ruiz and Ellen Carol DuBois (New York: Routledge, 1994), 80.

19. Ibid.

20. Sojourner Truth, "Ain't I a Woman," in *Feminist Frontiers*, 20.

21. Gloria Steinem, *Outrageous Acts and Everyday Rebellions* (New York: Henry Holt and Company, 1995), 141.

22. Alice Echols, *Daring to Be Bad: Radical Feminism in America, 1967–1975* (Minneapolis: University of Minnesota Press, 1990), 84.

23. See, for example, Evelyn Fox Keller, *Reflections on Gender and Science* (New Haven: Yale University Press, 1985) and Sandra Harding, *The Science Question in Feminism* (Ithaca: Cornell University Press, 1986).

24. Heidi Hartmann, "The Unhappy Marriage of Marxism and Feminism: Toward a More Progressive Union," in *Feminist Theory*.

25. Artie Russell Hochschild and Anne Machung, *The Second Shift* (New York: Avon Books, 1997).

26. Ann Ferguson, *Blood at the Root: Motherhood, Sexuality and Male Dominance* (London: Pandora, 1989), 77–99.

27. Betsy Hartmann, *Reproductive Rights and Wrongs: The Global Politics of Population Control* (Boston: South End Press, 1995).

28. Penelope Leach, *Children First: What Society Must Do—and Is Not Doing—for Children Today* (New York: Vintage, 1994), 19.

29. Ibid.

30. Aida Hurtado, *The Color of Privilege: Three Blasphemies on Race and Feminism* (Ann Arbor: University of Michigan Press, 1996), 18.

31. Angela Yvonne Davis, *Women, Race & Class* (New York: Vintage Books, 1983), 172–201.

32. Bell hooks, *Feminist Theory from Margin to Center* (Boston: South End Press, 1984), 14.

33. Ibid., 25.

34. Anne Koedt, "The Myth of the Vaginal Orgasm," in *Dear Sisters: Dispatches from the Women's Liberation Movement*, ed. Rosalyn Baxandall and Linda Gordon (New York: Basic Books, 2000), 158.

35. Adrienne Rich, "Compulsory Heterosexuality and Lesbian Existence," in *Feminist Frontiers.*

36. This phrase is attributed to Ti-Grace Atkinson.

37. US Census Bureau (2001), 452.

38. Michael Kimmel, *Angry White Men: American Masculinity at the End of an Era* (New York: Nation Books, 2015), 15.

Chapter 7

1. George Monbiot, *Heat: How to Stop the Planet from Burning* (New York: Penguin, 2006).

2. Bill McKibben, "Global Warming's Terrifying New Math: Three Simple Numbers That Add Up to Global Catastrophe and That Make Clear Who the Real Enemy Is," *Rolling Stone*, July 19, 2012.

3. Klein, *This Changes Everything*, 7.

4. Arne Naess and George Sessions, "A Deep Ecology Eight Point Platform," http://www.haven.net/deep/council/eight.htm.

5. Susan Griffin, *Woman and Nature: The Roaring inside Her* (New York: Harper and Row, 1978).

6. Val Plumwood, "Nature, Self, and Gender: Feminism, Environmental Philosophy, and the Critique of Rationalism," *Hypatia* 6, no. 1 (1991): 3–27.

7. Ibid., 13.

8. Vandana Shiva, "Colonialism and the Evolution of Masculinist Forestry," in *The "Racial" Economy of Science: Toward a Democratic Future*, ed. Sandra Harding (Bloomington: Indiana University Press, 1993) 303–14.

9. Ibid., 305.

10. Robert Bullard, "Environmental Justice for All," in *Unequal Protection: Environmental Justice and Communities of Color*, ed. Robert Bullard (San Francisco: Sierra Club Books, 1994), 5.

11. Ken Geiser and Gerry Waneck, "PCBs and Warren County," in *Unequal Protection*.

12. Mark Dowie, *Losing Ground: American Environmentalism at the Close of the Twentieth Century* (Cambridge, MA: MIT Press, 1995), 145–46.

13. E.K. Hunt and Howard J. Sherman, *Economics: An Introduction to Radical and Traditional Views* (New York: Harper and Row, 1990), 595.

14. Tom Athanasiou, *Divided Planet: The Ecology of Rich and Poor* (Boston: Little and Brown, Co., 1996), 196.

15. Klein, *This Changes Everything*, 7.

16. Alan Thein Durning, *How Much Is Enough? The Consumer Society and the Future of the Earth* (New York: Norton, 1992), 51.

17. U.S. Energy Information Administration, International Energy Statistics, Total Primary Energy Consumption, http://www.eia.gov/cfapps/ipdbproject/IEDIndex3.cfm?tid=44&pid=44&aid=2.

18. Jane Holtz Kay, *Asphalt Nation: How the Automobile Took Over America and How We Can Take It Back* (New York: Crown Publishers, 1997), 213.

19. Ibid., 214.

20. Ibid., 231.

21. Carlos Davidson, "Economic Growth and the Environment: Alternatives to the Limits Paradigm," *Bioscience* 50, no 5 (2000): 439.

22. Kay, *Asphalt Nation*, 320.

23. Hartmann, *Reproductive Rights*, 312.

24. Ibid.

25. Durning, *How Much Is Enough?*, 25.

26. Gilberto Gallopín et al., *Branch Points: Global Scenarios and Human Choice* (Stockholm: Stockholm Environment Institute, 1997), 13.

27. Ibid., 38.

28. Earthworks Group, *50 Simple Things You Can Do to Save the Earth* (Berkeley: Earthworks Press, 1989), 6.

29. John Robbins, *Diet for a New America* (Tiburon, CA: HJ Kramer, 1998).

30. Dowie, *Losing Ground*, 28.
31. Anders Hayden, *Sharing the Work, Sparing the Planet: Work Time, Consumption, and Ecology* (New York: Zed Books, 1999).

Chapter 8

1. Bruce Johansen, *Forgotten Founders: How the American Indian Helped Shape Democracy* (Cambridge, MA: Harvard Common Press, 1987).
2. John Keane, *The Life and Death of Democracy* (New York: W.W. Norton, 2009), xxvii.
3. Ibid., 691.
4. Peter Kropotkin, *Mutual Aid: A Factor of Cooperation* (New York: A.A. Knopf, 1919).
5. Adam Hochschild, *King Leopold's Ghost: A Story of Greed, Terror, and Heroism in Colonial Africa* (Boston: Houghton Mifflin, 1998), 46.
6. Ibid., 165.
7. Ibid., 166.
8. Jurgen Osterhammel, *Colonialism* (Princeton: Marcus Wiener Publishers, 1997).
9. Hochschild, *King Leopold's Ghost.*
10. Aimé Césaire, "Discourse on Colonialism," in *African Philosophy: An Anthology*, ed. Emmanuel Chukwudi Eze (Malden, MA: Blackwell, 1998), 222.
11. Personal communication.
12. Farewell address, January 17, 1961. Quoted in Ismael Hossein-Zadeh, *The Political Economy of U.S. Militarism* (New York: Palgrave, 2006).
13. Ibid., 13.
14. Ibid.
15. Ibid.
16. Hossein-Zadeh, *Political Economy*, 102.
17. David Cook, *Understanding Jihad* (Berkeley: University of California Press, 2005), 128.
18. Peter Mandaville, *Global Political Islam* (New York: Routledge, 2007), 261.
19. Ibid., 262.
20. Lenin in Robert C. Tucker, *The Lenin Anthology* (New York: Norton, 1975), 311.

21. Martin Carnoy, *The State and Political Theory* (Princeton: Princeton University Press, 1984), 61.

22. Ibid., 90.

23. Ibid., 94.

24. Ibid., 96.

25. Louis Althusser, *Lenin and Philosophy and Other Essays*, trans. Ben Brewster (New York: Monthly Review Press, 1971), 147.

26. Carnoy, *State and Political Theory*, 37.

27. Theda Skocpol, "Political Responses to Capitalist Crisis: Neo-Marxist Theories of the State and the Case of the New Deal," *Politics and Society* 10, no. 2 (1980): 157.

28. Samuel Bowles and Herbert Gintis, "The Crisis of Liberal Democratic Capitalism: The Case of the United States," *Politics and Society* 11, no. 1 (1982): 58.

29. Ibid., 65.

30. Ibid.

31. Ibid., 68.

32. Ibid., 69.

33. Christian Parenti, *Lockdown America: Police and Prisons in the Age of Crisis* (New York: Verso, 2000), 40–41.

34. Ibid., 44.

35. Antonio Gramsci, *Selections from the Prison Notebooks*, trans. Quintin Hoare and Geoffrey Nowell-Smith (New York: International Publishers, 1971), 229–35.

36. Frances FitzGerald, *America Revised: History Schoolbooks in the Twentieth Century* (New York: Vintage Books, 1980).

Chapter 9

1. John Stauber and Sheldon Rampton, *Toxic Sludge Is Good for You: Lies, Damn Lies and the Public Relations Industry* (Monroe, ME: Common Courage, 1995).

2. Edward S. Herman and Noam Chomsky, *Manufacturing Consent: The Political Economy of the Mass Media* (New York: Pantheon Press, 1988), 302.

3. Ibid., 2.

4. Ibid.

5.   Ibid., 31.

6.   James Curran, "Rethinking Mass Communications," in *Cultural Studies and Communications*, ed. James Curran, David Morley, and Valerie Walkerdine (New York: Arnold Press, 1996), 137.

7.   Ibid., 152.

8.   Ann E. Kaplan, "Is the Gaze Male?" in *Powers of Desire: The Politics of Sexuality*, ed. Ann Snitow, Christine Stansell, and Sharon Thompson (New York: Monthly Review Press, 1983).

9.   Antonio Gramsci, *Selections from the Prison Notebooks*, trans. Quintin Hoare and Geoffrey Nowell-Smith (New York: International Publishers, 1971), 152.

10. Ibid., 326.

11. Stuart Hall, "The Problem of Ideology: Marxism Without Guarantees," in *Stuart Hall: Critical Dialogues in Cultural Studies*, ed. David Morley and Kuan-Hsing Chen (New York: Routledge, 1996), 30.

12. Ibid.

13. Colin Sparks, "Stuart Hall, Cultural Studies and Marxism," in *Stuart Hall: Critical Dialogues*, 443.

14. Juliet Schor, *The Overworked American: The Unexpected Decline of Leisure* (New York: Basic Books, 1992), 117.

15. Marx in Tucker, *Marx-Engels Reader*, 93.

16. Nestor García Canclini, *Consumers and Citizens: Globalization and Multicultural Conflicts* (Minneapolis: University of Minnesota Press, 2001), 24.

17. Ibid.

Chapter 10

1.   Lenin in Robert C. Tucker, *The Lenin Anthology* (New York: Norton, 1975), 101–2.

2.   Max Elbaum, *Revolution in the Air: Sixties Radicals Turn to Lenin, Mao and Che* (New York: Verso, 2002), 333.

3.   Martin Carnoy, *The State and Political Theory* (Princeton: Princeton University Press, 1984), 64.

4.   Rosa Luxemburg, *Selected Political Writings*, ed. Robert Looker, trans. William F. Graf (New York: Grove Press, 1974), 98.

5.   Elbaum, *Revolution in the Air*, 238.

6. Wini Breines, *Community and Organization in the New Left: 1962–1968: The Great Refusal* (New York: Praeger, 1982), 6.

7. Many people refer to these movements as "new social movements." I don't use this term because, while there was a flourishing of attention to many of these issues on the period of 1950–1980, there have been movements around these issues for a long time.

8. Phillip S. Foner, *Helen Keller: Her Socialist Years* (New York: International Publishers, 1967), 14.

9. Joseph P. Shapiro, *No Pity: People with Disabilities Forging a New Civil Rights Movement* (New York: Random House, 1993), 41.

10. Ibid., 47–48.

11. Carolyn Gard, "How the Media Portray Mental Illness," *Current Health* 28, no. 1 (2001): 24.

12. Ann Bookman and Sandra Morgan, *Women and the Politics of Empowerment, Women in Political Economy* (Philadelphia: Temple University Press, 1988), 4.

13. Freire, *Pedagogy of the Oppressed*, 74.

14. Ibid., 129.

15. Frederick Douglass, "The Significance of Emancipation in the West Indies," Speech in Canandaigua, New York, on August 3, 1857; Collected in *The Frederick Douglass Papers. Series One: Speeches, Debates, and Interviews* (Volume 3: 1855–63), ed. John W. Blassingame (New Haven: Yale University Press, 1985), 2.

16. Martin Luther King Jr., *Where Do We Go from Here: Chaos or Community?* (Boston: Beacon Press, 1968), 37.

17. Ibid., 59.

18. Ibid.

19. Saul Alinsky, *Rules for Radicals: A Pragmatic Primer for Realistic Radicals* (New York: Random House, 1971), 127.

20. Michael Albert, "Why Protest the Conventions," http://www.thirdworldtraveler.com/Political_Reform/Protest_Conventions.html.

21. Frances Fox Piven and Richard Cloward, *Poor People's Movements: Why They Succeed, How They Fail* (New York: Vintage Books, 1978).

22. Miles Horton and Paulo Freire, *We Make the Road by Walking: Conversations on Education and Social Change* (Philadelphia: Temple University, 1990), 12.

23. Horton in Aldon Morris. *The Origins of the Civil Rights Movements: Black Communities Organizing for Change.* (Free Press, 1986), 142

24. Ibid., 155.

25. Center for Third World Organizing, http://ctwo.org.

26. Jo Freeman, "The Tyranny of Structurelessness," *The Second Wave* 2, no 1 (1972): 20.

27. Naomi Klein, "Reclaiming the Commons," *New Left Review* 9 (May–June 2001): 6.

28. Bernice Johnson Reagon, "Coalition Politics: Turning the Century," in *Race, Class and Gender: An Anthology,* ed. Margaret L. Andersen and Patricia Hill Collins (New York: Wadsworth, 1995), 542.

Index

"Passim" (literally "scattered") indicates intermittent discussion of a topic over a cluster of pages.

About the Author

Cynthia Kaufman is the director of the Vasconcellos Institute for Democracy in Action at De Anza College, where she also teaches community organizing and philosophy. She is also the author of *Getting Past Capitalism: History, Vision, Hope* (Lexington Books, 2012). She is a lifelong social change activist, having worked on issues such as tenants' rights, police abuse, union organizing, international politics, and most recently climate change.

FRIENDS OF PM

These are indisputably momentous times—the financial system is melting down globally and the Empire is stumbling. Now more than ever there is a vital need for radical ideas.

In the many years since its founding—and on a mere shoestring—PM Press has risen to the formidable challenge of publishing and distributing knowledge and entertainment for the struggles ahead. With hundreds of releases to date, we have published an impressive and stimulating array of literature, art, music, politics, and culture. Using every available medium, we've succeeded in connecting those hungry for ideas and information to those putting them into practice.

Friends of PM allows you to directly help impact, amplify, and revitalize the discourse and actions of radical writers, filmmakers, and artists. It provides us with a stable foundation from which we can build upon our early successes and provides a much-needed subsidy for the materials that can't necessarily pay their own way. You can help make that happen—and receive every new title automatically delivered to your door once a month—by joining as a Friend of PM Press. And, we'll throw in a free T-shirt when you sign up.

Here are your options:
- $30 a month: Get all books and pamphlets plus 50% discount on all webstore purchases
- $40 a month: Get all PM Press releases (including CDs and DVDs) plus 50% discount on all webstore purchases
- $100 a month: Superstar—Everything plus PM merchandise, free downloads, and 50% discount on all webstore purchases

For those who can't afford $30 or more a month, we're introducing Sustainer Rates at $15, $10, and $5. Sustainers get a free PM Press T-shirt and a 50% discount on all purchases from our website.

Your Visa or Mastercard will be billed once a month, until you tell us to stop. Or until our efforts succeed in bringing the revolution around. Or the financial meltdown of Capital makes plastic redundant. Whichever comes first.

About PM Press

PM Press was founded at the end of 2007 by a small collection of folks with decades of publishing, media, and organizing experience. PM Press co-conspirators have published and distributed hundreds of books, pamphlets, CDs, and DVDs. Members of PM have founded enduring book fairs, spearheaded victorious tenant organizing campaigns, and worked closely with bookstores, academic conferences, and even rock bands to deliver political and challenging ideas to all walks of life. We're old enough to know what we're doing and young enough to know what's at stake.

We seek to create radical and stimulating fiction and nonfiction books, pamphlets, T-shirts, visual and audio materials to entertain, educate, and inspire you. We aim to distribute these through every available channel with every available technology, whether that means you are seeing anarchist classics at our bookfair stalls; reading our latest vegan cookbook at the café; downloading geeky fiction e-books; or digging new music and timely videos from our website.

PM Press
PO Box 23912
Oakland, CA 94623
510-658-3906 • info@pmpress.org

Buy books and stay on top of what we are doing at:
www.pmpress.org